Study Skills for Social Workers

Study Skills for Social Workers

Chris Stogdon and Robin Kiteley

Los Angeles | London | New Delhi
Singapore | Washington DC

First published 2010

SAGE Publications Ltd
1 Oliver's Yard
55 City Road
London EC1Y 1SP

SAGE Publications Inc.
2455 Teller Road
Thousand Oaks, California 91320

SAGE Publications India Pvt Ltd
B 1/I 1 Mohan Cooperative Industrial Area
Mathura Road
New Delhi 110 044

SAGE Publications Asia-Pacific Pte Ltd
33 Pekin Street #02-01
Far East Square
Singapore 048763

Library of Congress Control Number: 2009943616

British Library Cataloguing in Publication data

A catalogue record for this book is available from the British Library

ISBN 978-1-84787-456-6
ISBN 978-1-84787-457-3 (pbk)

Typeset by C&M Digitals (P) Ltd, Chennai, India
Printed in India at Replika Press Pvt Ltd
Printed on paper from sustainable resources

Robin would like to dedicate this book in loving memory of Doreen (Rene) Kiteley, who is very much missed.

Contents

List of Boxes

List of Figures

List of Tables

Acknowledgements

Robin would like to say a HUGE thank you to Christian McGrath for his constant help and support, the endless cups of tea arriving on his desk and for being an all-round, lovely man. Love and thanks to my parents, Phil and Glenis Kiteley, who always make me feel better in stressful times! Thanks also to Ben Raikes and Dawn Beckett for helpful feedback, and Graham Ormrod for supportive words and diverting tunes. Finally, I would like to thank all of the students whom I've had the pleasure of teaching, and learning from, over the past eight years.

Chris would like to say thank you to her colleagues at the University of Huddersfield who have supported this project with enduring optimism and support which has not waivered even when hers did! I am grateful to the students, service-users and carers that I have worked with who have been the inspiration for this book and who continue to provide an important source of learning and understanding for me. I am especially grateful to my family and friends for their enthusiasm and support with a very special thanks and love to Guy, David and Anna and last but not least to my Mum.

We would both like to thank Emma Patterson and Susannah Trefgarne, at Sage, for their supportive comments and enthusiastic encouragement during the writing process.

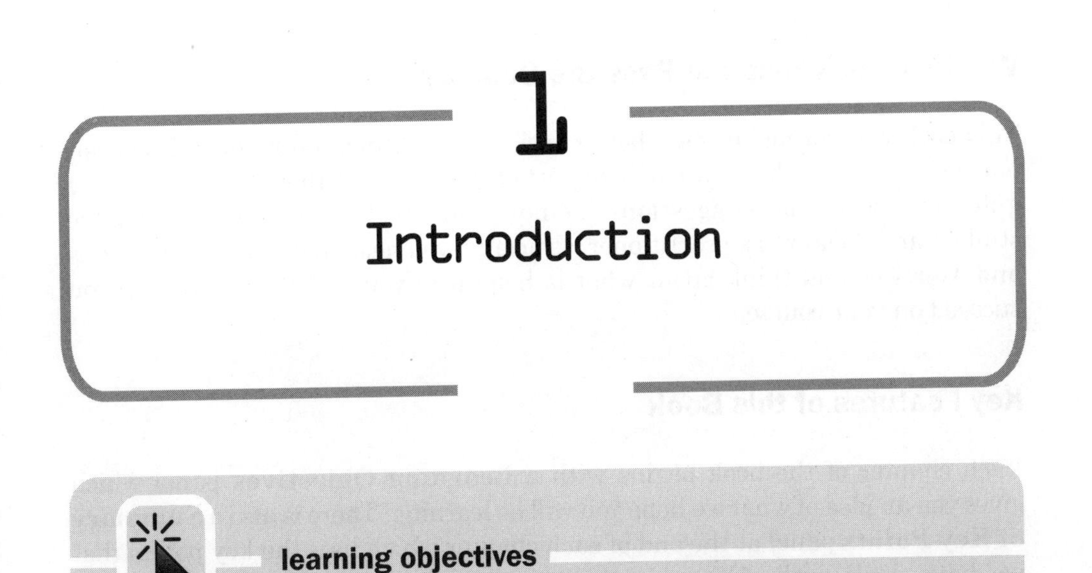

1 Introduction

learning objectives

- To gain an overview of the key learning features of this book.
- To introduce the main topics that the book covers through an active reading exercise.

What Does this Book Aim to Do?

This book will help you focus on the skills you will need to develop to succeed as a social work student and as a professional social worker. Our view is that study skills are most relevant if they are directly related to the subject area of social work practice.

We recognize that today's students are expected not only to learn about the specifics of social work practice during their degree or postgraduate courses. There is also an expectation, from employers in particular, that students learn about and appreciate the significance of becoming lifelong learners. This means that as well as studying specific modules/courses on topics such as social policy and law and human justice, you will also be expected to 'tune in' to what your particular learning needs are and to think imaginatively and creatively about how you can help yourself to develop as a learner.

Of course, learning is not all about just 'thinking' – especially within the context of a hands-on, people-oriented discipline such as social work – it is also, crucially, about translating thoughts into positive action. The key aims of this book are to get you thinking about your own learning performance, preferences and developmental goals and also to prompt you to think about practical ways in which you can develop both as a learner and as a social work practitioner.

Will this Book Help me Pass the Course?

This book will *not* make you a better social work student on its own. However, our point is – and this is a *really important point* – that this book can provide guidance, ideas and suggestions for how you can become a more effective student and social work practitioner. Crucially, you need to try out the activities and exercises and think about what is helpful to you and what can help you succeed on your course.

Key Features of this Book

Each chapter of the book begins with a **Learning Objectives** panel which gives you an idea of what we hope you will be learning! There is also a **Summary of Key Points** panel at the end of each chapter which lists the key points that we have dealt with. Alongside this you will find a 'Useful Resources and Further Reading' section which lists books and websites which we feel are useful for further developing your understanding of topics. You will find that many of these texts are available through your institution's library.

It is possible to work through the book in any order as each chapter is fairly self-contained. Where a topic in one chapter has links with a topic covered in another chapter, we have shown this in the text.

Reflection points

Throughout the book, we introduce **reflection points**.

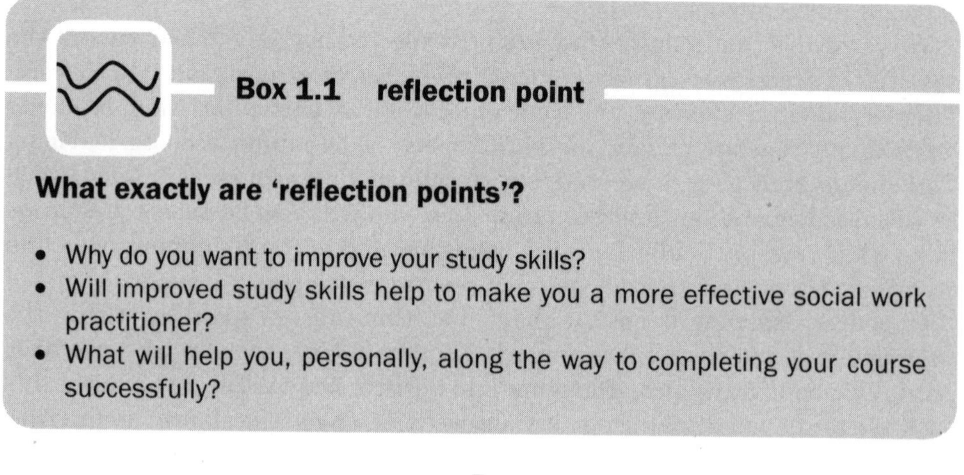

Box 1.1 reflection point

What exactly are 'reflection points'?

- Why do you want to improve your study skills?
- Will improved study skills help to make you a more effective social work practitioner?
- What will help you, personally, along the way to completing your course successfully?

These questions are examples of 'reflection points' which encourage you to think about your own responses to the key issues. You might decide that you want to record your responses in a journal or notebook – this is definitely something that we would encourage you to do. This is also something you would be expected to do when you go out on a social work placement.

Activities

We have developed activities to support the main topics and we would encourage you to complete each of them in order to get the most out of the book.

- Trying something out helps us to find out if we have understood it.
- Learning theory suggests that effective learning takes place when we take an idea that we have picked up from one context (e.g. reading about how to structure an essay in a study skills book), and apply it to another context (e.g. by actually having a go at writing and structuring an essay) (Petty, 2004: 29).
- We might also call this 'putting ideas into practice'.

activity 1.1

Getting intimate with this book!

Rather than provide you with a long description of the kinds of things covered in this book, we want you to GET ACTIVE and start investigating yourself!

1. Start by having a really good look through the **contents page** – what are the main chapter titles, and what are the topics within them?
2. Skim through the **index** at the back of the book – what are some of the key words here that might be of most use to you?
3. Browse the **Learning Objective** panels on the first page of each chapter to get a better idea of what each chapter focuses on.
4. Check out the **Useful Resources and Further Reading** sections on the last page of each chapter to get an idea of some of the other books and websites that will be of use to you.

This technique is a really useful way of quickly getting an overview of any new book, so try to make a habit of doing it whenever you pick one up.

Most of the activities in this book, including Activity 1.1, are based around fairly open questions. In other words, there is rarely a single 'right' or 'wrong' answer, so how well you respond to them will depend largely on the amount of thought and effort you put into them.

We have included some suggested answers which you can find at the end of the relevant chapters and which can be used as a guide. They are designed to encourage you to self-assess (i.e. mark your own work) which is proven to be a really good way of developing your own learning and understanding (Petty, 2006). As an alternative, you might want to consider partnering up with a 'study buddy' or even forming your own informal study group. You could each individually attempt the exercises and activities in this book and then get others in the group to peer-assess your work, and vice versa.

Useful Resources

As you would expect, the 'useful resources' boxes are designed to:

- Draw your attention to additional resources which could help with your study skills development.
- Encourage you to engage with a range of materials or learning environments including chapters in other books and websites.

Quick Tips

The 'quick tips' boxes contain useful pointers in relation to things that we know students can sometimes struggle with. For instance:

- Sometimes web addresses can change, so if you find a website is no longer accessible, try searching for it using key search words in a search engine.

Did You Know?

The 'Did you know?' boxes provide helpful summaries of some of the underpinning knowledge and background information.

Finally, at the end of the book, there is a glossary of key terms which should help if you come across any unfamiliar terminology or jargon.

summary of key points

- The more time and effort you are prepared to put into completing activities and exercises, the stronger your learning will be.
- Use 'Useful Resources' and 'Further Reading' to further develop your understanding of key topics.

2

Thinking about Learning

learning objectives

- To think about the ways in which adult learning is different to learning as a child.
- To consider the usefulness of models of learning, such as Kolb's (1984) experiential learning cycle.
- To understand the value and limitations of learning styles in helping you to develop your learning skills.
- To understand the difference between 'surface' and 'deep' learning.
- To identify common learning obstacles and consider strategies to overcome them.

Where are You Now as a Learner?

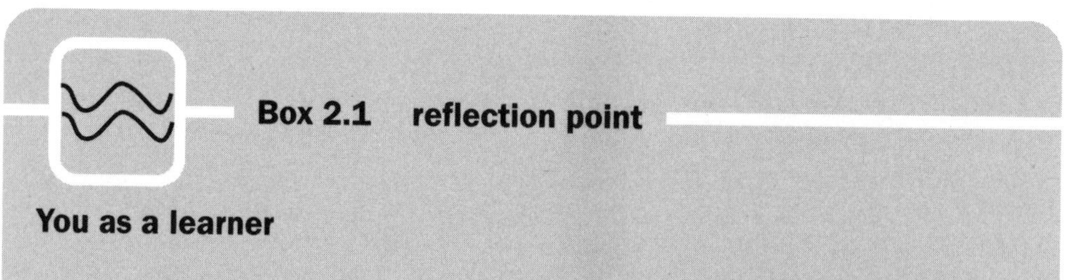

Box 2.1 reflection point

You as a learner

Spend a few minutes jotting down your responses to the following questions:

- How do you feel about learning? (What kinds of emotions do you experience in relation to learning, or the thought of learning?)

- What does learning mean to you – what is its significance or value?
- What kinds of messages have you received about yourself, as a learner, in the past?
- How have these messages shaped your view of your ability or potential to learn?

Our view of learning, and our ideas about ourselves as learners, can have a powerful effect on how ready, able and willing we are to engage in new learning experiences. This chapter gives you the opportunity to learn more about the learning process so that you can:

- begin to get to know your 'learning self' a little better
- feel better equipped to take control and responsibility for your own learning.

Learning as a Child or as an Adult?

Learning experts such as Malcolm Knowles suggest that the learning process is very different for us as adults, compared to our experience as school-children (Knowles et al., 2005). This is summarized by five main characteristics of adult learners:

Table 2.1 Five key characteristics of adult learners

1	As adults, we are used to taking control of our own lives and as a result **we prefer to manage and organize our own learning**. We will have a natural tendency to question things and will have our own thoughts about how we want to develop our learning.
2	**We bring a wealth of knowledge and life experience to new learning situations** and like to make links between new ideas and our existing knowledge. We are not 'empty vessels' waiting to be filled up with knowledge.
3	Generally, **we undertake learning because we want to change some aspect of our lives and this provides a high level of motivation.** This is different to when we were at school and were told to learn things because they would be useful to us in the future.
4	We tend to approach learning as a means of solving a problem or changing some aspect of our lives. This means that **we tend to be more drawn to learning about things that seem relevant to our own lives and our personal goals.**
5	**We are more motivated by factors from within ourselves**, such as the drive to develop self-esteem, increase our confidence or gain recognition for our achievements. This contrasts with the school child who is largely motivated by factors outside of herself, such as the authority of the teacher and peer group pressure.

activity 2.1

Applying Knowle's characteristics of adult learning

Think about and then write down some brief responses to the following trigger questions:

1 If adults, in general, learn best by being self-directed, what will you do during your academic course to ensure that you are an effective, independent learner?
2 What is motivating you to want to learn to be an effective social worker?
   a. How can you use this motivation to help you stay engaged with your studies?
3 What kinds of things from within yourself (internal processes) do you think are shaping your desire to learn and develop your skills?
4 What are the obligations and responsibilities that come with being an adult learner?
5 How will you ensure that you meet these obligations and take on board the responsibilities?

How does Learning Happen?

There is no one, simple explanation as to how people actually learn but several models of how learning takes place have been suggested. Before we go on to take a look at one of these models, complete the following activity.

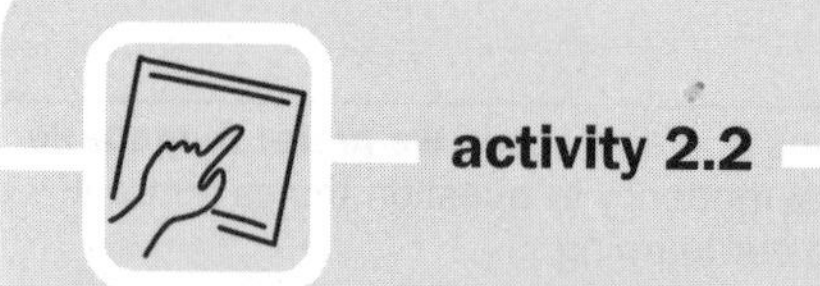

activity 2.2

How does learning work?

Make some notes, jot down some ideas or draw some kind of picture or diagram to show how you think learning takes place. Things that might be interesting to think about include:

- Does learning happen all at once – like having a sudden flash of inspiration – or do you think there are different stages to learning?
- How do you know when learning starts and finishes?
- Do you think you learn in the same way as your friends or members of your family?

David Kolb explores what he refers to as an 'experiential' cycle of learning (Kolb, 1984). 'Experiential' learning is where we learn from having an experience.

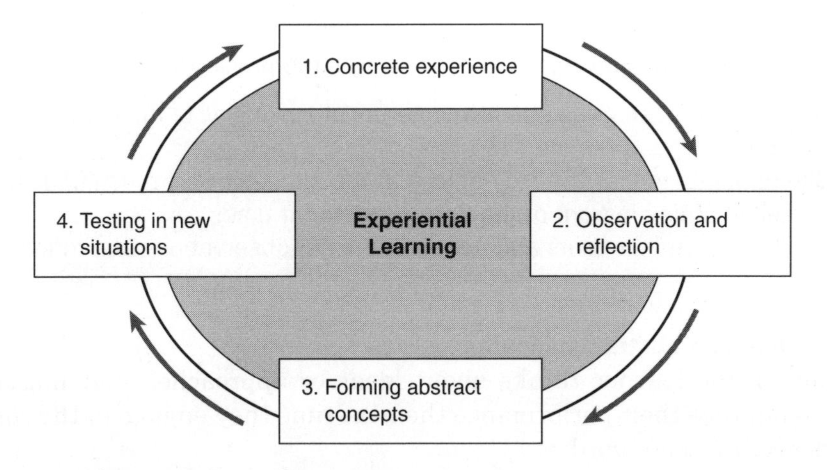

Figure 2.1 Kolb's Experiential Learning Cycle

Kolb's experiential learning cycle

Kolb's theory of learning can be represented in the form of a learning cycle which illustrates his idea that there are four main stages involved in learning from experience.

Stage 1: Concrete experience

Kolb says that learning involves having some form of 'concrete' experience. He uses the word 'concrete' to mean an experience that takes place in the real, physical world. A concrete experience could be:

- talking to a service-user
- reading a book
- putting together a care plan.

Stage 1 Example: Fozia has just **given a verbal presentation** to the rest of the students in her group.

Stage 2: Observation and reflection

In Stage 2, the learner enters a period of 'observation and reflection', in which they consciously think about what happened during their concrete experience. This 'thinking' can be triggered by their thoughts and memories of the event, or by feedback from others. For instance:

- What did they do well and what could have been better?
- What can they observe about their performance? Was it rushed or too slow? And so on.

Stage 2 Example: Fozia thinks about how well the presentation went.

- She thinks that she was effective in terms of making all of the key points she wanted to.
- She remembers that she did not look at the audience very much and caught herself shuffling in front of the data projector at times.
- Feedback from her peers and tutor confirm her observations and reflections.

Stage 3: Forming abstract concepts

In Stage 3, the learner thinks about ideas or approaches that might help them to improve their performance the next time they engage in the concrete experience. In other words:

- How could they do things differently in the future to achieve a more satisfactory outcome?
- Is there a theory, idea or technique that they have used previously, which might be useful in the current learning situation?

Kolb refers to this as 'forming abstract concepts'.

Stage 3 Example: Fozia thinks about how other people in her group delivered their presentations by using keywords and bullet points instead of a full script.

- She tries to imagine herself using bullet points to jog her memory in the future.
- In her mind's eye, she sees herself talking confidently and knowledgably to her audience, making lots of eye contact and communicating more directly with them.
- She decides it would be a useful idea to try this approach the next time she is required to deliver a formal presentation.

Stage 4: Testing in new situations

This stage is where the learner puts their new thoughts and ideas (the 'abstract concepts' from stage 3) into practice. It is a crucial stage because it allows learners to test out their 'abstract concepts' (ideas) to see if they actually work or make things any better.

Stage 4 Example: A few months later, Fozia gives a talk in the Students Union about the voluntary work she has been doing:

- She finds that using short bullet points on her PowerPoint slides helps her to maintain much better eye contact with the audience.

- However, there are also some occasions where she drifts a little off-topic and gets sidetracked. As a result, her talk runs 10 minutes over the agreed time slot.

So, overall:

- She is pleased that her new approach allows her to communicate better during the presentation.
- She makes a mental note that she will need to work on staying focused in future presentations.

What comes after Stage 4?

Kolb does not see his cycle stopping at Stage 4. In fact, he says that the cycle goes around again but this time the learner will continue to add to what they have already learnt. So, following the example of Fozia – she will go back round to Stage 1 where she repeats the concrete experience (i.e. she gives another academic presentation). However, this time around, she may receive feedback about other things she does well or could continue to improve. Kolb says that the 'learning process' is never fully finished, but simply continues to move around the stages of the learning cycle.

Learning Styles

Some learning experts suggest that we all have preferred ways of learning, which they call learning preferences or learning 'styles'. For instance:

The Visual-Auditory-Kinaesthetic (VAK) model of learning styles is very much concerned with how we process (take in and give out) information (Eicher, 1987). So it helps us to get a better understanding of how we most readily grasp or perceive things in learning situations.

Table 2.2 Learning preferences

When learning something new:	*We can call this learning:*
Ursula prefers to be able **to look at** written instructions, illustrations and diagrams.	**VISUAL** (involves *seeing* and *reading*)
Marvin prefers **to listen to** someone describing the topic and have them give verbal instructions and guidance.	**AUDITORY** (involves *listening* and *speaking*)
Gemma prefers to **physically try things out** for herself.	**KINAESTHETIC** (involves *doing* and *touching*)

activity 2.3

Quick Visual-Auditory-Kinaesthetic (VAK) Self-test

Imagine that you have just bought a flat-pack, self-assembly bookshelf for your home study area. When you come to put the bookshelf together, would you naturally prefer to:

A Read all of the instructions before starting, and closely follow the illustrations to see how each piece will fit together? ☐
B Have someone else read the instructions out to you as you go about assembling it, and ask them questions if necessary? ☐
C Ignore the instructions and just focus on working out how to build it yourself through handling the parts and discovering how they fit together? ☐

If you selected option A, you are probably more of a **visual** learner, option B would suggest you are more of an **auditory** learner and, finally, option C suggests you are a more **kinaesthetic** learner.

Why are learning styles useful?

Understanding your own learning style can help you to:

- recognize your current learning preferences and tendencies
- 'play to your strengths'
- identify areas of your learning where you could make further improvements, in order to become a more rounded learner.

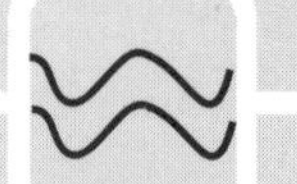

Box 2.2 reflection point

Learning styles can change!

The key thing to remember is that learning styles and preferences are not set in stone – they can change over time – and there are conscious things you can do to improve your skills and become a more rounded learner. For example – **use natural strengths to develop weaker areas**. If I am a student who finds it easier to learn from visual methods rather than listening to a lecturer talk for an hour, I could make a conscious effort to create my own set of lecture notes which use keywords, pictures, diagrams and concept maps. This may mean doing some more work on them after the lecture has finished but should be worth it in terms of helping me to learn more effectively.

Learning style tools and questionnaires

The value of learning styles activities and questionnaires is that they can help us to identify where our current areas of strength are, and equally importantly, alert us to areas where we might need to consciously think about improving our skills.

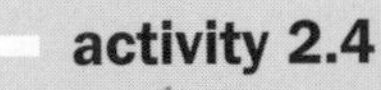

activity 2.4

Learning styles tools and questionnaires

Many people have developed their own different models of learning styles and they will usually offer some kind of questionnaire or activity to help you to work out what your learning preferences are (e.g. VAK Questionnaire, Honey and Mumford Learning Styles Questionnaire (1982)). We do not recommend using any one particular learning styles questionnaire or tool, but would encourage you to explore the range of free options that are available online. Try typing in the phrase **free learning style questionnaire** into your favourite search engine. Take careful note of how to interpret your result once you have completed the questionnaire or activity.

Limitations of learning styles

- Learning styles become less useful when they are simply used to 'label' or stereotype learners (Coffield et al., 2004: 51), e.g.:
    - '... oh, she's the type of learner who always wants to jump in and get started, so she won't be any good at doing anything that requires some thought and reflection'.
- Some critics claim learning styles can overlook the important social and political aspects of being a learner (Reynolds, 1997), which are shaped by race, gender and social class, as well as by age, disability and sexual orientation.

Figure 2.2 Emotional responses to learning

Our emotional responses to learning

Tools such as learning styles questionnaires may not tell us much about how we feel or what our emotions are in relation to our learning.

Emotional responses, such as those shown in Figure 2.2 above, clearly have the potential to affect how we view and approach our own learning. So, in helping you to consider your own learning style, we want you to use a method which draws on your own expertise and knowledge of your own previous learning experiences. This approach to thinking about your learning styles does not pretend to have the kind of scientific rationale associated with some of the learning styles questionnaires, but we hope it will be a valuable opportunity to explore your thoughts, feelings and responses.

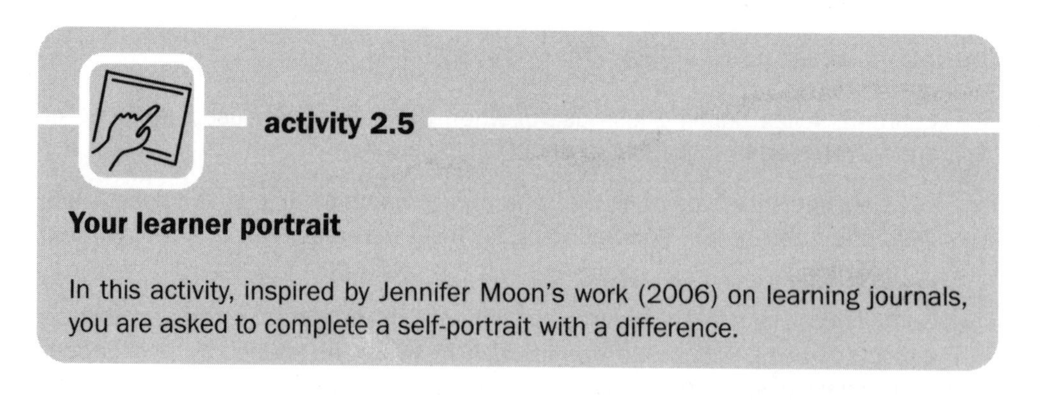

activity 2.5

Your learner portrait

In this activity, inspired by Jennifer Moon's work (2006) on learning journals, you are asked to complete a self-portrait with a difference.

STEP 1:

Produce something which represents what you think and feel about yourself as a learner. Be really creative and use any medium which you feel is most appropriate. You might decide to:

- **Produce a 'pen portrait'** – this is a written passage which describes and presents a narrative (or story) of you as a learner. This approach works well if you try to be specific and use real examples and memories to illustrate things.
- **Produce a drawing, diagram or collage** – use visual imagery to represent how you learn best and highlight the areas that you find challenging or feel that you may struggle with.
- **Produce an audio or video portrait** – you could use a mobile phone, mp3 recorder or video camera. This is similar to making an audio or video diary and the aim is to capture what you think and feel about your learning through the things you say, facial expressions and tone of voice.

Whichever method you use, try not to get too caught up in wanting to produce a 'masterpiece' – the most valuable part of this exercise is that you make some kind of record of your thoughts, feelings, hopes, desires, worries, concerns and beliefs about yourself as a learner.

STEP 2:

After you have completed your learner portrait, reflect back on it and write a short piece of 200–300 words in which you identify what your portrait reveals to you about your relationship with learning.

- Make links and draw your own conclusions – and if you feel comfortable, seek the creative input of peers and tutors.
- Keep your finished portrait somewhere safe as it records a useful snapshot of you at a particular point in time.
- Just like an old photograph of yourself, you can look back at it and acknowledge how you have changed and developed over time, with certain 'features' remaining constant.

Skim the Surface or Dive in at the Deep End?

Deep learning

Sometimes you may go into a lecture or teaching session feeling really motivated about what you are going to be doing because:

- you have a real interest in and passion for the topic
- you are curious about how there might be links between this topic and other areas you are interested in
- you have a number of questions in your mind about the topic, and look forward to the prospect that at least some of them will be answered
- you are keen to develop your broad understanding of social work ideas, in order to become a better social work practitioner.

Learning experts say the factors described above are more likely to be linked to **deep learning** (Biggs, 1999; Entwhistle, 1988; Marton and Säljö, 1976; Ramsden,1992). Deep engagement with a subject provides a really good grounding from which to do all of those things that are asked for in assignment guidelines and marking criteria, such as:

- critical thinking and analysis
- making links and connections to other ideas, theories and topics
- weighing-up the evidence
- providing a discussion or balanced view.

Surface learning

At other times, we may go into a lecture or teaching session planning to:

- just note down and remember those things which are relevant to our assignment
- focus on relevant facts which can be memorized and discard the rest
- not worry ourselves about how this topic might fit into the grand scheme of things.

This approach is often described as 'surface learning'. There are times where we all engage in surface learning in our daily lives. For instance, we may be told that a new records management system has been introduced into our workplace and our first response might be, '... just tell me about the bits that are relevant to what I do'. This kind of surface approach can help us to get by, and is often enough in the short term.

However, in relation to your academic assignments, you need to consider whether an entirely surface approach to learning is going to be enough to get you through your course, with the kinds of grades you are aiming for. To illustrate this, think about how many times in the past you have heard a tutor say:

- 'look *beneath the surface*'
- 'aim to examine the subject *in depth'*
- 'consider things from a *number of perspectives*'

- ‘examine the thinking that *underlies* a particular idea or belief’
- ‘try to *avoid giving a superficial view* of things’.

We are sure you can think of more. The point is that most of these phrases are directing you to think about the topic in some kind of depth.

Activity 2.6 below asks you to indicate whether each of the statements relates to your own approach to learning by indicating ‘Y’ or ‘N’. First, read the eight statements and tick whether or not they fit with your general approach to learning. Then go through the statements again and either write an ‘S’ for surface or ‘D’ for deep, depending on which style you think they are associated with.

activity 2.6

What’s your style?

1. **You just want to remember enough information in order to get the job done** (e.g. write an essay or assignment). Y: ☐ N: ☐
2. **You are not afraid to ask questions** about the things you are learning about, and some of these may be about the main ideas which make up the topic. Y: ☐ N: ☐
3. You are bored with the topic but **you just do enough to get through the assignment**. Y: ☐ N: ☐
4. **You are interested in the subject for the enjoyment and satisfaction that you get from studying it**. You are not just concerned with passing the assignment. Y: ☐ N: ☐
5. **You look for the main ideas which underpin the topic**, and have a depth of understanding which you can take to other learning situations. Y: ☐ N: ☐
6. **You try to make links** between new learning and those things you already know from previous learning occasions. Y: ☐ N: ☐
7. You have **scratched the surface of a topic** but do not know enough to apply the main ideas or principles to other learning situations. Y: ☐ N: ☐
8. **You learn things off by heart**, but don’t really think about the meaning of what you have learnt. Y: ☐ N: ☐

(summarized from Moon, 2007: 59)

Use this exercise to help you think about what you might need to do in order to develop the ‘deep learner’ within you.

Common Learning Obstacles

Barriers to learning

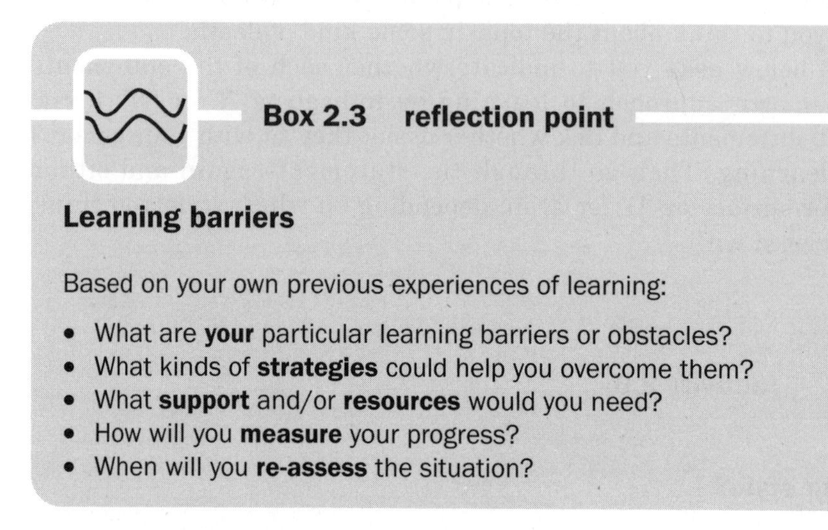

Box 2.3 reflection point

Learning barriers

Based on your own previous experiences of learning:

- What are **your** particular learning barriers or obstacles?
- What kinds of **strategies** could help you overcome them?
- What **support** and/or **resources** would you need?
- How will you **measure** your progress?
- When will you **re-assess** the situation?

Taking positive ownership of your own learning

Learning how to become self-directed, organized and self-motivated can be a real challenge in itself! That is, before we have even started to think about learning about the subject of social work. For instance, if you have previously been studying a course where your study was largely directed by the teaching staff, or if you have been in a job in which your work was closely supervised, it may come as a shock to suddenly have all of this freedom! The following chart uses the mnemonic (memory aid) 'EMPOWER' to help you to focus on the qualities required to take ownership of your learning, together with practical suggestions of how to develop these.

Table 2.3 EMPOWER

Quality:		*Characterized by:*	*Helped by:*
E	Enquiring	• Asking questions • Debating ideas • Following up your own areas of interest • Keeping an open mind	• Listening to the questions that others ask • Reading around the topic to see how issues are 'debated' and discussed • Making notes of interesting things to follow up and research
M	Motivated	• Being focused on own learning goals • Being clear about why you want to do the course	• Setting SMART learning goals which feel helpful and relevant to you

Table 2.3 (Continued)

Quality:		*Characterized by:*	*Helped by:*
			• Monitoring your progress and rewarding yourself for your efforts • Attending regularly and participating fully
P	Productive	• Completing work and developing your learning and understanding • Making best use of the time available to you • Seeing pieces of work through to their conclusion	• Avoiding procrastination using techniques suggested in Chapter 3 • Focusing on the bits you can do and coming back to the bits you know you struggle with • Avoiding unnecessary distractions (e.g. text messages, television)
O	Organized	• Being at the right place at the right time • Making sure you know what you have got to do • Thinking about the best order in which to do things	• Using simple tools like timetables, diaries and schedulers – these are invaluable • Writing down the tasks you need to do and prioritizing them • Keeping relevant handouts and notes together in files and folders
W	Well-prepared	• Having the materials, resources and equipment needed to do a given task • Being clear and focused about what you have been asked to do • Considering reading, research or other preparation before beginning to write your assignments	• Studying your timetable and getting a sense of what topics will be covered – if possible doing some preparatory reading • Always using assignment guidance • Using lectures notes and reading lists to guide your background reading • Taking equipment you will need along to taught sessions (e.g. pens, paper, laptop, memory stick, etc.)
E	Engaged	• Contributing to sessions • Taking part in activities • Finding points of personal interest, even in the sessions that may seem dull or irrelevant	• Pushing yourself to make contributions where invited to do so – do not wait for someone else to speak first • Looking for the interesting point, angle or perspective – it can be found in even the dullest of topics!
R	Resilient	• Being able to accept constructive criticism • Being able to cope under pressure (i.e. family commitments, work commitments, looming assignment deadlines) • Accepting that learning can sometimes involve 'getting it wrong'	• Using feedback on your work to guide your learning development goals • Factoring in relaxation time or stress-busting techniques (see Chapter 4) • Trying to think of 'mistakes' or failures as important learning opportunities

Your Learning Goals

We know that you want to be a qualified social worker. But what about delving into it in a little more detail? For instance:

- if you have always had a dread of public speaking, what about using your time at university to purposefully develop these skills?
- perhaps you feel that you have never been 'any good' with IT systems?

You will have plenty of opportunities to practise and develop these skills but you need to be actively taking hold of these rather than shying away from them, or even worse, avoiding them altogether.

activity 2.7

Putting together a learning development plan

Strengthening your skills can be a lot easier if you record your plan, methods and progress, using a personal 'learning development plan' similar to that shown in Figure 2.3. They encourage you to be very clear about:

1. Your **learning goals** (what is it that you want to achieve).
2. The **actions** that you need to take in order to achieve your goals or improve your performance.
3. The **resources** (equipment, material, time, support from others) that you will need to help you do this.
4. A **review date** which makes you reflect back on your progress, and gives you the chance to make any changes to your plan.

Using a learning development plan may just seem like yet another task to do, but unless you record this kind of information, it is very hard to be accurate and honest about your progress, or share this information with others.

You will almost certainly be asked to use some kind of learning development plan during your course in order to record and chart your personal development. The types of skills involved in this tie in very closely with Key Role 2 which requires social workers to '**plan**, **carry out**, **review** and **evaluate** social work practice, with individuals, families, carers, groups, communities and other professionals' (TOPPS UK Partnership, 2002).

Learning Goal	Action Required	Resources	Timescale

Figure 2.3 **Learning Development Plan**

Be SMART!

Make sure that your learning goals are 'SMART'!

Did you know? SMART Goals

'SMART' is a convenient mnemonic to help you remember the various factors that you should aim to take into account when planning, carrying out and evaluating your own learning goals. For instance, if my learning goal is to 'improve my referencing', I could apply SMART in the following way:

S	**specific**	e.g. I will aim to strengthen my referencing and citation skills in my academic work.
M	**measurable**	e.g. I will aim to get 90% of my references absolutely correct in my next essay/assignment.
A	**achievable**	e.g. I will focus on book, journal and web referencing to begin with and then look at other kinds at a later date.
R	**relevant**	e.g. I will make sure that I use resources which focus on the Harvard Reference system, as this is used at my institution.
T	**time-bound**	e.g. I will aim to have developed this for when I do my next essay on 18 November 2010 (two months away).

Using SMART helps you to be much more specific about your intentions, so that you can actually translate them from positive intentions into **positive actions**.

Tackling Boredom and Frustration – Head On!

No doubt we have all had experiences of sitting in a classroom or a lecture theatre and listening to someone who has completely baffled us within the first 10 minutes of their lecture. We might have then spent the rest of the hour-long lecture:

- doodling
- checking out our fellow students' fashion sense
- mentally devising shopping lists
- imagining ourselves reclining on a tropical beach!

By the end of the hour, we were probably none the wiser about the topic of the lecture than at the beginning! This is not to say that traditional lectures do not have their place, and like them or not, they are still used extensively on many social work courses. Many people find it incredibly interesting to be able to sit and listen to an academic develop a particular theory or idea over the course of a lecture.

Quick Tip: Lectures provide an opportunity to ...

- develop your **listening skills**
- sharpen your **critical thinking skills**
- work on your **summary and note-taking skills**.

Quick Tip: Emergency Recovery Plan for Dull or Difficult Lectures

If you find that you often lose concentration or focus in dull or difficult lectures, seminars or workshops, try to note down:

- anything you do not feel you understand fully
- the questions you would ideally like to ask if you could put the lecturer on 'pause'
- those things you do understand, or are confident about
- those things which you might need to go away and do some further reading or research on
- anything that would make the topic more interesting or accessible for you.

You can use these notes to help you focus your independent learning or even to help you talk about your specific learning needs in tutorials.

Box 2.4 reflection point

Transferring these skills

In social work practice, we will need to sit and listen to service-users for extended periods of time. They will have vital information and issues to share with us and may not always present things in the way that we might prefer. For instance, they may:

(Continued)

- **make assumptions about what we already know**
- use **language and terminology that we are not always familiar with**
- **present things in an order that makes sense to them**, but which might not appear to be organized or sequential to you.

As professional social workers, we will still be expected to:

- **pick out relevant details**
- **identify key themes or concerns**
- take a **flexible and responsive approach to note-taking** and information recording.

summary of key points

- Models such as Kolb's experiential learning cycle can help us to gain a better appreciation of how learning actually takes place.
- Understanding our own learning styles and preferences can help us to identify our strengths and weaknesses and set ourselves appropriate learning goals.
- Learning styles should not be used in a self-limiting way.
- Many student social workers face learning obstacles but these can be tackled with the right attitude and appropriate support.

further reading

Burns, T. and Sinfield, S. (2008) *Essential Study Skills: The complete guide to success at university*. London: Sage.

Clegg, B. (2008) *Studying Creatively*. London: Routledge.

Cottrell, S. (2003) *The Study Skills Handbook*, 2nd edition. Basingstoke: Palgrave Macmillan. (especially Chapters 2, 3 and 4).

Hargreaves, S. (2007) *Study Skills for Dyslexic Students* (Study Skills Series). London: Sage.

Hoult, E. (2006) *Learning Support for Mature Students* (Study Skills Series). London: Sage.

3

Self-management and Organization

learning objectives

- To understand the skills involved in managing yourself and your time effectively, including:
  - timekeeping
  - working independently
  - organizing your study space.
- To understand what procrastination is and how you can deal with it.
- To develop an awareness of what stress is, how it can be recognized and why it is particularly significant for social workers.

Timekeeping

Social work courses tend to focus on the importance of regular and punctual attendance which links in with the required level of attendance set by the GSCC. This recognizes that in order for you to be successful in your studies, there does have to be a level of input which gives you the necessary information and knowledge to meet the assessment requirements, and prepare you for professional practice. Teaching sessions are time limited and even with the use of e-learning systems, to support the face-to-face teaching, they are still of relatively short duration.

Box 3.1 time keeping

Do any of the following sound familiar?

- You usually arrive at college just as the lecture starts but stop to pick up a coffee and this means that you are only five minutes late. ☐
- You avoid catching the early train as this will mean you arrive fifteen minutes before the lecture. By catching the later one, you arrive ten minutes after the lecture starts, but people are still arriving with coffee at that point so you do not see it as a problem. ☐
- You are usually ten minutes late after the mid-lecture break because you have to queue for coffee but as most other students in your session, were late at the start of the session, you can justify being a bit late back. ☐
- You regard yourself as someone who misses either the start, the middle or the end of a teaching session. ☐
- You are punctual but get annoyed by the disruption caused by latecomers. ☐
- You want to develop the skills of timekeeping to enhance your experience in both academic and practice settings. ☐

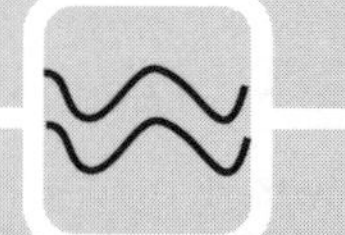

Box 3.2 reflection point

The consequences of being late

Being late for:

- a lecture is disruptive and distracts the whole group
- a visit to a service-user is rude and assumes that your time is more important than the service-user's
- a visit is an invasion of privacy as a service-user may well have a visitor who has no knowledge of your social work input with their host.

The importance of timekeeping as a sign of courtesy is well established in most societies and as a social worker you will have a responsibility to act in a courteous manner with service-users and colleagues. The skill of good timekeeping connects to the Value Requirements for social work, as being on time provides a good opportunity to show respect towards a service-user or colleague. The GSCC position respect, trust, dignity and privacy as high on the agenda of the Value Requirements for professional practice, so how do they apply to time keeping in both university and practice settings?

activity 3.1

Timekeeping and organizing yourself

Jasmine is often late for university lectures. Her lecturer raises this as a point of concern. She thinks about why she does not often manage to get in on time, and it occurs to her that:

- she has never bothered using an alarm clock as she can normally rely on one of her housemates to get her up
- she is normally too tired to sort her university notes out in the evening, so is often searching around for her bag, notes, pens and other equipment first thing in the morning
- when she leaves the house in the morning, she rarely factors in the time taken to walk from the bus station to the university and the time to grab some coffee or breakfast
- she knows that on some mornings the journey can take almost twice as long as normal due to adverse weather conditions or really heavy traffic
- she does not carry a timetable around with her so is sometimes unsure about which lecture room she should be in.

1. What aspects of her time management and organizational skills would you advise Jasmine to reconsider so that she can become more punctual?
2. What are the general principles of time management and organization you begin to draw out from this?

Timekeeping and social work practice

In practice, timekeeping has a particular significance in relation to working respectfully with service-users. You may have come across the urban myth that social workers are always late. The truth of this criticism is not rigorously evidenced but we do have feedback from service-users who clearly are unhappy with the lack of respect shown through the lateness of social workers. Undoubtedly, there will be occasions when you are unavoidably late for both lectures and appointments with service-users and it is important to make every effort to warn the person that you will be late. If it is in relation to an appointment with a service-user, you will need to check out if it is convenient for you to arrive late or whether you need to rearrange the appointment time.

Working Independently

Developing the skills to work independently is not only crucial for the successful completion of your social work course, but is also key to performing effectively and professionally in a social work role.

Did You Know? Working independently and NOS

The National Occupational Standards (NOS) for social work, key role 5 requires social workers *to manage and be accountable for their own social work practice* (with appropriate supervision) (TOPPS UK Partnership, 2002).

activity 3.2

Rating your independent working skills

You are asked to rate your effectiveness in the kinds of tasks that are involved in working independently.

Rate yourself using a scale from 1 to 5, where 1 = not very effective and 5 = very effective skills.

Working independently

How effective are you at:	1	2	3	4	5
Motivating yourself?					
Planning your time effectively?					
Avoiding distractions?					
Setting targets?					
Completing jobs?					
Working things out for yourself?					
Coping when things become difficult?					

Study timetables

Of course, you should spend the early part of your course developing and enjoying your new social network, but this does not have to be at the expense of beginning to develop a steady and regular study pattern which will set the foundations for a successful time at university. One of the simplest yet most effective tools you can use to establish this study pattern, and take ownership and control of your learning, is the use of a study timetable.

activity 3.3

Planning a study timetable

The useful thing about timetables is that they allow you to be more purposeful and objective about how you *actually* use your time.

When devising a study timetable, you should:

- **Be realistic** – will you really have the energy to study when you come home from just having worked a late shift at the Students' Union Bar? Do not forget to factor in family commitments, employment commitments, socializing, travel time, shopping, domestic chores and so on.
- **Be specific** – what will you focus on in each of your weekly study sessions? For instance, you might choose to have at least one study session per week for each of the modules you are currently studying.
- **Give yourself a break** – you actually need to get a balance between working, studying and relaxing in order to be at your best and most productive!
- **Stick to it** – even if you do not consider yourself to be a 'timetable' person, have a go at sticking to a timetable for *at least a week*. You will hopefully feel motivated to carry on with it when you review how effectively you have used your time!
- **Review it** – our priorities and commitments very often change at short notice. You may need to reflect this by tweaking or revising your timetable.

There are many different ways to structure your timetable but the key is to find something that suits you. Figure 3.1 shows our version of a study timetable which you can photocopy and use to plan your own study time.

Organizing Independent Study Space

As a lot of your time will include independent study hours, it is a great idea to establish a study space within your own home or student accommodation.

Time	Monday	Tuesday	Wednesday	Thursday	Friday	Saturday	Sunday

Figure 3.1 Individual study timetable

If you do this, you will need to think about how you will use this space and how you will negotiate access with any other members of your household.

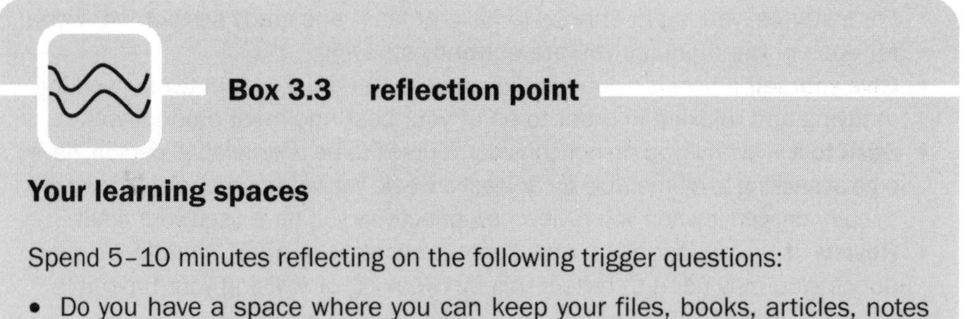

Box 3.3 reflection point

Your learning spaces

Spend 5–10 minutes reflecting on the following trigger questions:

- Do you have a space where you can keep your files, books, articles, notes and other study materials? It is easier if you can put everything in one place, rather than having to search around for the relevant resources every time you want to start a study session.
- Does your study space allow you to study in ways that you prefer? For instance, if you prefer a quiet environment, is this attainable in the space that you have got?
- Do you have to share your study space with others in your household? If so, how will you ensure that this arrangement works for everybody? Perhaps you will each have a drawer to store your study materials.

Do not forget that if establishing a study space within your own home is difficult, then there are public alternatives. For instance, your own institutional library or local lending/reference library will have a number of study spaces available for you to use. Having identified a suitable study space, devising an effective study timetable and setting some study objectives is surely just a matter of getting down to it, isn't it? Things are not always that straightforward when it comes to focus and motivation as the next section describes!

Avoidance Strategies and Procrastination

For many of us, the idea of getting down to doing some academic work on our own can be rather daunting. In fact, we may suddenly become uncharacteristically conscientious about:

- doing the housework
- sorting out our filing
- taking the dog for a walk
- carrying out any number of 'crucial' errands.

Most of us will recognize the strategies involved in this scenario as belonging to a finely honed toolkit of avoidance strategies! If you know, or suspect, that you do this when it comes to completing assignments or essays, it is worth thinking about why you do this and whether you would like to change any of these behaviours.

Tick any of the following that ring a bell with you or add any others which are not listed below:

activity 3.4

Reasons for putting things off (procrastination)

Statement	✓
It will be too difficult for me!	
I'm just too scared of failure!	
I don't want to find out that I can't do this task I have been set.	

(Continued)

I know that I'm not in the best frame of mind to do this – I'll leave it until another day when I might feel more like it.	
Doing this task will be boring – there are more interesting things to do right now.	
I work best when my adrenalin is pumping, so that's why I leave it until the night before the hand-in.	
I don't know how to begin so I'll wait until some of the others in my group have made a start.	
I really don't understand the topic so it's not worth starting yet – if I leave it a while, maybe it will all start to make sense and fall into place.	
I want to produce a perfect piece of work, and I'm not feeling on top form today, so I'll leave it until I'm feeling really productive and creative.	
I've got too many other time commitments – this will have to wait until I have a chance to squeeze it in to my schedule.	
If I leave this work until the last minute and make a bad job of it – I can always tell myself that I probably would have got a better grade if I had had more time to do it.	
Add others:	

We all avoid things and procrastinate about them at various times. For a small number of people, this approach may work very effectively for them. These are the kinds of people who are probably very confident about being able to complete the task that they have been set, but need the adrenalin rush of a deadline in order to galvanize them into action.

But for most people, the whole expense of emotional and physical energy involved in avoidance tactics and procrastination is draining. It makes the entire process of completing a task seem about ten times harder than it really needs to be! However, there are some very genuine concerns and anxieties that underlie such avoidant behaviour. So, if you are the kind of person that engages in avoidance tactics from time to time (or even regularly), the best approach to changing this is to not beat yourself up about it. Instead, try to understand why you might do this, and assess what you think you gain from doing it.

Example: Dan procrastinates because he worries that he will not do a very good essay and that this will only confirm his suspicion that he 'shouldn't have been given a place on the course as he's not up to it'. However, by putting things off, he:

- gives himself less time to focus on the essay
- often ends up rushing to finish his pieces of work, and sometimes only just makes the deadline
- feels he does not do himself justice.

Dan realizes that this kind of behaviour is in many ways counter-productive, but somehow always seems to slip back into the same pattern.

Whatever your reason is for delaying or putting things off, once you understand what is behind this, then you are in a better position to weigh-up whether the 'pay-offs' of procrastination are greater than the possible benefits from doing things differently in the future.

Box 3.4 reflection point

The 'pros' and 'cons' of procrastination

For you personally:

- What are the advantages (the pros) of delaying or avoiding working on essays and assignments?
- What are the disadvantages (the cons) of delaying or avoiding working on essays and assignments?
- What could you do differently to ensure that you were not always leaving things until the last minute? Think about what the advantages would be of doing things in this new way, but also list the disadvantages as well.
- Do you think there is any benefit for you in changing your approach to getting work done? If there is, what would you need to think about doing now in order to make this a reality?

The advantages of making an early start on assignments

As educators, and ex-students ourselves, we know that there are a number of compelling reasons why it is always a good idea to avoid leaving things until the last minute.

Box 3.5 reflection point

Reasons to avoid procrastinating

A gradual, planned and structured approach to completing assignments means that:

- **If you do not understand an aspect of what you are reading or writing about**, you can:
  - look for clarification from further reading, or revisiting your lecture notes
  - ask one of your tutors for help or guidance.
- **If you fear that you will not produce your best work,** then getting a draft version completed fairly early means that you can continue to develop and strengthen your work before the final version is submitted for assessment.
- **If your original choice of assignment topic was difficult to write about** because there was not much published work on it, then you have a chance to change the focus of your work.
- **There is plenty of time for proofreading** and even re-writing sections of your work. Often students miss the 'checking and evaluation' stage of essay writing purely because they have not given themselves enough time to do it properly.

Stress and Stress Management

During any learning experience, there will be times when things begin to get a little stressful.

Example: Jo is struggling to cope with three assignment deadlines which just happen to have coincided with her taking on a new role in the Parent Teacher Association at her daughter's school and caring for her partner who has is temporarily incapacitated due to a back injury. She worries about how she will keep everyone happy!

Dealing with stress, or 'stress management', is not only a part of being a student on a higher education course but can affect our performance in our jobs and our daily lives. So, this would be a really good opportunity to gauge how effectively you think you deal with stress. You can then begin to develop some useful and effective strategies which you can use to manage stress during the rest of your career.

Box 3.6 reflection point

Beyond 'the knowledge'...

Being a social work student is:

- about so much more than simply 'learning the social work knowledge' – it is also about the realities of day-to-day working
- an ideal opportunity to develop your skills and abilities to be an effective practitioner and lifelong learner
- a chance to strengthen the skills that are also helpful in managing your personal life.

What is stress?

Pressure is part and parcel of all work situations, including the work involved in studying, and this helps people to maintain motivation and get the job done (HSE, 2008a). However, constant, excessive pressure can lead to stress.

Did You Know? The difference between 'pressure' and 'stress'

- **Pressure** can be understood as a stimulating sense of urgency which can help us to get things done and meet our obligations and responsibilities.
- When pressure becomes intense or unmanageable, we may experience a sense of loss of control and have an adverse reaction which may affect our mental, physical and emotional health. **This is the point at which pressure tips over into stress.**

Access this online video of Professor Cary Cooper, an expert on management and work-related stress, as he explains the difference between pressure and stress: http://www.hse.gov.uk/stress/standards/before.htm

Table 3.1 Common symptoms of stress

Mental/Emotional Symptoms	*Physical Symptoms*
Anger	Chest pains
Depression	Constipation or diarrhoea
Anxiety	Cramps or muscle spasms
Changes in behaviour	Dizziness
Food cravings	Fainting spells
Lack of appetite	Biting finger nails
Frequent crying	Nervous twitches
Difficulty sleeping	Pins and needles
Feeling tired	Feeling restless
Difficulty in concentrating	Tendency to sweat a lot
	Sexual difficulties
	Breathlessness
	Muscular aches
	Difficulty sleeping

Taken and adapted from: NHS Choices (n.d.)

Symptoms of stress

- Different people will respond to stress, and display symptoms of stress, in different ways.
- This is important for considering both your own individual responses to stress and being aware of the range of stress factors and symptoms experienced by the service-users and carers that you work with.
- There are a range of commonly experienced symptoms which may be indicative of stress and these are indicated above in Table 3.1.

NOTE: Remember that not everyone experiences stress in the same way, and in particular, stress symptoms may vary for children and young people. It is important for social workers to be sensitive to the symptoms of stress in others as you will be working with carers and service-users who will be under significant pressures.

Stress triggers

So, what usually causes stress? Greener (2002) explains that the factors that commonly cause stress can be grouped together into six broad categories:

Table 3.2 Greener's six categories of stress triggers

Category	*Example*
1 Conflicting motives or priorities	Time spent studying may be time that has to be sacrificed with family and/or children.
2 Internal conflict	Working in a situation where a manager asks you to behave in a way which is unethical or which contravenes the 'Codes of Practice'.
3 New or unfamiliar situations	Beginning a new course or starting a new job and not knowing what to expect.
4 Unpredictable events	Receiving exam results or having a new system introduced into the workplace.
5 Loss	Experiencing a bereavement, losing one's job or experiencing the break-up of a friendship or relationship.
6 Frustration	Not obtaining the assignment results you feel you deserve or getting stuck in a traffic jam and being late for an appointment with a service-user.

Note: We have adapted elements of Greener's original categories and examples.

- There are many different stress triggers and some people will be affected more by certain events or situations than others.
- Stress triggers may not always be associated with unpleasant events or experiences – for instance, getting married or having a civil partnership ceremony ranks as one of the highest scoring events on the 'life stress scale' (Greener, 2002: 24).

activity 3.5

Stress triggers

Drawing on your past life experiences, try to identify four of your own, recurring, personal 'stress triggers':

1

2

3

4

Stress and social work

The social work profession can be particularly stressful (Asthana, 2008; HSE, 2008b) due to a number of factors including:

- difficulty gaining wider recognition and sometimes acceptance of the social work role.
- conflict when working with other professionals and/or service-users.
- the regular requirement to respond to changes in legislation and social policy (Lloyd et al., 2002).

Did You Know? Social workers should take stress seriously

Results from the Labour Force Survey (LFS), in respect of self-reported illness data for 2006/07, shows that health and social work sector employees are at a higher than average risk of experiencing work-related stress (HSE, 2008b: 25).

Dealing with the negative effects of stress

Did You Know? Stress and supervision

- A good supervisory relationship can be of significant value in terms of helping to combat the negative effects of stress, and guard against the risk of burnout (Lloyd et al., 2002).
- This is why effective supervision is seen as being such a key part of successful social work practice.

In some cases, it may be that your relationship with your supervisor is 'not great', and may itself be one of the contributing causes of stress. If this is the case, you would need to think about identifying strategies for dealing with this, preferably through having an open and honest discussion with your supervisor. However, if this relationship had completely broken down, the supervisor's line manager should normally be involved in helping to resolve any issues, and in some cases, where agreed upon, using the services of an impartial third party.

Quick Tip: Tackling stress

If you are experiencing the symptoms of stress, there are things that you can do to try to reduce the negative impact of these.

For instance:

- Seek guidance from your employer's occupational health unit or your academic institution's student services.
- Try to identify what you could do to reduce the stress factors in your life:
  - What things are in your control?
  - What are those things that are beyond your immediate control?
- Draw up your own stress management plan:
  - Identify things that you could do differently.
  - Plan a review date so that you can see whether they are having any beneficial effect.
- Plan some relaxation time into your day – even if it is only for a short while:
  - Some people like to do a relaxing activity or hobby.
  - Try using aromatherapy oils, listening to relaxing music or simply chatting with friends.
  - You will probably have ideas about what works best for you.

There is evidence to suggest that social work students make use of humour to help deal with stress, but it is probably the social element of humour as opposed to the humour itself which is the important factor (Moran and Hughes, 2006). It is even suggested that appropriate humour should be considered more within the social work curriculum – you may be able to identify lecturers who already seem to subscribe to this view!

However, on a more serious note, if you feel that stress is prolonged or is having an adverse effect on your health and well-being, you should consult your General Practitioner, who should offer helpful advice and support.

Useful Resource: *Working together to reduce stress at work* (HSE)

- *Working together to reduce stress at work*, from the **Health and Safety Executive** website, contains information and guidance for those experiencing stress in the workplace.
- It outlines the roles that all employees should play in protecting their rights, discusses the significance of the HSE's Management Standards and the responsibilities of employers.

See http://www.hse.gov.uk/pubns/indg424.pdf

activity 3.6

Social care-related case studies from the Health and Safety Executive

These case studies describe interventions designed to reduce stress in social care environments. Read through them and identify:

1 The factors that contributed to stress within the work environment.
2 How the interventions that were introduced aimed to address the situation.

Case Study A: Care Home

See http://www.hse.gov.uk/stress/casestudies/rsrp-demand.pdf

Case Study B: Social Services

See http://www.hse.gov.uk/stress/casestudies/rsrp-control.pdf

summary of key points

- Focusing on time management, organizing yourself and organizing your study space can help you to become a more effective student and practitioner.
- Procrastination can prevent us from using our time more effectively but there are positive steps we can take to avoid procrastinating.
- Stress is a big issue for those in the social work profession, so it is important to be able to recognize the symptoms of stress in ourselves, and others, and be able to take steps to reduce the negative impact of it.

useful resources

Student Social Workers (a site for student social workers set up by student social workers). Available at: http://www.studentsocialworkers.org.uk/
Web discussion forums contain a range of topics, such as information on:

- getting into social work
- academic issues

- financial issues,
- resources.

further reading

Fanthome, C. (2005) *The Student Life Handbook*. Basingstoke: Palgrave Macmillan.
Levin, P. (2007a) *Conquer Study Stress*. Maidenhead: Open University Press.
Levin, P. (2007b) *Skilful Time Management*. Maidenhead: Open University Press.
McMillan, K. and Weyers, J. (2006) *The Smarter Student*. Harlow: Pearson Education.
Rugg, G., Gerrard, S., and Hooper, S. (2008) *The Stress-free Guide to Studying at University* (Study Skills Series). London: Sage.
SWAP (2007) *The Social Work Degree: Preparing to Succeed* – SWAP Guide 3 [online]. Available at: http://www.swap.ac.uk/docs/swapguide_3.pdf

4

Learning in the Workplace

learning objectives

- To understand how to work effectively with colleagues, tutors, mentors and managers.
- To think about making the most of the work base and the university.
- To develop an awareness of how to survive the strain.

Work-based Social Work Courses

In this chapter, we want to explore some of the challenges and opportunities of being a student on a work-based social work course.

Did You Know? Routes into social work

- There are many undergraduate and postgraduate courses in the UK that have been developed in partnership with social care agencies in both the statutory and independent sectors. Many of the agencies will have drawn upon funding from central government to support the initiatives of 'Grow Your Own Social Workers' (DOH).

- Some employers have chosen to support their existing staff through professional social work courses and others have looked to recruit externally to introduce new trainees to their workforce.
- Some employers have chosen to do a mixture of both by offering internal staff the opportunity to apply for sponsorship alongside external candidates. This has been viewed by many employers as a positive and productive way of addressing some of the more complex aspects of workforce planning.

Whichever route you have travelled in relation to arriving on the course as a work-based student, it is likely that you will have managed to overcome several obstacles to reach the point of enrolment on your social work course. The areas that we will consider here will include:

- working with colleagues
- the differences between university and the workplace
- accessing support
- the roles of mentors and tutors
- making the most of your learning
- what to do when things go 'pear-shaped'
- managing work and study
- survival skills for you and your loved ones.

Working with Colleagues

As a new student, you will probably be in uncertain surroundings which seem very strange to you and may raise thoughts such as:

'What am I doing here?'

Or:

'Why did anyone think I was capable of this?'

Or:

'Is social work the right choice for me, or should I get a proper job?'

These may be the thoughts of all students starting on a social work course, whether work-based or not, but there is one overriding anxiety that work-based students often identify and this takes shape as:

'All eyes are on me' – the eyes of family, friends, tutors, other students and, worst of all, *employers and work colleagues.*

If we focus on the eyes of colleagues first of all, we will note that many work-based students have been through a competitive process to be selected by employers. This selection process may well have included colleagues who also applied for support to do the course but were unsuccessful. Human nature being pretty unpleasant at times may well display the less flattering aspects of jealousy and it may well be that just at the time when you are feeling at your least able and lowest in confidence that colleagues are reinforcing your insecurities by being unhelpful because of their own lack of success.

Skills for Managing Change

Skills for managing change come from a variety of sources. For instance, it may be that you use your **ability to communicate** to convey to your colleagues the impact of their disappointment in not being selected for the course. To discuss in an open and non-threatening way will be a good starting point for your professional practice, so if you were to raise the situation in a team discussion, it may well alert colleagues to just how hard it is to be the 'chosen one' when others have not been successful. The way that you conduct yourself in this discussion will be determined by your clarity of communication and your understanding of addressing contentious issues in a productive way.

Assertiveness skills

One method of approaching areas that are difficult to discuss is to use some of the basic skills in assertiveness. This can be in the form of clearly owning the difficult area and not apportioning blame.

Example: Nisha is upset by the negative responses to her success. She knows that a positive way of dealing with this would be to avoid blaming others and to frame her concerns by taking responsibility for her own feelings.

This could take the form of:

'I am upset by the way you have treated me since I got a place on the course and I do know that it can't be easy for you.'

Rather than:

'Why have you been hostile to me since I got a place on the course?'

The first response is much more about Nisha:

- **taking ownership** for her responses
- offering an olive branch of **understanding** in the recognition that she would have felt the same way if the boot had been on the other foot.

The second response clearly:

- **denies any ownership** for Nisha's reactions, and as such
- puts the **blame** on her colleagues.

Colleagues' expectations

As you are not going to be in work for the same amount of time that you were before going on the course, it is important that colleagues are clear about when they can expect you to be available. It is equally important that they know that when you are away from work, you are actually either attending university or studying. Your clear communication on this will be important and will help colleagues to understand the differences between university and the workplace.

Managing transitions – many hats!

Before coming on the course, you may well have had a significant amount of time in practice so the transition from the workplace to the university will be a challenging one. This is more of a challenge because you may well be making this transition on a weekly basis. It may be for instance that you have two days each week in university and one day for study with two days in your work base. If this is the case, you will probably be conscious of wearing many hats but also be acutely aware that you only have one head!

On the other hand, it may be that you are new to the social work environment and also new to the university setting. If this is the case, you will be going through a process of change in which you will be absorbing the two new worlds and trying to make sense of them both concurrently.

In the two new roles of worker and student, you will no doubt be faced with masses of information which may feel overwhelming. The introduction to the world of social work in your workplace and the world of social work education in the university will exercise your powers of adaptability to the extreme. It may be appropriate here to consider the skills that you will need to use to deal with this transition time, whether you are experienced in social work or completely new to it.

Communication, Confidence and Understanding

In order to understand the complexities of the two worlds that you will inhabit as a work-based student, it is important that you can **ask any questions** that may come up for you. To ask these questions, you will need to:

- have a certain level of **confidence**
- be able to **recognize that you may be worried** about admitting that you have not understood something in case your manager or tutor will think that you should not be in the job/on the course.

Quick Tip: Wise Words!

He who asks a question looks a fool for a moment but he who does not understand and does not ask stays a fool forever (anon Chinese proverb).

The newness of the situation may have made you feel less confident so the process of admitting that you do not understand something could be daunting for you. You are not alone!

A common feature of observed human behaviour is that when people are thrown into new situations that pose a threat to their existing way of making sense of the world this can be debilitating in the extreme.

Did You Know? Ontology

A common term for the way that we make sense of the world is ontology. Ontology has a significant part to play in social work practice and therefore it is important that, as a student social worker, you are able to identify your own way of making sense of the world on both personal and professional levels.

The way that you make sense of the world will no doubt be influenced by your view of how you and your behaviour impacts upon other people.

Think about:

- the signals that you send out through your appearance
- the music you like
- the politics you hold.

Now consider the signals that you want to send out regarding your role as a worker and as a student. It may be fair to assume that you would like to send out the signal that shows you know what you are doing – even if that is only true for some of the time!

The process of change that you are experiencing may have shaken your confidence and this may make it harder rather than easier for you to ask the pertinent questions when you have not understood something connected to either work or university. Recognizing that your way of making sense of the world may include being 'regarded as competent at all times' may help you with the shift that will need to occur in order for you to admit that there are some things that you do not understand.

Self-perceptions and colleagues' perceptions of your work

There is a particular issue to be negotiated for work-based students who have had lengthy experience in practice before starting the course. This is the perception that others will have had of you whilst working alongside you over a period of time. For instance:

- It may be that you developed a good reputation for specific areas of work and that your work has been heralded as a showcase of good practice.
- It may also be that although you have been successful in a particular way of working that you have never understood why your work has been effective.

As a student, you will be asked to look critically at your practice but as you are still a worker, it may be more difficult for you to ask questions which will highlight that the perceived competence was built on sand.

Box 4.1 reflection point

A solid foundation for practice

Would it really be devastating to say that you have been confused about your practice for a long time, and that you now relish the opportunity to develop understanding and knowledge that will mean your future practice is built on solid granite?

Making connections between this perception of yourself and how others see you will contribute to your increased confidence and ultimately your ability to communicate the questions about the areas of your work and study that you need to explore. This awareness will also assist you to access the necessary support and guidance from the appropriate people.

activity 4.1

Working on your confidence

- Start to consider situations where you are confident and look at why you can be confident in one situation and not another.
- Consider how you adapt to the different roles of worker and student.

Connecting university and practice learning

One of the real advantages of being work-based is that you will be in a prime position to make the connection between your learning in university and your work in practice.

- Theoretical understanding will be quickly connected to its application to practice – for example, you may be surprised to find that you have been using a social work intervention as part of your practice without realizing that it has a particular name and that it comes from a recognized theoretical perspective.
- Your skills in thinking through and evaluating your own practice will be really important to your overall learning.

Independence

Another aspect of the difference between university and the workplace will be in relation to the expectations of you in your role as a student. In university, you will be given guidance about the areas of relevant study but you will not be expected to adhere rigidly to the recommended reading and will be encouraged to develop your own individual approach to your learning and development. This is sometimes perceived as a lack of direction and compared to the more structured environment of the workplace can be quite unsettling. Being completely in control of how you use your own study time can be overwhelming at the start of the course and your understanding about how you learn and organize your time can be helpful to you in your management of these sometimes conflicting needs.

Support and Guidance

Social work concerns itself with the serious intention of enabling people to access support and guidance but it does not always 'practise what it preaches' in relation to the people who work within it. However, it is expected that student social workers may need to access support and both your manager and your tutor will be working closely with you to ensure that the mechanisms are in place for you to be fully supported. As a work-based student, it may be that there is someone in the staff development section of your agency who has a specific role in relation to offering you support whilst you are studying on your social work course.

But where do you start? The key is to have the mechanisms set up as soon as possible when you know that you have a place on the course.

It is helpful to define these mechanisms in a tangible way using the mnemonic 'SUPPER':

S	Supervision
U	Understanding
P	Prioritizing
P	Planning
E	Evaluation
R	Review

And we are not expecting you to sing for it!

Supervision

As an employee, you should be used to having regular supervision with your manager regarding your workload and other related aspects of your practice and development. As a student, you will be faced with trying to balance a whole variety of needs, including those of:

- service-users and carers
- the agency or organization you work for

- the course at university
- your family and friends
- and last, but importantly, your own needs both personally and professionally.

We have talked in detail about the importance of organizing your time in order to meet the demands of work and study but this can be easier said than done.

Did You Know? Supervision

- **Supervision** has the primary purpose of ensuring that the work of the agency is being carried out in a *competent and professional way.*
- An important part of this primary purpose is to evidence that the work is being done in line with the legal and procedural requirements of the particular agency.
- **The well-being of service-users and carers is the essential starting point in supervision**. As a student and a worker, you may feel that your own personal needs should be prioritized and in order for your manager to access the effectiveness of your practice, it is important that your needs are considered. However, it is worth remembering that they do not come above the needs of the service that you are employed to deliver.

Workload issues and supervision

- In the work context, it may be that you need to **look closely at your workload** in relation to your reduced availability and to **review this on a regular basis** with your line manager in the formal setting of supervision.
- Your workload will need to reflect the needs of the agency as it may be that you are only going to be replaced when you go on placement. Some employers of work-based students will not be able to find the resources to fully cover the gap when the student is in university and taking study time.
- This places an obvious demand on your colleagues and although they may be fully supportive of your opportunity to study, it will invariably mean that they take on additional work.
- The measure of this work will be the responsibility of your manager but it would be wise to consider colleagues' workloads the next time you are tempted to moan about an outstanding assignment.
- Using supervision as a forum in which you can be open and honest about the pressures and the positives of your new and complex roles of worker and student will mean that you have a productive outlet which will assist in your progress both at work and on the course.

Understanding

It is now time for some tough talking in relation to the understanding that you will need to demonstrate if you are going to access appropriate support in the workplace – you are not the first and hopefully not the last work-based student who is studying on a qualifying course in social work. It may well be that your colleagues have been on a similar route and as such can fully understand the hectic schedule that you have taken on. Your own understanding of the demands on your colleagues will play an important part in the way they respond to your need for support.

Example: Your understanding of the sometimes conflicting needs of the workload in relation to academic work will be tested in relation to your flexibility. For example, you are likely to have a regular study day allocated to you for the duration of your course but there may be times when the demands of work are such that you need to be willing to offer to reschedule in order to help out your colleagues. Obviously, if this became a regular occurrence, your studies would be compromised but occasional changes should not pose a significant problem for you but will encourage your colleagues to reciprocate when the pressure is on for you.

Finally, the understanding that you develop about your own social work practice will be a significant part of your experience as a work-based student. You will be introduced to theoretical perspectives in university which will challenge some of your work with service-users and carers, as it may be that you have worked in an intuitive way in the past. You may now suddenly realize that the work that you have been doing has a theoretical base which you can discover through your reading.

Example: Ivan has worked as a support worker in a mental health context and has effectively supported people when they have experienced periods of acute illness. Some service-users required intense support for specific periods of time and Ivan's role diminished when the person became well again. His course helped him to consider this support in relation to Crisis Intervention theory – he was able to link his understanding of his practice to his new understanding of theory.

One of the real strengths of learning in the workplace is that you will have ample opportunity to dovetail this understanding throughout your course rather than purely on the formal placement of assessed practice.

Prioritizing

It may well feel as if you are spinning too many plates and living with the fear that they will come crashing down at any moment. Developing your skills around prioritizing will became an important part of your repertoire whilst on the course. You will need to be able to decide on those tasks that can be done later or respond quickly to the ones that require your immediate attention. Supervision will give you the opportunity to discuss how you can be supported in achieving a balance between the conflicting demands on your time. On a course in higher education, it is usual for there to be a requirement to do significant amounts of reading in order to complete the assessed work. Many courses will stipulate that for every hour of direct contact in lectures and seminars, you will need to match with at least three hours of reading. When you start to add this up on a weekly basis, you will quickly realize that ten hours of lectures in a week should be accompanied by 30 hours of reading and research. For some, this comes as a harsh realization that the days away from university were not in fact days off for leisurely pursuits but were in fact a crucial part of the course.

This means that you will need to allocate enough time to prepare for pieces of work and prioritize your commitments to enable you to read sufficiently in order to complete the assignments successfully. It is best to prioritize the reading time *before* you consider how much time you will need to actually write the assignment.

Equally, if you have a report that has to be completed as part of your practice, you will need to ensure that you prioritize this above the other demands in order to meet the required deadline. Developing an overview of all the work you need to complete, both from your agency and from your university course, is key to prioritizing and planning.

Quick Tip: How to prioritize

Think about three simple questions to ask yourself around prioritizing:

1 **What** have you got to do?
2 **When** do you have to do it by?
3 **How much time** do you need?

Your response to the above will lead very neatly into the consideration of your skills in planning.

Planning

A fundamental part of your work as a social worker will hinge on your planning skills. The Key Roles in social work, which are based on the National Occupational Standards for social work, rely heavily on both the understanding and application of the key roles as a basis for safe social work practice. The planning skills that you develop during your course will not only be important to you as a student and worker but will also form the basis for your effective practice as a qualified social worker.

So why is planning so key to social work practice?

Box 4.2 reflection point

Planning

It is perhaps useful to think about planning in the context of **the scarcity of resources** and when we have a limited amount of:

- time
- money
- opportunity

it is wise to consider the most effective use of them.

Thinking in this way will encourage a more strategic view of how you will manage the limited resources that you have in relation to the two worlds of employment and the university.

How you plan your time as an employee

The agency that employs you may have a strict policy in relation to mileage payment and needs to be satisfied that your journeys in the car are both necessary and suitably arranged in relation to limited resources of both time and money. Consider how you might apply this skill of planning your travel at work to think about the assignments and coursework that you need to complete for university.

***Example*:** Applying planning skills to an assignment

Imagine you are asked to detail your understanding of Care Management processes as part of an assignment. It would make good sense to look at the areas of your practice where you are using these processes on a day-to-day basis. Your assignment can then be based on a piece of your practice which has been totally removed of all personal details of the service-user and carer. It may be appropriate to change details in order to ensure confidentiality (COP).

In relation to your planning for this piece of work, you will draw upon your ability to take the overview that:

- If you are familiar with the assignments that you will need to complete (the course handbook always makes good bedtime reading), you will be able to request the allocation of a specific piece of work which will form the basis of the work for your written assignment for your coursework for university.
- If you have looked at this as part of your supervision with your line manager, then you will have demonstrated your forethought and skill in planning to meet the needs of both the employer and the university work.

Evaluation

Box 4.3 reflection point

Evaluation

The ability to evaluate your work and your progress is another important aspect of the Key Roles for professional social work practice:

- Why do social workers need to evaluate their work?
- Why do you, as a student social worker, need to evaluate your work?

In very straightforward terms, we evaluate to check out if the job has been done effectively. You will be aware of the scrutiny that surrounds social work practice when things go badly wrong and in these instances the evaluation is done either by other professionals through the courts, serious case reviews or through the media.

The professionals involved in externally evaluating the effectiveness of social work practice have a serious mandate to identify both responsibility and messages for future practice. The results of external evaluation often lead to significant changes in both practice and legal perspectives. Social work is externally evaluated when things go wrong but it also has rigorous methods of internally evaluating practice in a routine way.

So, how does the evaluation of professional social work practice connect to the skills that you need to acquire as part of your experience in employment and on the course? As a worker, you will be familiar with the way in which your practice is evaluated on both an individual and agency basis. Evaluation as a skill for your study takes on a different flavour as you will be expected to:

- look critically at the theoretical concepts that you are discovering
- examine your practice in a detailed way which fits in with the requirements for assessment of your suitability to become a qualified social worker, i.e. GSCC, COPS, key roles and value requirements.

Developing the skill to look critically at your development will prepare you to work in a reflective way, and reflection skills are considered in more detail in Chapter 11.

Box 4.4 reflection point

Assessing appropriateness and effectiveness

As social workers, when we are looking at why we followed a particular course of action, we will no doubt be assessing the effectiveness of the action at the same time. We can think about this in terms of:

- Why did we do it?
- Did it work?
- If so, why did it work?

It may be appropriate to ask the above in relation to a piece of academic work that you have completed which focuses on evaluating your own practice. The understanding gained from this will point to another question around the learning that has occurred from the evaluation, which leads us on to the 'review' process.

Review

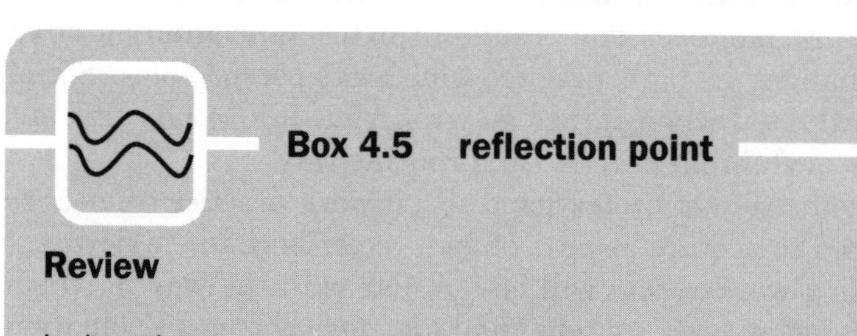

Box 4.5 reflection point

Review

In broad terms, the process of review is retrospective and encourages the opportunity to look at learning from evaluation and to plan a future activity.

- Consider how you might review your activities on the course in relation to how they have complemented or conflicted with your experiences as an employee.
- Consider how you have managed the role of student alongside that of your personal commitments and try to highlight the hot spots of demands when you have not had enough hours in the day to meet deadlines.

It may be that part of the review process for you is to revisit the time management skills that we discussed in Chapter 3 and look at why the demands have become excessive. For example, it may be that your workload has increased due to staff shortages or an increase in the demand for the service overall – it is not always your fault so try to avoid an assumption of personal responsibility for uncompleted tasks. Alternatively, if you have spent your study days accessing retail therapy, then you will know you are to blame!

summary of key points

- Key issues that are important for work-based learning students are:
  - learning to work with colleagues
  - developing skills for managing change
  - dealing with your expectations and those of co-workers
  - developing assertiveness skills.
- The skills needed for effective practice-based learning include:
  - clear communication, confidence and understanding
  - connecting university learning to practice learning and experiences.
- Remember your 'SUPPER' (Supervision, Understanding, Prioritizing, Planning, Evaluation, Review).

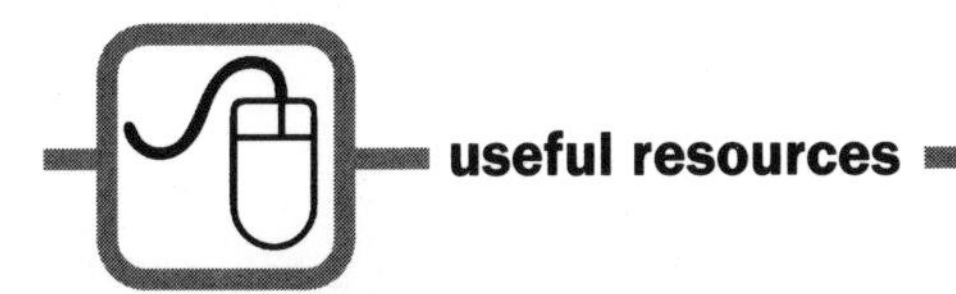

useful resources

Practice Learning. Available at: http://www.practicelearning.org.uk/default.html

- Contains useful resources for supporting practice learning in social work education.
- Is aimed at lecturing staff, practice-based mentors and assessors, and social work students.

Making Practice-based Learning Work. Available at: http://www.practicebased learning.org/home.htm

- Contains a 'Student Materials' section with resources designed to support the learning of students on health and social care work-based placements.

A Virtual Placement: Preparing Students for Practice. Available at: http://www.hcc.uce.ac.uk/virtualplacement/

- Is designed to prepare students for going out onto placements.
- Has an emphasis toward social work students.

further reading

Beverley, A. and Worsley, A. (2007) *Learning and Teaching in Social Work Practice*. Basingstoke: Palgrave.

Brotherton, G. and Parker, S. (eds) (2009) *Work-based Learning and Practice Placement: A textbook for health and social care students*. Exeter: Reflect Press.

Durrant, A., Rhodes, G. and Young, D. (2009) *University-level Work-based Learning*. Hendon: Middlesex University Press.

Parker, J. (2004) *Effective Practice Learning in Social Work*. Exeter: Learning Matters.

Shardlow, S. and Doel, M. (2005) *Modern Social Work Practice: Teaching and learning in practice settings*. Aldershot: Ashgate Publishing.

5

Learning Online

learning objectives

- To develop an understanding of what 'e-learning' is and the kinds of learning technologies that you might encounter on your course.
- To appreciate how to make the most effective use of online learning environments and how to do 'advanced' web searching.
- To build confidence in assessing the quality of online resources.
- To prepare you for independent online learning, online collaboration and e-assessment.

What is E-learning?

Quick Definition: E-learning

E-learning is 'the use of technology to enhance learning practice' (Mayes and de Freitas, 2004: 4).

This definition is helpful as it emphasizes the role of technology to enhance learning practice, rather than suggesting that e-learning in some ways replaces 'traditional learning'.

- 'E-learning' tends to refer to the range of technologies that really began to emerge in UK schools, colleges and universities in the 1990s.
- The popular form of 'e-learning' really began to become established in the mid-to-late 1990s when more learning organizations became connected to the World Wide Web.

Online orientation

For some learners, particularly those who may have been out of formal education for some time, the use of computer-based technology may seem a bit bewildering at first and possibly a little intimidating. The message to those students is: DO NOT PANIC!

Most online learning environments (sometimes referred to as Virtual Learning Environments) are easy to use once you have been given an introduction. In fact, an effective learning environment should, by definition, be fairly user-friendly. Getting up to speed with online learning mainly involves getting used to various processes like how to:

- log in
- open and download files
- participate in things like discussion boards
- send email.

Try to think about the process of getting to know your way around online learning environments in a similar way to how you would approach getting to know a real, physical place.

Often your institution will put supporting documentation online which is designed to help you do most of the things that you need to do in virtual learning environments. If you know the name of the learning environment that your institution uses, you could also try searching for guidance or help sheets yourself (e.g. Blackboard, WebCT, Moodle, Sakai and others).

What Sort of Technologies Might You Be Using?

Today, e-learning or 'technology enhanced learning' implies more than the use of computers to access learning materials and online learning environments. More and more opportunities are becoming available to use technology within learning contexts. It is possible that you will encounter all or some of the technologies described in Table 5.1 during your social work course, but also in years to come when you are engaged in post-qualifying education and professional development.

TABLE 5.1 An overview of learning technologies

Learning technology	*What it is typically used for*	*Examples*
Virtual Learning Environment (VLE)	• Accessing electronic lecture notes and resources. • Communicating with students and lecturers via email, discussion boards and chat tools. • Completing online assessments. • Submitting assignments and receiving assignment marks.	• Blackboard • WebCT • Moodle • Sakai
Social networking	• Forming specific interest groups or online networks of people. • Socialising and making new friends/contacts. • Sharing digital photographs or music files. • Blogging.	• Facebook • Bebo • MySpace • Ning
Blog (short for 'weblog')	• A blog is a type of website that allow users to keep an online journal or diary. • Blogs may be focused on specific interests (e.g. digital photography, politics, e-learning) or they may be more like a personal diary. • 'Bloggers' are people who write blogs. • Blogs are often used in education for reflective journal work.	• Blogger • Wordpress • LiveJournal • Twitter
Wiki (from a Hawaiian word meaning 'quick')	• Wikis are websites (or web pages) which allow anybody to edit the content of the site. • Wikis are collaboratively written by a potentially unlimited number of people, with the theory being that this ensures that they will be accurate and up to date. • You may be aware of one of the most popular examples of a wiki site which is 'Wikipedia' – an online encyclopedia where anybody can change an update the subject entries. • Wikis are often used in education to support group work and peer collaboration.	• Wikipedia • Wikiversity
Podcasts	• Similar to short 'radio' programmes they are 'broadcast' online. • They usually consist of audio files (can be video in which case they are known as vodcasts) which users can download onto mp3 players, computers and other mobile devices. • Users can subscribe to podcasts which allows them to download a new podcast episode automatically. • Podcasts are often used within education to make audio lectures available to students.	• Institute for Research and Innovation in Social Services Podcast (IRISS)
Immersive environments	• Simulated three dimensional environments allow users to interact with the environment and other users using 'avatars' (similar to character in computer games). • You can normally control your avatars' movements and actions. • In some immersive environments, you can create your own resources (even create a new house), set up a virtual business or even attend virtual lectures and seminars. • Some colleges and universities have set up their own campuses in immersive environments such as 'Second Life ' and some are using them for learning and teaching.	• Second Life

How Will E-learning Be Used?

You will almost certainly find that e-learning is used to some extent on your social work course. You may be a work-based learner who is required to complete a lot of their independent learning online or you may simply be a student who is attending an institution that has invested a lot in terms of developing methods of online learning. E-learning approaches can, if designed appropriately, be much more accessible for students with disabilities.

Blended learning

Many courses will follow a pattern of 'blended learning' which mixes the use of face-to-face and e-learning, based on their respective strengths and weaknesses. For instance, you may be required to attend a lecture on campus but may then be set the task of discussing some of the issues arising from the lecture in online, group discussion forums. Or you may be required to attend a seminar which provides guidance on a group work assessment and then work with a group of others to create a collaborative, wiki-based resource. You might then be required to attend another face-to-face seminar during which you and your group present your findings to the rest of the student group.

Effective Use of Online Learning Environments

Your institution will usually provide some kind of induction into the use of their online learning environment. This may be in the form of a demonstration, help sheet, practical session in a PC lab or a combination of any of these.

Quick Tip: Preparing for online learning

When you first begin to use online learning environments, it is important that:

- you are clear about how you would access the learning environment both on and off campus (if you have access to a computer with internet access off campus):
  - o Do you need to use a particular web address to get to the login page?
  - o Do you know what your username and password are?

(Continued)

- you check to see if you can access things from off-campus without any difficulties (sometimes browser cookie settings can prevent you from accessing virtual learning environments).
- you know who to contact if you are having any technical difficulties:
  - What is the telephone number or email address of your institution's IT support desk?
  - What are the opening hours for the IT support desk?

If your course is likely to involve a significant number of e-learning activities, it would be a good idea to think about what kinds of computing resources are available for you to use.

Box 5.1 reflection point

Computer access issues to consider

- If you already own a computer or are able to negotiate access to a computer within your home, you may find that getting access is not a problem.
- If you have a computer that is shared amongst several members of your family, or any other people who may live with you, you may need to think about the likely availability of it.
- If you have children who need to use the computer for homework or recreation, you might consider likely times of the day or evening when they will not be using it.
- If you are making use of both a computer at home and computers on campus, bear in mind that you may be using slightly different versions of the software. This becomes particularly important in relation to any work that you produce on a machine off-campus that you later need to present using a university machine (e.g. PowerPoint presentation).

Quick Tip: Software compatibility issues

If you have any concerns about whether the software that you use on an 'off-campus' computer is compatible with 'on-campus' computers, check with your departmental or institutional computing support officers.

Using on-campus computing facilities

Many institutions have some PC labs that are available on campus on a 24-hour access basis. You should make sure you know what is available early on in your course so that if you need to rely on the institution's facilities, you will know exactly where to go and when you can access them.

These facilities tend to be in heavy demand around the time of assignment hand-in dates and exams. If you do intend to rely on your institution's computing resources, think about some of the practicalities, such as:

- How do you intend to save your work? You may be given an allocation of storage space on the institution's servers which is normally accessed by logging into your institution's computer network. USB memory sticks and flash drives come in a range of sizes and can often be a convenient way of saving your work. Remember to **always back your work up** (in other words, take a copy of your work) just in case you lose or damage a USB memory stick.
- If you are intending to work late on campus, think about issues of personal safety, particularly in relation to travelling to and from the campus. Contact your Student Union if necessary to see if they operate a 'Safety Bus' service.
- You may consider buying a computer to help you with your studies. Laptop computers are becoming increasingly cheaper and the cost of investing in a computer might be offset against the travel expenses incurred through having to travel to the campus several times a week.

It is certainly possible to get through a course without buying a computer yourself but there can be some serious drawbacks to relying on institutional computing facilities, such as:

- not always being able to find a 'free' computer
- noisy computing labs
- a lack of flexibility.

Some institutions run schemes which loan laptops to students for the duration of their studies, but this does involve a rental fee. If you are interested in this type of scheme, contact your institution's IT support desk or helpline.

Doing Research Online

The World Wide Web (WWW) has made it much easier for students to search for materials to help them research topics that relate to their assignments. However, most people have developed a fairly simplistic way of using WWW search engines which often means that search results can run into the tens of thousands, making it seem impossible to pick out something that is genuinely relevant and useful. Most people's solution to this problem is to just 'go with something' that appears on the first page of results. However, this is not the smartest way of using the web for academic study. So:

- How do you cut through the seemingly endless list of web results in order to find something that might be more useful to your assignment research?
- How can you tell what is a source of quality information and what is biased, unsupported and subjective?

This section will outline some of the practical ways in which you can begin to develop and hone your web-searching skills.

Becoming an 'advanced' web searcher

Almost all search engines (such as 'Google', 'Yahoo', 'MSN LiveSearch') will allow you to click on a link that takes you to some **advanced search** options. Just look for a link that says something like '**Advanced**' or '**Advanced Search**'.

Did You Know?

Advanced searching will often allow you to do most of the following:

- **Include specific words** – the search engine will only return results for pages that contain all of the words you specify e.g. social *and* exclusion.
- **Search for an exact word or phrase** – only pages that contain the exact word or phrase will be returned in your search results. For instance, you might need results that contained the phrase 'domestic violence' rather than the separate words 'domestic' and 'violence'.
- **Exclude words from the search** – this is often a way of narrowing down your search if you notice that you get lots of irrelevant results.
- **Search for particular file types** – for instance, you can restrict your search to only look at PDF files or Word documents.

From search engines to subject gateways

Search engines are the tool of choice for most people when it comes to searching for information and resources on the web. However, there is another breed of website known as a 'subject gateway' that can be particularly useful to students and researchers (Dolowitz et al., 2008). In order to appreciate why, it is useful to briefly consider how most search engines work.

Did You Know? How search engines work

- Most search engines use programmes called 'spiders' or 'robots' to automatically trawl around the web and bring back details of new web pages and sites that have been created.
- When you get results back from a search engine, there has been no attempt to identify quality sources of information from the wealth of commercially driven, or downright bizarre, resources that are also out there on the web.
- Search engines do a very good job of cataloguing new pages on the web, but do not attempt to do any 'quality control' of what is useful, reliable, up to date and so on.

By contrast, subject gateways:

- bring together a range of specially selected resources that all relate to a particular subject area – they are intended as a guided way into a particular subject area.
- are like specialized online directories and search engines rolled into one.
- contain resources which are specifically selected by subject specialists.

Example: **Subject Gateway**

For students studying on social work courses, a really good example of a subject gateway is 'Intute: Social Sciences', which can be found at the following web address: http://www.intute.ac.uk/socialsciences/

When to use the search box and when to use the subject headings

In general, you would probably use the search box if you already had a pretty good idea of the particular topic that you wanted to search on. So, if you were asked to complete an essay on the factors that may contribute towards social exclusion, you might begin by typing the words '**social exclusion**' into the search box. This would allow you to quickly identify what specific resources were available on this topic. However, if you were about to begin a module or unit with the title 'Social Welfare and Social Provision', and you wanted to find out more about the kinds of things that this might involve, you could use the topic browsing lists to help you get a broad overview of the topic.

Assessing the quality of online resources

Whilst subject gateways, such as Intute, can provide really useful starting points for research, there will obviously still be occasions where you need to search more broadly. In these cases, you will need to exercise your own judgement as to whether something is a quality online source of information or not. The reason that you need to take much more care with online resources is that, unlike with books and journals, literally anyone can publish more or less what they want online.

Academic books and journal articles usually go through a process of **peer review**, which means that:

- Suitably qualified experts or professionals in the field review the quality of material and make constructive suggestions, before it even gets into print.
- Although we may not agree with everything that is written in academic books and journals, we can be fairly confident that the material has been properly prepared and researched.

Compare this with the material that might be presented on someone's personal blog site. This may reflect someone's own personal beliefs and opinions but is unlikely to be backed up with research and evidence (unless the blogger is very conscientious or a professional researcher). But even in this case, if the material is posted to a blog site, you can be certain that no kind of peer-review process has taken place.

activity 5.1

Criteria for assessing the quality of information

Think of at least five features that you could look for in order to gauge the quality or reliability of material that you find on the web. Note these five features down in the space below:

1
2
3
4
5

Now that you have got something to help you evaluate online sources of information, try to apply these criteria in relation to the following web resources (or find a selection of your own sites):

1. Social Care Online – better knowledge for better practice
   http://www.scie-socialcareonline.org.uk/
2. Political correctness – the awful truth (Children)
   http://www.politicallyincorrect.me.uk/children.htm
3. National Children's Bureau
   http://www.ncb.org.uk/

activity 5.2

Internet for Social Work Tutorial

Go back to the '**Intute: Social Sciences**' web page (http://www.intute.ac.uk/socialsciences/) and then:

1. In the left-hand menu of options, there is a link called 'Virtual Training Suite'. Select this link to access a new page with a list of tutorials.
2. Look for the link called 'Social Worker' and select it.
3. This should take you to a tutorial called 'Internet for Social Work'.

(If you have problems, you can try this direct link which was current when this book was written: http://www.vts.intute.ac.uk/he/tutorial/social-worker)

Complete this tutorial – you may find that you wish to complete it in separate 'sittings' as it does involve quite a lot of reading from the screen. The tutorial itself is divided into four main sections:

1. **Tour** – gives an overview of the social work and social care resources that are available online.
2. **Discover** – helps you to hone your web-searching skills.
3. **Judge** – encourages you to be more critical and discerning in respect of online information.
4. **Success** – gives case examples of how social work students, lecturers, service-users and carers make productive use of the Internet.

Independent Learning Online

How do you manage your learning online?

Many students, and even some tutors, assume that online learning is basically the same as more traditional, face-to-face methods, but is simply engaged with

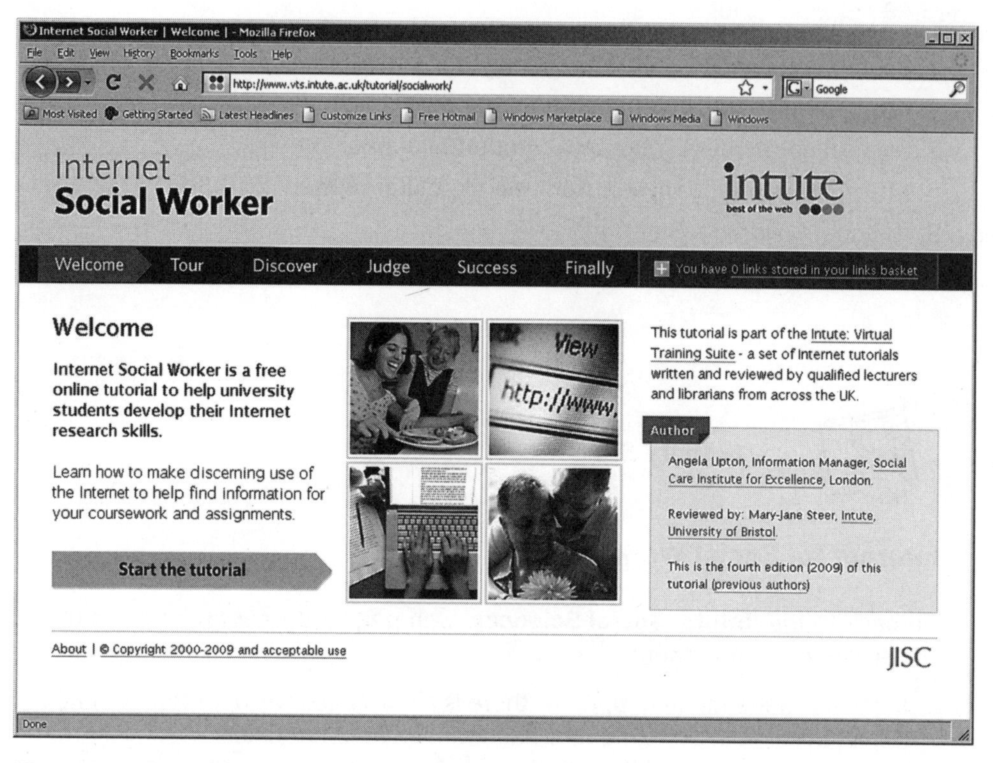

Figure 5.1 Screenshot of Internet Social Worker Tutorial used by permission of Resource Discovery Network (RDN)

in a different way using a computer and an Internet connection. For some students, it can be very difficult to remain motivated when studying online. There is always the potential distraction of:

- countless other websites
- engaging in online chat
- instant messaging with friends or family
- listening to online radio or watching online television.

There is going to be nobody standing over you pointing out that you are supposed to be writing an essay about child development or participating in a course-related online discussion board. Although you may find that your tutor provides prompts and support to help facilitate your online learning, it will be largely up to you how you choose to respond to these. The circumstances of online learning and the greater degree of freedom and flexibility can encourage some learners to view it as being much more informal. They may begin to assume that what happens online is not all that important or does not really matter. In those circumstances, it is not surprising that they may begin to lose interest and not fully engage with it.

Box 5.2 reflection point

Remaining focused and engaged with online learning

Think carefully about the following:

- Is the online element a key part of the course delivery?
  - If so, which aspects of the work done online are either formatively or summatively assessed?
  - Which parts do you need to actively prioritize?
- What kinds of tutor guidelines have been issued in terms of levels of participation?
  - Make sure you know what is expected of you and if you are not clear, seek clarification from your course tutors.
- Think about how you will incorporate online learning activity into your own personal study timetable (see Chapter 3 for study timetables)?
  - When and where will you be able to access a computer in order to complete the work?
  - Do you need to be online all the time, or is it possible to work offline, perhaps using a word-processor, and then later copy and paste your work into the learning environment?
  - If you have access to a computer at home, when will be the best time for you to access and use that computer?
- Set your own personal online learning goals. These should relate specifically to the learning tasks and activities that you are being required to complete.
  - Make a plan based on these requirements and check things off as you complete them.
  - For instance, you might set a goal to overcome your inhibitions about posting something to an online discussion board because of your worries about your spelling and grammar skills.
  - Practical ways of achieving this might be to spell-check your work beforehand using your word-processing software, ensuring that you proofread your work (possibly with the assistance of proofreading software) or getting a trusted friend to read over your work before posting it.
- Be clear about the difference between 'work time' online and 'leisure time' online.
  - If you have logged on in order to complete an online learning activity, try to remain focused on the task, even if that involves reading and searching for information on other websites.
  - If you are someone who likes to have multiple windows open at the same time (e.g. email, a social networking site and an instant messaging window), is this likely to impede your concentration?

Responsibility

Many people are familiar with the experience of losing a sense of inhibition whilst working online as we feel that we are in some way distanced or protected from the situation. Things sometimes do not 'feel' as real or immediate when we are online, even if we are using some form of real-time communication such as online chat or video chat. The consequence of this is that we may sometimes behave in ways which we would not dream of doing in a face-to-face situation.

We have all probably had the experience of sending a hastily typed email, full of raw emotion, which we may have regretted sending in retrospect? We may have criticized or ridiculed something or someone in the 'heat of the moment' or perhaps been downright rude or offensive?

For you, as social work students, there is clearly an additional responsibility in terms of behaving in a professional manner and this does not magically disappear when it comes to online interaction. This not only involves being mindful of the rights and diversity of your peers but also involves thinking about the use of anti-oppressive forms of language and participation. Remember, 'bullying' and 'harrassment' are not just things that take place offline.

Things that you do or 'say' online tend to remain available for other people to access long after the point at which your interaction or participation occurred. In other words, a hasty comment made verbally may cause some temporary upset and embarrassment – but is often soon forgotten. This is not the case with upsetting or rash comments that are made in online environments.

Box 5.3 reflection point

Online etiquette and ethics

- Is it really appropriate to post intimate details of your personal life within a course-related discussion board (unless of course this is part of a particular activity where this level of disclosure might be appropriate)?
- Is it appropriate to make judgements or assertions about the behaviour or conduct of others?
- Is it appropriate to discuss specific, personal details of service-users?
- If you want to take issue with or question something that has been posted online, are there ways of doing so without making it seem like a personal attack or provocation?

- Is it appropriate to engage in a dispute or squabble with another course colleague in a semi-public online, learning environment?
- Are there times when one-to-one email communication is a more appropriate vehicle for discussion, than semi-public discussion boards and forums?

As Gregor (2006) notes, there are various ethical issues and dilemmas raised by the increased use of computing systems to record personal data, particularly in relation to social work practice.

Clarke (2008: 6) condenses many of the points raised above into a list of six qualities required for successful online learning:

1. Confidence
2. Positive attitude to learning
3. Self-motivation
4. Good communication skills
5. Willingness to collaborate, share and work with others
6. Confidence in using ICTs

Acting professionally online (managing your identity online)

As more and more people are using websites and online services for professional, social and entertainment purposes, it is important to bear in mind that each of us is creating a 'digital footprint'.

Did You Know? Digital footprints are ...

the records or 'traces' of the things that we have been doing online, whether that is:

- posting photographs of our holiday in Spain
- blogging about the latest Star Trek film
- uploading the fruits of our latest karaoke efforts on a MySpace page
- engaging in heated political debates on open discussion forums
- other types of professional and social online activity.

An increasing number of employers are using web searching as a means of checking out potential employees. You can check your own digital footprint by entering your name into a search engine and checking what kinds of results are returned.

Quick Tip: Managing your online identity

- Be thoughtful and careful about the kinds of information that you make available about yourself online.
- Many people do not think twice about including their date of birth, address and phone number on online profiles, despite the fact that this is precisely the kind of information used by identity thieves.
- Beware of email requests to confirm details of passwords and bank accounts – most organizations will have a clear policy about never approaching customers in this way.

In the workplace, there are additional considerations around the use of the Internet and email and you should make sure that you are clear about your organization's policy in relation to this. Think carefully before forwarding on funny or humourous emails, particularly if you recognize that certain types of humour may cause offence. Forwarding on material which could be considered to be discriminatory is clearly unacceptable. Also, be sceptical and questioning about the kind of information that is sent to you, especially in unsolicited emails.

Did You Know? Hoax Emails

- Common email hoaxes or scams try to encourage people to part with money or personal data.
- Some create unnecessary fear around issues such as personal safety through hoax accounts of car-jackings, muggings and worse.
- Websites such as **www.hoax-slayer.com** and **www.snopes.com** can help in identifying hoax and scam email.

If you receive offensive email through your work email account, you should always make sure that you report this to your employer. This will help your organization to block such email in the future but also makes it clear that you did not solicit or wish to receive such offensive material.

Online Collaboration and Group Work

Some universities are beginning to make use of e-learning methods to help students to work together and collaborate on aspects of their learning (Clarke, 2008). The following case study gives you a flavour of the way in which this has been done within the context of social work education in our own institution. You may find that some similar approaches are used within your institution.

Example: **Case Study 1 – Use of online discussion boards to support group work on a 'Working in Organizations' module, as part of a BSc in Social Work course.**

As part of this module, first-year social work students were required to work together in groups to investigate a particular problem. The importance of this activity was that they had an opportunity to come together and work as a group, and the learning was mainly focused on how the group dynamics worked, rather than the group's progress in terms of solving their problem.

The groups had a 12-week period in which to complete this project and they were given an online group discussion space within which to work. They were told that they could use their own discussion spaces in any way that they thought was most suitable to achieving their aims. At the end of the 12-week period, the students were required to give a group presentation based on how they how worked together as a group. They were expected to draw on evidence from their group discussion boards in order to illustrate their presentations.

The groups reported that they found this to be a very useful way of being able to keep track of their progress. They were able to record minutes of face-to-face group meetings in the discussion space and were also able to use it to clarify decisions and further action points. Many of the groups reported that they sometimes found it hard to meet face to face because their group members came from all parts of the region and often had commitments outside of formal university teaching, including family and childcare commitments.

activity 5.3

Discussion board collaboration

With reference to the case study outlined above, try to answer the following:

- What advantages do you think there are in working with other group members in online spaces?
- What kinds of skills do you think you would need to use as an individual to ensure that you participated fully in this kind of activity?
- What kinds of difficulties or problems do you think might crop up in this kind of situation? How could those difficulties be resolved?

E-assessment

Some institutions are using e-assessment methods which can include:

- online testing
- assessment of online activities, for example discussion board comments, wiki contributions or blog entries
- e-portfolios.

At the very least, many institutions are now requiring students to submit assessed work electronically, most usually through the virtual learning environment. As part of this process, assignments may be fed through an electronic plagiarism detection service such as TurnitinUK. This software compares the work that has been submitted by students against a vast database of electronic sources and previous student submissions from institutions across the United Kingdom, in order to help identify any instances of copying or plagiarism. If electronic submission is being used, it is also common for tutors to return grades and feedback electronically.

Your institution will prepare you for any methods of e-assessment that are being used on your social work course.

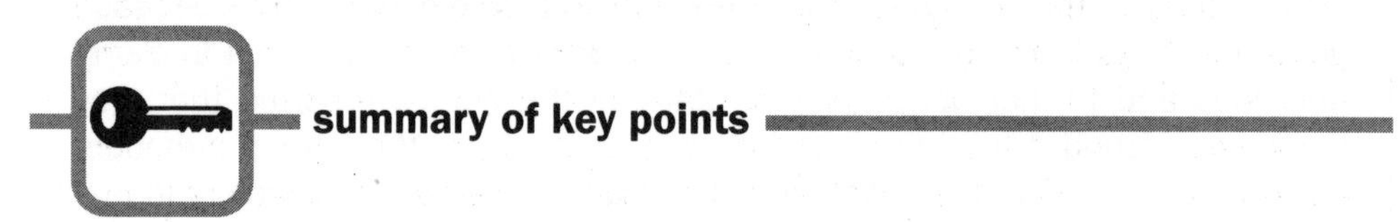

summary of key points

- E-learning is used in a variety of ways on social work courses and will probably be focused on the use of a virtual learning environment.
- There is a wealth of research material and learning resources on the WWW but you need to be discriminating about the kinds of information that you find there. Online material is rarely peer-reviewed.
- Skills required to be an effective e-learner include managing your own learning, remaining motivated and retaining focus.
- You may be required to engage in online collaboration or e-assessment (including use of plagiarism detection software).

useful resources

The following document is really useful as it contains real-life accounts of four social work students' experiences of online learning:

SWAP (2007) *Does online learning work for you? Student Case Study Competition Entries*. [online]. Available at: http://www.swap.ac.uk/docs/eltep_studentcase studies.pdf

Internet for Social Workers Tutorial
http://www.vts.intute.ac.uk/he/tutorial/social-worker

Internet Detective Tutorial
http://www.vts.intute.ac.uk/detective/

Social Care Institute for Excellence (SCIE) e-learning resources
http://www.scie.org.uk/publications/elearning/

This provides interactive learning materials on the following topics:

- Series 1: Law and social work
- Series 2: An introduction to the mental health of older people
- Series 3: Poverty, parenting and social exclusion
- Series 4: Children of prisoners
- Series 5: An introduction to residential childcare
- Series 6: Communication skills

Learning Exchange Open Search. Available at: http://www.iriss.ac.uk/openlx/
This is the IRISS's digital library of learning objects relating to social work education and social services. It provides a search box to allow users to enter search terms.

Open Learning (OU). Available at: http://openlearn.open.ac.uk/
This is the Open University's bank of freely accessible learning materials. It contains tutorials and learning packages on social care subjects and study skills.

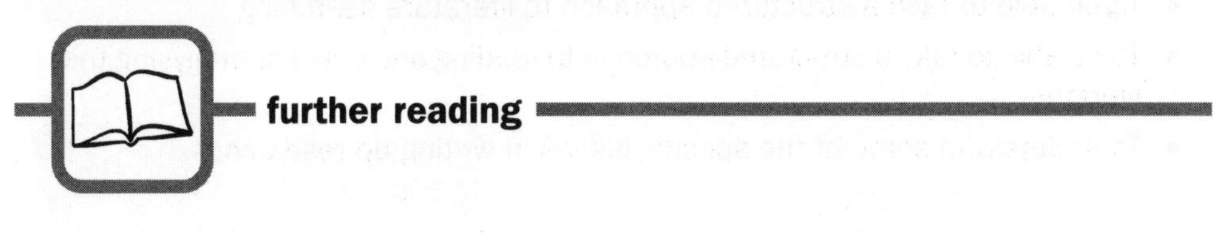

Clarke, A. (2008) *E-learning Skills*. Basingstoke: Palgrave Macmillan.
Dolowitz, D., Buckler, S. and Sweeney, F. (2008) *Researching Online*. Basingstoke: Palgrave Macmillan.
Santy, J. and Smith, L. (2007) *Being an E-learner in Health and Social Care*. Abingdon: Routledge.

6

Researching, Reading and Critiquing

learning objectives

- To understand what research is and why it is significant in the study of social work.
- To recognize the basic types of research approach.
- To develop your skills in reviewing the literature for essays, assignments and research projects or dissertations.
- To be able to take a structured approach to literature searching.
- To be able to take a structured approach to reading and critically analysing the literature.
- To understand some of the specific issues in writing up research.

What is Research?

Good question! In a broad sense, research can be described as:

> *a 'planned, cautious, systematic and reliable way of finding out something or deepening understanding'* (Fink, 1998: 5).

So the key idea here is that:

Research helps us to find out more about things ...

– in order words, as Fink says, it helps us to *deepen our understanding*.

But, as Fink suggests, the way that we go about developing this 'new' or 'deeper' understanding is key to the research process. So, for example:

- The fact that research is planned and cautious should alert us to the fact that it is something more than just waffling on about our pet theories or promoting our own biased points of view.
- If research involves finding a systematic and reliable way of trying to deepen understanding or create new knowledge, then there is an idea that it should be able to stand up to critical analysis and review.

One of the ways in which researchers aim to be systematic about their research is to identify a **research methodology** before they begin their research project.

Quick Definition: Research methodology

This is the approach, methods and strategies employed in collecting data and carrying out the research process.

Research carried out within the social sciences tends to:

- involve direct work with other human beings
- focus on issues that are relevant to people and society.

The main stages of research are:

1. Establishing the research question or topic

During this first stage, the researcher focuses on defining exactly what it is that she is wanting to research. Often a question or hypothesis is used to help to narrow the focus.

2. Carrying out a literature review

A literature review is basically a critical summary of what has previously been published on the topic under consideration. Literature reviews help to establish:

- what is already known
- what is still to be explored
- where significant gaps exist
- what has worked in terms of previous research approaches (... and what has not!).

3. Data collection

Researchers can use a variety of methods to collect raw data including:

- questionnaires
- interviews
- focus groups
- case studies
- participant observation.

4. Data analysis

This is a period of analysis during which the researcher:

- considers all of the material that she has collected
- attempts to understand or interpret the data.

5. Writing up findings

The researcher will usually write up her findings in the form of an article, report or dissertation. She will also come to some kind of conclusion based on the available evidence. For instance, the results may suggest that:

- there is a need to do things differently in the future (e.g. new practices or procedures)
- further research needs to be carried out
- the situation is more complicated than was initially suspected.

How is Research Relevant to Your Course?

During your social work course, you will regularly be asked to look at the research that has been done by others in relation to a particular topic. This will form some of the background reading and research that you will need to do in order to successfully complete your assignments. Many of the research papers that you read will mention the different stages of the research process described above.

Projects and Dissertations

You may also be required to undertake a research project or dissertation yourself based on your own particular interest in the field of social work. If you are a student on a masters level social work course, it is more likely that you will be asked to complete a dissertation, and possibly undertake a research methods module to prepare you to do this. You will usually be expected to demonstrate how you have addressed issues of research ethics, and in some cases you may need to submit a request for ethical approval to your school or faculty's research ethics group.

Did You Know? Research ethics

- Research ethics are about ensuring that any research that you are involved in is well thought-out in relation to any ethical issues that may arise during the research process.
- Institutions and faculties often have their own Research Ethics Panel which considers proposals for new research projects from an ethics standpoint.
- Some of the key principles of ethical research are:
  - Research must avoid harming participants (including researchers).
  - Research participants must be fully informed about the intended uses and outcomes of research, and must be clear about what their involvement entails including any possible risks. This ensures that they can give 'informed consent' to take part.
  - Participation is on a voluntary basis and participants are clearly informed that they have the right to withdraw at any stage.
  - Confidentiality and anonymity should be safeguarded.
  - Research should be well designed, independent and quality ensured.

Quantitative and Qualitative Research

There are two broad types of research method which you will regularly come across during your social work education:

Did You Know? Quantitative approaches

- **Quantitative** research tends to focus on data which can be measured in some way (or quantified).
- This type of research approach usually seeks to establish some kind of objective, measurable statements about the world.

Example: Roni asks service-users of a local youth club to complete a questionnaire which asks them to rate their satisfaction with the services they access. After having collected the questionnaires and analysing the data, she is in a position to state that:

- 76% of service-users felt the service that they received was 'very good'.

Did You Know? Qualitative approaches

Qualitative research tends to focus on data which allows the researcher to explore people's:

- views
- attitudes
- beliefs
- emotional responses
- 'lived experience'

in relation to the research topic/question.
Qualitative data collection methods include:

- in-depth interviews
- focus groups
- personal accounts.

This type of approach is generally far less concerned with asserting quantifiable, objective statements about things, but much more interested in investigating the subjective experiences of people.

Example: Omar researches asylum-seekers' experiences of racism and discrimination. He does this by:

- conducting 10 in-depth interviews with asylum-seekers
- transcribing the interviews into a written format
- analysing the interview transcripts for common themes.

He presents his findings in the format of a written report which uses quotes from the interviews in order to support the main findings.

Sometimes researchers use a range of both quantitative and qualitative research approaches which is known as a '**mixed-methods**' approach.

Searching the Literature

Did You Know? What is a 'literature search'?

Gash describes a literature search as being 'a systematic and thorough search of all types of published literature in order to identify as many items as possible that are relevant to a particular topic' (2000: 1, cited by Ridley, 2008).

Systematic searches

- 'Systematic' means doing something in a planned, structured and organized kind of way (Oxford Reference Dictionary).
- This tends to rule out the way that most of us search for things, especially when we are online, plucking random words out of the air in the hope that we will eventually hit on the 'right' combination of words at some point.

Thorough searches

- A **thorough** search means applying attention to detail and aiming for completeness.
- We are not being thorough if we only look at the first page of results from a search engine, following some links but not others, based on fairly non-existent criteria.

The range of literature

- This means that we should not just restrict ourselves to only looking at books *or* only looking at journals *or* only looking at conference proceedings – consider the full range.
- Quality information sources tend to come from academic research and professional reports and studies – so focus on these kinds of areas.

Relevant searches

- Keep it focused and relevant.

Example: If you were carrying out a literature review on the **recent provision** of **statutory services** in the **United Kingdom**, for **adults** with **learning difficulties**, then gathering research resources on *voluntary services* for *children* with *physical disabilities*, in *America*, during the *1960s*, would clearly be of very limited value.

Box 6.1 reflection point

Research and relevance

- It is not always easy to find relevant information but then in many ways this is the point of research.
- If the 'answer' to your research question was glaringly obvious from the start, then there would not really be much point in doing any research into that topic!
- Research, by its very nature, involves:
  - looking, searching, scrutinizing
  - uncovering, revealing, exposing
  - detecting, probing, analysing
  - explaining, discussing, summarizing ... and so on.
- All of the above takes time! This is often why students struggle when they leave assignments until the last minute.

The Six-step Search Strategy

If you want to make sure that you do a thorough and systematic search, you will need to put together some kind of **search strategy**. This should help you to:

- carry out the search in a planned and considered way
- give yourself the best possible chance of finding relevant, quality information.

The left-hand column of Figure 6.1, headed '**Search Stages**', shows the different stages of the search and these are numbered from 1–6. The central column headed '**Tools & Resources**' gives you an indication of the resources that you should expect to be using in order to carry out each of the stages.

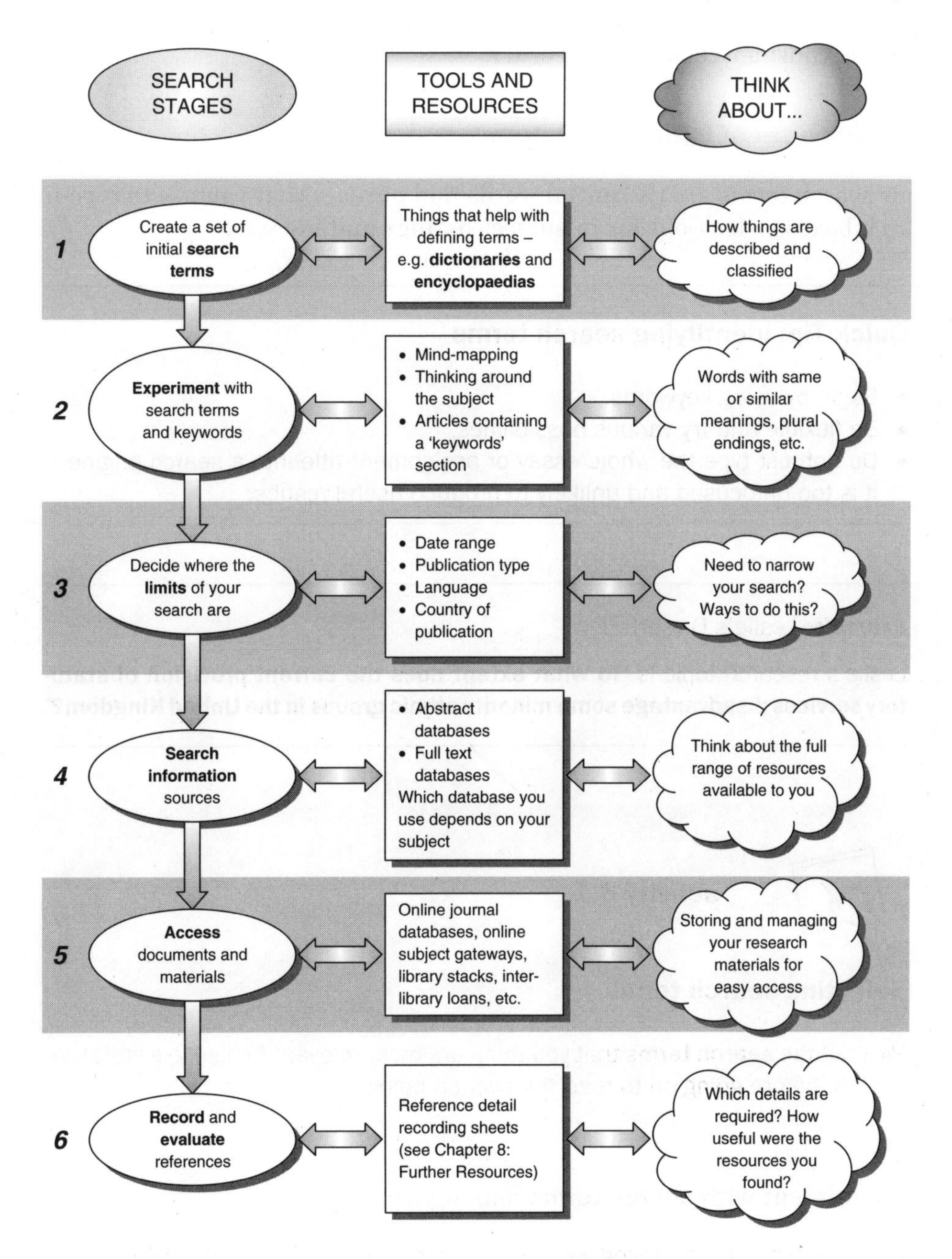

Figure 6.1 Flow chart showing the process of doing a literature search

Finally, the right-hand column, headed **'Think About ...'**, flags up the kinds of things you should aim to think about at each stage.

Let us consider each stage in order:

1. Create a set of initial search terms

Your search terms are the initial words and phrases that you use to type into search boxes or look out for in subject listings and indexes.

Quick Tip: Identifying search terms

- Begin by using keywords.
- Be flexible and try various possibilities.
- Do not just type the whole essay or assignment title into a search engine – it is too unfocused and unlikely to produce useful results.

Example: Leslie's Dissertation

Leslie's research topic is **'To what extent does the current provision of statutory services disadvantage some minority ethnic groups in the United Kingdom?'**

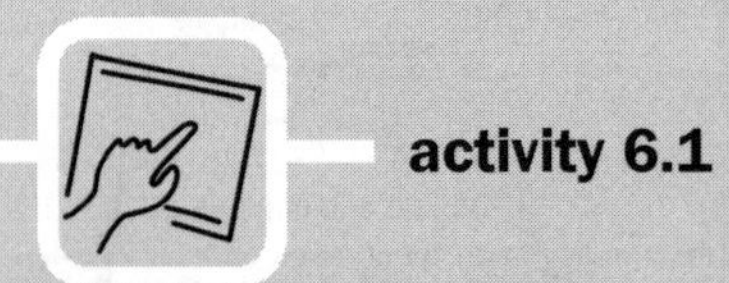

Selecting search terms

Pick out the **search terms** that you think are most relevant for Leslie's literature search, before going on to read the section below.

2. Experiment with search terms and keywords

- Try to think about varying your initial search terms by thinking of as many other words as possible which have the same or similar meanings (e.g. try 'BME' or 'ethnic minority' as well as 'minority ethnic').
- Think about using both the singular and plural versions of words (e.g. minority, minorities).
- You could identify a series of keywords by just writing a list on a piece of paper, or try using visual tools such as 'mind-maps' or 'spider diagrams'.

activity 6.2

Generating keywords for literature searching

Using the earlier example of Leslie's project title ('To what extent does the current provision of statutory services disadvantage some minority ethnic groups in the United Kingdom'):

1 Identify what you think the **keywords** are in Leslie's title and list these below.
2 Think of *at least* **three alternative words** that could be used in place of the broad search terms you identified in step 1. These should be words that mean the same or similar things.

Compare your list of keywords that you came up with in response to Leslie's research topic with a suggested keyword list in Table 6.4: Leslie's keyword and key phrase list, which is at the end of this chapter.

Wildcards

Some words can have a variety of different endings, e.g. child, child's, children, childcare. To avoid having to search for all of these variations, you can make use of something called a *wildcard* search to make the process easier.

Quick Tip: Wildcard searches

If we take the word 'child', and add the wildcard character *, the search engine we use will look for any words which begin with the root word 'child', e.g.:

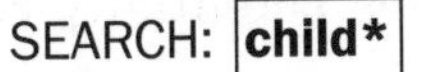

If we ran this search, it would pick up results which include the word 'child' or words that begin with 'child' such as 'child**ren**', 'child**ren's**', 'Child**line**', 'child**like**', etc. Try this out for yourself using the 'Intute: Social Sciences' website search facility.

3. Decide where the limits of your search are

Students sometimes struggle when doing their literature search because they cannot seem to find anything relevant. Sometimes the opposite is the case and they become overwhelmed by the sheer volume of search results.

In this case, you may need to think about consciously limiting your search:

Table 6.1 Techniques for limiting searches

Range of Dates	• Is your search currently including information sources which are out of date? • Aim to access research published within the last 5 years if possible.
Range of publications	• Are you considering too broad a range of publications or documents? • Have you considered focusing your search on particular social work or social policy journals, or using a subject gateway web site like 'Intute: Social Sciences'?
Country of publication	• Are you getting a lot of results returned which focus on countries other than the United Kingdom? If so think about extending your keywords to include 'UK' or 'United Kingdom' or 'British' etc. • There are differences in the kind of terminology that is used in different countries. For instance, the term 'handicapped' is still used in the USA whereas 'disabled' is the term more commonly used in the UK.

You should make sure that you have completed stages 1 and 2, before beginning to limit your search.

4. Search information sources

This is the stage where you really get stuck in with the process of searching for relevant literature. Think about:

- **primary sources** (a primary source is something that provides raw research data and could be something like local authority statistics, results from a questionnaire, transcripts from interviews, case study material)
- **secondary sources** (pieces of work which provide discussion or commentary on primary research data)
- **peer-reviewed academic journals** (these contain more cutting-edge and up-to-date research than books, as the publishing process is quicker)
- **books** (including electronic books)
- **reference resources** such as dictionaries, encyclopaedias or specialized glossaries (an example of a specialist glossary is included at the end of this book).

When using electronic database services to search for potentially relevant journal articles, try to make effective use of **abstracts**.

Did You Know? Abstracts

An **abstract**:

- appears at the beginning of an article or piece of research
- is a summary of the key arguments, ideas, principles, approaches and findings that are examined in an academic article or piece of published research
- is a quick way of discovering if the article or research is relevant to your topic; or not – if it seems relevant, then go on to read the entire article or report.

Library resources

Your institutional library will have a specialist academic librarian (or possibly a team of academic librarians) who focus on particular subject areas. They may be able to make some constructive suggestions about alternative ways that you could search the library databases or carry out your online searches.

> **Quick Tip: Links with other subjects**
>
> A lot of research these days tends to be interdisciplinary and your research topic could have links with other subjects as well as with social work. For example, think about:
>
> - health
> - psychology
> - sociology
> - law
> - counselling
> - anthropology
> - cultural studies
> - human geography etc.

5. Access documents and materials

Clearly, many of the resources described in stage 4 are available for you to access electronically using a computer with Internet access. Your institution will make you aware of any systems provided for this purpose, and the username and password you would need to use in order to access them.

If you find that a book looks like it is potentially very useful, but it is not part of your institutional library's book stock, you can always think about putting in a **Inter-Library Loan** request.

Table 6.2 Other useful online resources

Name of Resource	*Features*
Google Scholar http://scholar.google.co.uk	Provides access to a range of academic material including some journal articles, books and conference proceedings.
Google Books http://books.google.co.uk	Allows you to 'preview' parts of books, including contents and index pages. This helps to establish whether a book could be useful to you.

Did You Know? Inter-library loans

- Inter-library loans allow you to borrow books, or obtain copies of journal articles, that your library does not normally hold in its stock.
- There is usually a minimal fee for this service.
- It can sometimes take up to six weeks for inter-library book loans to become available so it is important that you check this out with an academic librarian well in advance.

6. Record and evaluate references

It is a really good idea to keep a record of your literature searching process. Some people find it easiest to do this in the form of a 'research diary'. This is simply an ongoing record of your progress as you move through the different stages of your research process.

Box 6.2 reflection point

Recording your research process

The kinds of things to think about are:

- What kinds of **keywords** did you identify?
- Which **online sources** did you use to search for materials?
  - Did they provide many useful results?
  - What could you try doing differently next time?
  - What ideas do you have for other resources that you might use to help with your search?
- What information do I need for my references? (e.g. author's surname and initial, date, title, place of publication and publishing company for a book)
  - Where will you record these details so that you can access them easily when you come to write your reference list?
- Did one set of references and resources lead you to more useful material?
- What lessons have you learnt about what is most effective when doing a literature search?

This kind of information can be extremely useful when it comes to writing up the methodology part of your research project.

The Snowball Technique

The 'snowball technique' is based on the idea that the more you begin to research your topic, the more you will begin to pick up additional ideas for other things to consider, and that this will create a 'snowball' effect.

Example: **The 'snowball technique' in action**

Mel is doing a literature review on how the social model of disability has helped to shape policy and legislation in relation to disability issues within the UK.

- She begins her search using her institution's electronic databases.
- She finds six articles that look like they will be relevant.

She skim-reads the abstracts for each of these six articles:

- She rejects three as they are looking at the situation in the USA (so are less useful). ☒
- One is from 1976 and focuses on the medical model of disability – she decides that this article is not relevant. ☒
- The remaining two articles are incredibly useful and provide her with a valuable insight into the social model of disability. ☑ She goes on to find that:
  - **The author of one of these two articles has an international reputation for writing on that particular topic**. She searches his name and finds he has written a book and three other articles on this topic. She makes a note to try to get hold of these. ☑
  - **Each article has approximately 25–30 references listed at the end in the references list** – at least 15 of these seem to relate to the topic she is researching. Of these 15 resources, she finds that 11 are available through the university library (some are on the shelves and others are available electronically). ☑
- Mel reads through these 11 new sources and realizes that:
  - Each of them has a reference list which contains, on average, two useful pointers to other articles, books and websites that she might consider (so in total that is 22 new possible leads). ☑
  - She is picking up even more clues as to who has written widely on her topic. ☑

So, to recap:

- Mel began with two useful articles, and through using the snowball technique, she found 11 additional sources and ended up with 22 new leads that she can follow up.

Box 6.3 reflection point

Start making snowballs!

The snowball technique can be as useful as experimenting with different search words, as Diana Ridley points out:

'... extending the scope of your reading by the snowball technique tends to be more common than key word searches as the research becomes more focused and the researcher becomes more familiar with the literature in the field' (Ridley, 2008: 40).

Table 6.3 Academic journals related to the study of social work

Journal Title	*Print Version*	*Electronic Version*
Age and Ageing	✓	✓
British Journal of Criminology	✓	✓
British Journal of Social Work	✓	✓
Community Care	✓	✓
Child and Family Social Work	✓	✓
Child Welfare Review	✓	
Critical Social Work	✓	✓
Health and Social Care in the Community	✓	✓
International Journal of Sociology and Social Policy		✓
Journal of Social Policy	✓	✓
Journal of Social Work Practice	✓	✓
Practice	✓	✓
Professional Social Work	✓	
Social Policy and Administration	✓	✓
Social Policy Review	✓	
Social Work		✓
Social Work Education	✓	✓
Sociology	✓	✓
Welfare Rights Bulletin		✓

Effective Reading and Note-taking

When you are reading for study purposes, there should be some more sophisticated processes going on in your head than if you are simply reading a lightweight novel or a magazine.

The SQ3R reading technique

The '**SQ3R**' technique (Robinson, 1970) aims to make you more productive in your reading, resulting in:

- less time spent re-reading material
- less time going over the same ground twice because you did not pick up all of the important stuff the first time
- more ideas generated for things that you can write about in your assignment or project
- a better understanding of the material.

'SQ3R' stands for:	
	Survey the text to ascertain the gist or general idea
	Question Think about questions that you would like the text to answer
	[1]**Read** the text carefully if you think it is relevant for your research
	[2]**Recall** the main points after you have read the text
	[3]**Review** the text to confirm that you have recalled all the main points that are significant for you and your

Let us consider each stage in turn:

Survey

When you 'survey' the text (journal article, chapter of a book or report etc.), you should:

- aim to get the basic gist of the document
- use skim-reading and scanning (or speed reading) to get a quick overview
- read the 'introduction' and 'conclusion' sections to gain an overall feel for what was explored and what was discovered.

Surveying the text is useful in giving you a good general sense of what the author is attempting to communicate, before you get too involved in the details of the piece.

Question

As you are surveying the document, you should also aim to:

- think about what you already know about the subject
- identify the remaining gaps in your knowledge

- formulate any questions that you want answering about the topic
- establish what you want to know as a result of reading the piece.

This purposeful probing or questioning is very different from a 'passive' form of reading where you literally just let your eyes wander over the text and hope you are absorbing what is written.

Read

Having identified the questions that you want to focus on, you are now ready to read through the material properly. As you read through the text:

- try to make connections with other things that you have read
- link the reading material with things you already know something about.

Learning is really all about developing your ability to make connections and link things together in meaningful ways.

Recall

After you have finished reading the piece, you should test your ability to recall the material by noting down the key points on paper or in a word-processed document (bullet points are fine). If you end up with very few bullet points or words written down, you will realize that for whatever reason, you have not 'taken in' much of the content. Again, this may be a cue to you to go back and re-read parts of the document to improve your understanding and recall.

Recall helps you to:

- establish your own understanding of the subject in the language that is most familiar (and therefore likely to make most sense) to you
- avoid inadvertently incorporating large chunks of others' material into your work, by encouraging you to paraphrase (but remember that even paraphrased material requires a citation).

Review

The process of reviewing is about:

- briefly skim-reading the document again to check that your notes are accurate and complete
- identifying anything that has been missed out and adding it to your notes.

Writing about Research

> When you are ready to write up your work, you have one major task: how do you adequately, appropriately and interestingly describe, explain and justify what you have done and found out? (Hart, 1998: 172)

Quick Tip: Planning work

You may have already developed a personal approach to developing writing plans from having completed academic work in the past.

One technique for doing this is to write a series of headings and sub-headings in a new document and then to begin to type in:

- bullet points
- short notes
- keywords
- other reminders to serve as a memory jog or prompt for what you want to write about at that point in the project, dissertation or assignment.

Based on the research and reading of the literature that you have done at this point, try to find the best way of structuring what you have got to say. For instance, is it best to begin with a chronological overview of the topic, or a broad presentation of the main strands of thinking that are currently associated with your topic?

How do I write 'critically' about what I have read?

Some students struggle with the idea of writing 'critically' in academic work. This is partly because in most of the work that we produced at school, we were encouraged to use description, where we simply wrote an account based on what others told us. However, at higher education level, you are expected to develop a 'critical discussion' of what is reported in the literature. This means writing in a way that goes beyond the descriptive style of 'x said this ...', 'y said that ...' and 'z said the other'.

So, how can we start to write more critically?

Box 6.4 The main ingredients of critical writing (taken from Ridley, 2008: 119)

➢	Comparing and contrasting different theories and concepts
➢	Synthesizing and reformulating arguments from two or more sources to create a new or more developed point of view

(Continued)

➢	Agreeing with, confirming or defending a finding or point of view through an analytical focus on its merits and limitations
➢	Acknowledging that a certain point of view may have some strengths, but qualifying your support of the position by highlighting certain weaknesses
➢	Rejecting certain points of view and giving reasons for the rejection
➢	Developing a case for a particular approach, methodology or viewpoint by presenting a body of evidence (cited and referenced)

Learn by example

This process of writing critically involves some active engagement with the subject matter which is very different to just providing a descriptive overview. A great way of developing your understanding of how to do this kind of thing is to look at a well-written journal article and try to identify how the author has written in a critical way. If you cannot find a suitable article, you could ask your tutor for a recommendation.

Box 6.5 reflection point

Critical issues!

In academic work, being 'critical' doesn't have to mean being 'negative' or picking holes in something, which is often the way we use this word in everyday speech and conversation. You can, and should, also aim to 'critically' examine and reflect on the strengths and positive aspects of a piece of research.

Foregrounding your 'Writer Voice'

Students sometimes think that writing objectively and supporting arguments with evidence means that they cannot put 'anything of themselves' into their work. However, this is not strictly the case. As Ridley (2008: 131) writes, it is possible to make the reader aware of your own stance in relation to the material you are discussing in a number of ways:

- establish a solid body of evidence for the position you feel is most convincing
- structure your discussion in such a way that you are guiding the reader towards the conclusion you feel is most plausible
- provide examples that help to illuminate the strengths of the points of view you agree with, and also provide evidence which casts doubt on the positions which you feel are less convincing.

It is also worth remembering that most of the decisions you make about:

- what is important
- what is significant
- what is persuasive
- what is weak
- the connections you make between key ideas and concepts

will all go some way toward communicating your own position.

Planning a Research Project

> Plans are only good intentions unless they immediately degenerate into hard work. (Drucker, n.d., cited by Cryer, 2006: 139)

Most of the processes and techniques that we have discussed in this chapter relate to both general research for essays and assignments and situations where you may be required to undertake larger research projects. However, one of the additional considerations with research projects is the importance of establishing a project timetable or plan. Often students are given longer periods of time in which to complete research projects, in contrast to regular assignments, and there is a good reason for this. A research project is usually a substantial piece of work which requires careful planning, development and execution – and lots of stamina! It is also usually a self-directed piece of work which means that you will have to take individual responsibility for how it progresses.

The key to successful planning and time management is finding a method of doing it which works for you! Many people like to draw up a checklist of things to do and then set themselves deadlines. Others prefer to use diagrams or charts such as Gantt Charts which allow them to keep track of multiple areas of activity as they develop over time. You do not need to use a highly sophisticated process of time management (we all know of people who spend more time preparing and 'prettifying' timetables than they do in actually carrying out their timetabled activities!).

Table 6.4 Leslie's keyword and key phrase list

Research Title: To what extent does the current **provision** of **statutory services** **disadvantage** some **minority ethnic groups** in the **United Kingdom**?

Original Search Terms

'provision'	*'statutory services'*	*'disadvantage'*	*'minority ethnic groups'*	*'United Kingdom'*
Keywords:	**Keywords:**	**Keywords:**	**Keywords:**	**Keywords:**
supply	mandatory services	detriment	ethnic minority groups	UK
offer	required services	held back	ethnic minorities	Great Britain
make available	local authority services	denied	BME	England
services provided	core services	disservice	Asian	Scotland
	social welfare services	unfavourable treatment	Afro-Caribbean	Wales
	social services	discriminate against	Bangladeshi	Northern Ireland
	health care services	disfavour	Black	
	social work services		Chinese	
			Indian	
			Pakistani	
			South Asian	

NOTE: This is the list of keywords that Leslie generated from her original search terms. You can see that from five original search terms, she has now generated 33 keywords or phrases, which she could try using in various combinations when it comes to searching databases. Some of these keywords will probably prove to be more useful than others, but it's good to have a wide set of keywords to begin with.

You will notice that some keywords are synonyms of Leslies original search terms – in other words, they are words that mean roughly the same thing as the search terms. However, some of Leslie's keywords are more general or more specific in meaning – and some are related terms or concepts. Try to think laterally when developing your list of keywords. As Bhopal (2004) notes, there is still considerable debate around terms relating to ethnicity and race in the study of health and welfare issues for minority ethnic and racial groups, and some of the keywords and phrases shown here reflect words that are in common usage. From a research perspective, this does open up a useful debate about how concepts are defined and developed and leads to its own set of associated terms.

Quick Tip: Project planning

Whatever form of project planning you use, you should aim to incorporate the following factors:

- How much time do you have overall?
- What are the main tasks that need to be completed?
- In what order do tasks need to be done?
- Which tasks are likely to take longer than others?
- How can you divide the available time up in the best way?
- What needs to go into my short-term plan(s)? (You are likely to put together several short-term plans as you progress through each stage of the literature review process.)
- What needs to go into my longer-term plan? (This is your overall project plan – you could think of it as 'the bigger picture'.)
- What about if something unexpected happens? This might be absence or illness. Have you thought about building in any 'buffer' time into your plan?
- What can you do to avoid procrastination (see Chapter 3 for more on this)?

As the quotation at the beginning of this section states, it is pointless to have a beautifully worked-out plan if you then file it away and do not do anything with it. It is important to think about being realistic with your planning and your time management. Commitments such as work, family life, socializing and other activities should not be ignored. However, you will need to try to find ways of being most productive with the time that you have available.

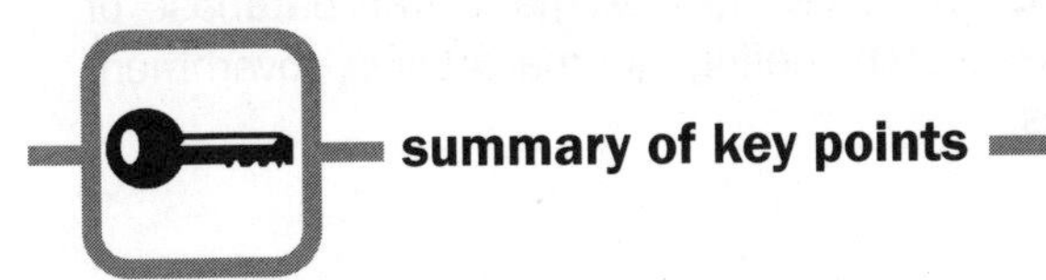

summary of key points

- Research is significant for social work students as you will need to:
  - search for it and read it in order to complete your essays and assignments
  - use it to develop a greater understanding of evidence-based social work practice
  - possibly carry out a research project or produce a dissertation if you are on a postgraduate social work programme.
- Helpful tools for successful literature searching include the 'six-step search strategy' and the 'snowball technique'.

- The effectiveness of reading and note-taking can be dramatically improved through the use of the 'SQ3R' reading technique.
- Writing about research in a more critically analytical way can be developed by focusing on the main ingredients of critical writing, and reading the published work of others.

useful resources

Methodology.co.uk – The Research Methods Resource Centre
Available at: http://www.methodology.co.uk/

IRISS (Institute for Research and Innovation in Social Services)
Available at: http://www.iriss.ac.uk/audio
The aim of IRISS is to promote a 'world-class, knowledge-based social services sector in Scotland'. It provides access to a range of resources and learning materials.

Joseph Rowntree Foundation
Available at: http://www.jrf.org.uk/
The Joseph Rowntree Foundation works to develop a better understanding of social problems and how they can be overcome in practice. The website contains a range of academic research and publications.

Research Mindedness in Social Work and Social Care
Available at: http://www.resmind.swap.ac.uk/
This website helps students to be more 'research minded' in their studies and social work practice.

Social Care Online – better knowledge for better practice
Available at: http://www.scie-socialcareonline.org.uk/
Social Care Online describes itself as 'the UK's most extensive free database of social care information'. It contains research briefings, journal articles, government reports and links to useful websites.

further reading

Cottrell, S. (2005) *Critical Thinking Skills*. Basingstoke: Palgrave Macmillan.
Dolowitz, D., Buckler, S. and Sweeney, F. (2008) *Researching Online*. Basingstoke: Palgrave Macmillan.
Metcalfe, M. (2006) *Reading Critically at University* (Study Skills Series). London: Sage.
Ridley, D. (2008) The *Literature Review: A step-by-step guide for students*. London: Sage.

7

Writing Effectively

learning objectives

- To understand why writing is important in relation to studying social work.
- To develop an awareness of different forms of writing and writing style.
- To develop an awareness of the support that is available for students with specific learning difficulties such as dyslexia.
- To understand what an essay is and how it is structured.
- To gain an awareness of other types of academic writing including reflective writing, writing for presentations and writing projects and dissertations.

Why is Writing so Important?

Writing is particularly important in terms of university courses as it is still the most frequently used method of getting you to demonstrate your knowledge and understanding when it comes to university assessments. Some of you may feel extremely confident in your writing skills and ability, and the thought of having to write a 2000-word essay on an aspect of social policy might not seem at all daunting. However, for the vast majority of people, the ability to write clearly and coherently does not come naturally and needs to be practised, developed and cultivated over time. Trust us – we know this from experience – and it can be done!

Improving your Writing Skills

It is possible to learn how to improve your writing skills, no matter at which point you feel you are starting from. The time you spend at university is the perfect opportunity to try to strengthen your general writing skills as much as you can, and make use of the support that is available to you. Although you will probably be very focused on getting through each individual assignment as it crops up, it is worth remembering that the writing skills that you use (and hopefully develop!) in the course of studying will be very valuable in terms of your own professional practice when you become a fully qualified, independent social worker, and indeed in terms of your own lifelong learning.

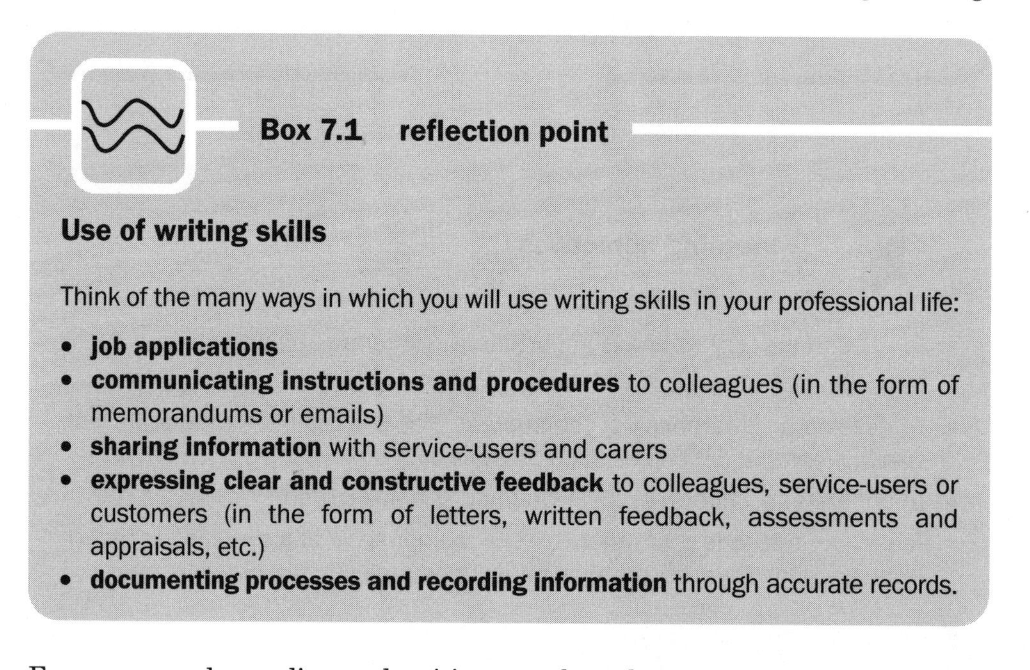

Box 7.1 reflection point

Use of writing skills

Think of the many ways in which you will use writing skills in your professional life:

- **job applications**
- **communicating instructions and procedures** to colleagues (in the form of memorandums or emails)
- **sharing information** with service-users and carers
- **expressing clear and constructive feedback** to colleagues, service-users or customers (in the form of letters, written feedback, assessments and appraisals, etc.)
- **documenting processes and recording information** through accurate records.

For some people, reading and writing may have been a struggle in the past – particularly through school years – and if you feel that you yourself are in this position, then you will not be alone. Be honest with yourself about what you think your current difficulties are in relation to writing and do not be afraid to share these with people who can support and help you. This might include lecturing staff as well as specialized study support tutors who may be based within your own university school/faculty or within a central study support unit.

Support for Students with Specific Learning Difficulties

Some students with specific learning difficulties such as dyslexia may require additional support and it is worth remembering that universities and colleges have a legal obligation (as well as a moral duty) to ensure that this support is provided. This is usually done by helping students to:

- obtain a **dyslexia assessment**
- access financial support from the **Disabled Student Allowance (DSA)**
- access **supportive materials** and other resources.

Did You Know? Types of support for dyslexic students

Some of the sources of support that are available for dyslexic students include:

- coloured overlays to use with books or paper-based reading materials
- advance access to lecture notes and handouts in an electronic format enabling customization of font style, size and background colour
- proofreading services (including specialist software packages)
- specific arrangements for examinations
- support during lectures from professional note-takers.

More information about the kinds of software and assistive technologies available to help students with reading, writing and other study skills are discussed in Chapter 13.

Your Previous Experience of Writing

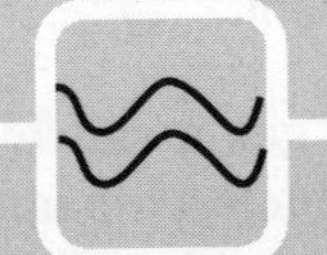

Box 7.2 reflection point

Your experience of writing

Think about a past experience where writing has played an important role for you in communicating something to others (for instance, this could be your experience of sitting an exam at school or college, writing creatively or writing in the context of previous employment).

With this situation in mind, try to answer the following questions:

1. Was this a positive or negative experience of writing?
2. Did you receive any feedback on this writing? If so, did you feel it to be negative or positive? Justified or unjustified? Helpful or unhelpful to you?

(Continued)

3 What did you do differently (if anything) as a result of receiving this feedback?
4 What are your own personal hopes and aspirations in terms of developing your writing skills?
5 What goals could you set yourself in order to help you achieve your hopes and aspirations?
6 What sort of milestones could you set for yourself?
7 How might strengthening your writing skills make a difference to other areas of your life? How might it have an affect on your own personal confidence?

Getting Used to 'Academic Writing'

For many students, one of the hardest aspects of getting to grips with university work is being able to produce 'academic writing'. When the dreaded first essay or assignment is due to be handed in, you may find that you struggle to find the 'right words'. You may feel under pressure to try to sound more intelligent than you think you are or be concerned that your spelling and grammar skills may let you down.

Practice essays

Some courses in social work will try to ease you in to the process of writing academic work by setting you a 'practice' essay to complete. These are normally:

- shorter pieces of work than the standard assessed essays
- on a topic that helps to prepare you for an upcoming assessment.

Lecturers will usually collect them in and 'mark' them to get a sense of your current knowledge of 'academic writing conventions' (which translates as the rules of how university work is normally written, structured and presented). You may be asked to fill out a self-assessment sheet before you submit this practice essay. This is intended to get you thinking about how well you have completed different aspects of it (including presentation, referencing, structuring and other elements). Lecturing staff will normally use this opportunity to provide extensive written feedback on your work so do not be too disheartened if you see that lots of comments have been written on your work.

Essay feedback

Understandably, many students see lecturer's critical comments as a 'negative' thing – they tend to think that it means that they are 'rubbish' at doing academic work. However, we would strongly encourage you to try to get into the habit of always viewing feedback (both negative and positive) as a valuable learning opportunity. After all, if you never receive feedback on your work, you are never going to develop a good understanding of where you do things well and where you could aim to improve your skills and performance. It is also true to say that on occasion you may receive feedback which you feel is unjustified but even in these cases it is useful to try to think how or why someone has formed a particular opinion of your work.

Writing at Higher Education Level

Did You Know? Writing at HE Level

Writing at higher education level is slightly different from the kinds of writing that people do at school or college. There is usually more of a focus on:

- encouraging you to write in an objective style which takes account of a number of possible viewpoints;
- 'developing an argument' or 'discussing an issue' which is different to getting up on your own personal soapbox and simply 'emptying your head' on the page.

For some people, getting the feedback from the first formally marked piece of work can be a bit of a shock as they may have felt that they had already developed a good writing style at school or college.

activity 7.1

Essay feedback as a learning tool

Samir is just beginning the second term of his first year of a BSc in Social Work at the University of Northerntown. He has just been handed back the first essay that he has produced for this course and is rather disappointed to see several paragraphs of feedback which he interprets as being fairly 'negative'. He is also feeling a little bit annoyed as previous feedback from tutors on his Access Course suggested that he could already write very well.

(Continued)

Look at the tutor feedback page below and try to identify any positive 'learning points' that Samir could focus on.

Samir – you have clearly identified a relevant social issue and have begun the process of thinking about how policy and legislation have been developed in response to it. However, some areas of your work require further development in order to bring it up to a passing standard. Please contact me for a tutorial and we can discuss this feedback further and try to identify things that may help you to develop your essay-writing skills. I have provided specific feedback on the separate aspects of essay writing below:

Structure and relevance

Overall, the essay has some elements of structure but it could be further improved. Your introduction is very brief and really needs to outline for the reader exactly what you are intending to cover in your essay. Similarly, your conclusion is extremely short – it needs to summarize and draw together the key issues that you have discussed. At other times in the essay, you tend to jump around a bit from topic to topic, and it is not always clear how things are linked. Try to make sure that there is a logical thread that runs throughout the entire essay.

Content and argument

You have obviously done some background reading and this helps you to focus on your chosen topic. It is also good that you are using statistics to help you to support your points. On some occasions, your writing becomes a little subjective and you slip into giving personal opinions. Also, try to be wary of making simplistic conclusions from the information you have gathered – remember that there could be a number of factors that contribute to the situation that you have described.

Sources and their use

It is very encouraging that you are drawing on the information that you have read in order to support your comments. However, you are not currently using the Harvard referencing system correctly. Unfortunately, this means that you are not showing where your background information comes from, in the main body of the essay itself (citation), and your reference list is missing key bits of information. Also, you have taken large, direct quotes from websites and have not shown these as being quotes, or referenced them. Please be EXTREMELY careful to avoid doing this in future, as it could appear as if you are attempting to plagiarize material.

Style and presentation

Overall, your writing style is reasonably good although there are some occasional spelling and grammar issues. Please try to proofread your work (even read it aloud to yourself) before you hand it in – this should help you to pick up some of these errors. A couple of your paragraphs are a little short – try to make most of your paragraphs of a similar length.

- What practical steps could he take to avoid repeating the same kinds of things in future assignment submissions?
- What kind of support could he seek from his tutor?
- What are the current strengths that he should aim to build upon?

Responding to the assignment question or title

It is really important that you are clear about the details of the particular assignment that you have been given. For instance, if you are asked to write a 2000-word essay on a social issue of your choice and the ways in which social policy has developed in response to this issue, then *you must*:

1 Keep to the word limit by writing **2000 words** (although it is a standard academic practice to allow you to write either 10% over or under a word limit).
2 Write about a **social issue** (e.g. anti-social behaviour).
3 Write about **social policy** (e.g. legislation, anti-social behaviour orders, etc.
4 Discuss **how the policy links with the social issue**.

This may seem completely obvious but it is surprising how many students will fail an assignment because they have not followed the instructions they have been given. Always make sure that you have access to the specific assignment guidance and that you fully understand what is being asked of you. If in doubt, *ask* your tutor!

Academic writing style

The ways in which we write in informal contexts (such as email, texting or 'blogging') are not appropriate for formal academic work. This means that you should avoid using text abbreviations such as '4' for the word 'for', or 'u' instead of 'you'. For some people, it can seem as if the academic writing style required in course work or essays is a million miles away from how they would normally write. In many ways, academic writing can seem like a completely alien language, with its own bewildering set of conventions. One of the best ways of developing your understanding of writing in a more formal way is to invest some time each week engaging in some 'quality reading'. Observing how the 'professionals' write can be extremely useful in helping you to absorb some of the good habits you will need to develop.

Box 7.3 reflection point

Different styles of writing

What are the key features of, and differences between, the following styles of writing?

- Tabloid newspaper article (e.g. from the *Sun*)
- Broadsheet newspaper article (e.g. from the *Guardian*)
- An academic article (e.g. from the *British Journal of Social Work*)
- A blog page
- An entry in a hard-copy encyclopaedia
- An article from the Wikipedia website

Types of Academic Writing

Writing lecture and/or seminar notes

Sometimes lecturers give out their own set of notes to students and often these are 'print-outs' of their PowerPoint slides. Also, your lecturers may make their entire set of lecture notes available on a virtual learning environment (VLE). This can be useful for:

- helping you to develop an overview of the ground that will be covered in the session, so you can start to formulate your own thoughts and questions
- students with dyslexia or other specific learning disabilities who may benefit from a pre-prepared set of notes which outlines the structure of the session, and places less pressure on them to create a full set of notes during the session
- some disabled students who may use assistive technology such as screen-readers.

Limitations of lecturers' notes

However, you should remember that:

- lecturers' notes are basically *their own* set of prompts
- they may have less meaning for you in six weeks', or even six months' time
- they may not be effective in reminding you of what *you* thought was useful or important about a particular session.

For these reasons, we would **always** recommend that you make your own set of notes if possible, or at the very least add to and annotate a pre-prepared set of notes that have been given to you by a tutor.

Skills involved in taking notes

There is a definite skill to writing useful lecture or seminar notes. This is because it is really quite difficult to:

1. **listen** to someone talking
2. **process** the information that they are putting across
3. **translate** their words into words/phrases that mean something useful to you
4. **decide** what really needs to be written down
5. **write** your notes WHILST continuing to listen to the lecturer

... *and all before the lecturer has moved on to the next topic*!

Table 7.1 Tips for producing useful lecture notes

Use abbreviations and shorthand	• Do not attempt to get down every word that the lecturer is saying. • Abbreviate words and use your own shorthand, e.g. 'sw' for 'social work'.
FOCUS on key words and concepts	• Note down specialist terms or phrases. • Ask for confirmation of the spelling of specialist terms or names if you are not sure.
Write down what you DO NOT understand!	• Note down those things you are not clear about or do not understand, rather than simply 'switching off'. • Use these notes to seek clarification from peers, tutors or through extra research.
Notes are a STARTING point (not the finished article)	• Use them to help you to write more expansive notes soon after the session has taken place (whilst recall is fairly fresh). • This is also a good exercise for improving your memory and recall.

Table 7.1 ***(Continued)***

Use books or web resources	• Follow up suggestions for further reading to help to develop your understanding of a topic. • Most lectures simply scratch the surface of a subject – it is down to you to build on this in your independent study time.
Create your own SUMMARY	• Add a 'summary' section at the end of your notes, in which you pick out the main themes, arguments and debates. • This will help when you revisit the notes in the future, particularly for exam revision.
Put a date in your diary to REVISIT your notes	• Revisiting your notes helps you to remember the material. • Do this within a week of writing them, and then again within a month of having written them.
USE your notes	• When you come to prepare for essays and assignments, or exam revision, remember that your notes are a very useful resource.

Writing Essays

Did You Know? What is an essay?

An essay is a piece of writing which responds to an essay question or title. It has a specific structure, is written in paragraphs, and is normally written in a formal style (Cottrell, 2003).

Preparing to write an essay or academic assignment should involve more than powering up your computer and opening a blank word-processing document! There are several stages of preparation that should come before you even begin to write anything.

Table 7.2 **The five stages of essay writing (from Greetham, 2001: 2)**

1. **Interpreting and understanding the essay title or question** – make sure you understand what is being asked of you and what each key term refers to. If you are not sure, then try using a dictionary or asking your tutor for clarification.
2. **Researching the topic of your essay** – it is a cold, hard fact of life that the more you have read around your subject, the more material (facts, figures, examples, points of view, arguments, etc.) you will have to work with when it comes to writing.
3. **Putting together an essay plan** – a good plan helps you to stay on track, avoids you repeating things, gives your work a clear structure and helps you to shape your discussion in such a

Table 7.2 ***(Continued)***

way that it actually answers the question. Please, NEVER embark on an essay or assignment without having first done some kind of plan!

4. **Writing the essay** – if you have done each of the three previous steps, the process of actually writing the essay should be considerably easier, and should help you to avoid 'SAABS syndrome' (**s**taring **at a b**lank **s**creen)! Not only that, but you will not be going to the word count button constantly to see how many words you need to conjure up!
5. **Revise and redraft** – it is vitally important that you do leave yourself some time to read back through your work thoroughly, so that you can pick up any spelling/grammar issues and any inconsistencies or inaccuracies in what you have written. Even professional writers end up producing many drafts of their work before they come up with the final, polished product! So, do not expect to be able to churn out perfection with your first attempt.

Essay structure

Always begin with an introduction

All academic essays will begin with one or two paragraphs of 'introduction'.

Box 7.4 Introductions SHOULD ☑:

☑ Tell the reader how you intend to provide an answer to the essay question OR how you intend to respond to the essay title.
☑ Outline the main areas and/or issues that you intend to discuss and briefly indicate why these areas are relevant.
☑ Define any key terms.
☑ Be somewhere in the region of about 8–12% of the total word length of the essay. So if you are writing a 1000-word essay, your introduction would normally be of about 80–120 words in length.
☑ Demonstrate to the marker that you have thought about how to structure your assignment.

Box 7.5 Introductions SHOULD NOT ☒:

☒ Launch straight into a discussion of the essay/assignment topic.
☒ Go into forensic detail about how you are going to approach the essay – you have the rest of the essay itself to develop your lines of discussion or argument.
☒ Drift off into discussing irrelevant issues.
☒ Go on for too long – brevity and conciseness are required.

activity 7.2

Analysing Introductions

Read the following introductory paragraph, from a real academic article, and answer the questions below:

> Issues of Alcohol Misuse among Older People: Attitudes and Experiences of Social Work Practitioners
>
> Catherine Shaw and George Palattayil
>
> *Introduction*
>
> Alcohol misuse appears to be adversely affecting the quality of life of older people, and the literature demonstrates evidence that alcohol use among older people is increasing and significantly impacting on their health and well-being. Data from the Health Education Board for Scotland's Health Education Population Survey (2002) indicate that around 13 per cent of adults aged 55–64 and 6 per cent of those aged 65–74 may be drinking more than the recommended amounts. We feel that Social Work has an important role to play in providing support to these vulnerable service users.
>
> This study explores the experiences of social work practitioners in an Older People's Team based in the west of Scotland, with the issues related to alcohol misuse among older people. The goal is to provide insight into some of the complexities and vulnerabilities that older people face. The study also explores the attitudes of practitioners towards the available services and considers possibilities for developing newer services, including a more age-appropriate service.
>
> *Source: Shaw, C. and Palattayil, G. (2008) 'Issues of Alcohol Misuse among Older People: Attitudes and Experiences of Social Work Practitioners',* Practice – Social Work in Action *20(3): 181–93.*

- What 'problem' or 'issue' is the article focusing on?
- What is the aim or goal of the piece or work?
- What other broad areas or issues will be discussed?
- What might be the implications of this piece of work?

Notice how this introduction is giving the reader an overview, or a kind of mental map of the 'ground' that will be covered in the article.

The main body

The main 'body' of the essay is where you develop your 'argument', 'answer' or 'response' to the essay title or question.

Box 7.6 The main body SHOULD ☑:

☑ Make up the largest section of your essay and be roughly 80% of your entire word count.
☑ Develop a discussion of the essay topic in a logical and planned way. The reader should be able to understand why you have moved from talking about one topic to another.
☑ Consider different ways of thinking about and discussing the key areas of your topic.
☑ Include definitions, specialist terms or vocabulary – you should also use the full written version of any acronyms the first time you use them in your essay e.g. 'The issuing of **anti-social behaviour orders (ASBO)** in relation to socially excluded, young people will be discussed'.
☑ Include the main arguments for and against the various points of view that you discuss in your essay.
☑ Show that you can look beyond your own opinion (however well-informed that opinion might be), in order to be able to discuss all angles of the debate. The more background reading you can do, the better able you will be to do this.
☑ Make use of evidence to support the points that you are making in your essay, i.e. citations to published work (books, journals, reports, websites and so on), statistics, case studies, direct quotations, diagrams, charts, tables and other kinds of information.
☑ Show that you can engage in critical analysis of the topic (see Reflection Point below).

Box 7.7 The main body SHOULD NOT ☒:

☒ Be random and unstructured. Proper essay planning will help you to avoid this.
☒ Simply present your own unsupported opinion as if it were fact (e.g. 'Young people today do not have enough respect for authority').
☒ Use direct quotes without you commenting on why they are useful or helpful.
☒ Assume that your reader is familiar with specialist terms.
☒ Repeat things that you have already said.

Box 7.8 reflection point

What is critical analysis?

For some people, the word 'critical' suggests **mainly negative things** such as being told that they were not very good at something or perhaps being negatively judged (criticized) for their behaviour, language or even physical appearance at school.

However, in relation to academic writing, 'critical' is better understood as referring to the really important, meaty issues which are at the heart of a thorough understanding of a particular topic. This will involve:

- arguing for and against particular viewpoints
- pointing out both strengths and weaknesses of various arguments or 'positions'.

Why do students sometimes find critical analysis difficult?

Bringing critical analysis into your essay is not always easy as it tends to require a *very good general overview* of the topic that you are writing about. You are only likely to have this kind of grasp of a topic if you have:

- studied it (or a related topic) before
- done some extensive reading around the topic.

So, consider the development of your critical thinking skills as being a long-term learning objective that stretches throughout the duration of your studies and beyond.

Quick Tip: Demonstrating critical analysis

There are probably very few university lecturers in any academic subject that would not welcome more critical analysis in the work that they mark.

You can demonstrate critical analysis in your work by:

- showing that you have thought about underlying ideas and concepts
- attempting to weigh up the usefulness of certain points of view
- looking closely at the evidence to see if it 'holds water'
- showing that you have started to make links with other blocks of learning
- avoiding simply describing things or paraphrasing chunks from recommended textbooks.

activity 7.3

Situation critical?

- Find an article from a social work journal (Table 6.3 in Chapter 6 lists some of the key social work journal titles) and read through it, paying particular attention to how the author(s) have critically analysed aspects of their topic.
- Make a note of the kinds of things that the writer has done in order to achieve a critically analytical style of writing.

The conclusion

Your essay should always finish with a conclusion.

Box 7.9 Conclusions SHOULD ☑:

☑ Be somewhere in the region of about 10–15 % of the overall essay length.
☑ Provide a summary of the key points that you have made in your essay.
☑ Draw together the strands of your discussion.
☑ Evaluate the weight of evidence for the things that you have discussed.
☑ Provide indications of where possible answers might lie.
☑ Acknowledge areas which require further thought or research.

Box 7.10 Conclusions SHOULD NOT ☒:

☒ Include any new material that you have not already discussed in your essay:

- If it is important enough to include in your essay, it should have its own paragraph(s) within the main body and not just be mentioned in passing in the conclusion.
- You should be pulling all of your essay strands together, not wandering off in new directions.

☒ Include over-generalisations or rush to provide simplistic 'answers', where they may not exist.

Example: In an essay about social exclusion and poverty, Halima concludes by stating that '*increased education is the answer to fighting social exclusion and poverty*'.

From a marker's point of view:

- This is a weak statement as there are a number of factors that feed into the process of social exclusion, *one* of which includes access to education.
- To pick out this one factor and claim that this alone would 'solve' the problem of social exclusion comes across as being rather simplistic and naïve.

Learning to assess the quality of your own work is a really useful skill to develop, as you can start to identify the areas of your essay or assignment that might require further work and development, before handing the work in for marking. Use Table 7.3 below to help you to consider how you have done in each of the key areas:

Table 7.3 A useful form for the self-assessment of essays (adapted from Cottrell, 2003: 173)

Organization and Relevance	
Clearly organised and planned work which includes a title, an introduction and a conclusion	☐
The assignment provides an effective overview of the topic – I have responded to the essay question/title	☐
I have referred to sources and material that clearly relate to the topic of the assignment	☐
Content and argument	
I have introduced the topic of the essay	☐
I have defined key terms	☐
I have used sources of evidence to support my points	☐
I have tried to analyse what I have been discussing, rather than just describe things	☐
I have tried to be critical (e.g. evaluating the work of others, comparing and contrasting views etc.)	☐
I have remained objective, and have avoided simply presenting my own personal point of view	☐
Referencing skills	
I have been clear about my sources of information	☐

Table 7.3 ***(Continued)***

I have used in-text referencing (citation) correctly	☐
I have produced an accurate and correctly presented reference list	☐
Writing skills and proofreading	
My writing is clear and concise	☐
I have used correct spellings and grammar in my writing	☐
I have written in paragraphs	☐
My work is readable and neatly presented	☐
I have kept within the assignment word limit (normally 10% over or under is acceptable).	☐

Other Types of Writing

There are many other types of writing aside from note-taking and essay/assignment writing that you will be expected to do as a social work student, and a social work professional.

Reflective writing

You will be required to engage in reflective thinking about your own ideas, beliefs, performance and practices. 'Reflection' is a central part of continuous professional development and will be a core part of your work as a social work practitioner (see Chapter 11). As part of this, you will be required to engage in reflective writing, which is essentially one way of demonstrating to others that you are thinking reflectively.

> **Quick Tip: Aspects of reflective writing**
>
> Reflective writing tends to be quite different to standard academic writing because:
>
> - you would normally refer to yourself using the 'first-person' (e.g. use 'I', 'me', 'my') as you are reflecting on your own experiences
> - you are encouraged to explore your own thoughts, feelings, 'conflicts' and learning development

(Continued)

- it is difficult to back up our own, individual, subjective experiences with references drawn from the published literature. So, reflective writing tends to include less citation and references.

Writing presentations

There are likely to be a number of occasions during your social work course when you will be expected to put together presentations.

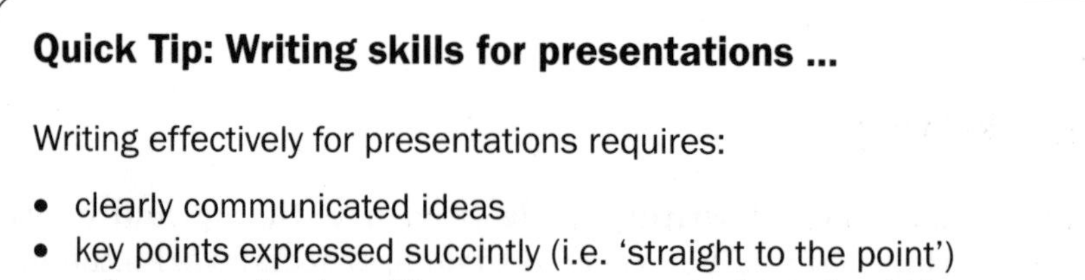

Quick Tip: Writing skills for presentations ...

Writing effectively for presentations requires:

- clearly communicated ideas
- key points expressed succinctly (i.e. 'straight to the point')
- a focus on structure (like essays, presentations should have an introduction, main section and conclusion).

In practice, the vast majority of student presentations that we see are delivered using electronic presentation software (see Chapter 14 for a brief guide to using Microsoft PowerPoint). Presentation software positively encourages you to:

- write using brief bullet points which makes written material easier for an audience to take in and digest (avoid writing a full script on your slides)
- summarize using a few keywords with the intention of 'fleshing out' your points when you deliver the presentation.

Citations and references in presentations

Occasionally, students seem to feel that citations and references are not necessary in a verbal presentation but they are, in the same way that we would expect to see citations and referencing in written assignments. Add brief citations to your bullet points and include full references on a slide at the very end of the presentation (see Chapter 8 for more on referencing).

Writing projects and dissertations

Many social work courses will require students to complete a project or dissertation, usually towards the end of the programme.

> **Did You Know? Projects and dissertations**
>
> A project or dissertation differs from standard academic essays in that they:
>
> - tend to be longer pieces of work
> - have a structure which usually incorporates specific elements such as an 'abstract', 'literature review', 'methodology', 'results', 'discussion' and so on
> - are normally researched, carried out and written over a longer period of time – this gives you time to develop your thinking and ideas, but it also requires more sustained effort and engagement than a standard assignment
> - will usually include substantially more citations and references than would normally be required in a standard assignment.

If your course requires you to complete a project or dissertation, you will be given guidance and support around what needs to be included and how the work needs to be written. Another really useful starting point can be found at the following website:

> **Useful Resource: Dissertation website**
>
> *Companion for undergraduate dissertations* – Sociology, Anthropology, Politics, Social Policy, Social Work and Criminology: http://www.socscidiss.bham.ac.uk/

Writing skills for professional practice

Whilst it may be true that the hands-on nature of working with people may be what attracts you most to a career in social work, it is worth thinking at this very early stage about the ways in which your ability to write clearly, coherently and accurately will impact on your own effectiveness and professionalism.

Did you know? Writing skills and NOS

The **National Occupational Standards (NOS) for social work** (Topps UK Partnership, 2002) explicitly mention the use of writing skills in relation to meeting certain occupational standards, and the use of effective written and verbal communication is implied in many of the other standards.

Let us briefly consider the 'performance criteria' for some of these NOS:

***Excerpt 6.2a:* Write plans** to meet objectives and outcomes, ensuring that they:

- are sufficiently clear to be evaluated.

***11.1c:* Prepare reports and documents** that:

- are accurate, understandable and accessible
- identify gaps and conflicts of evidence, professional judgement and opinion
- contain clear summaries and recommendations in a format appropriate to the task.

***16.2a:* Document:**

- professional judgements and decisions accurately
- the evidence on which the professional judgements have been based
- where professional judgement is based on informed opinion.

19.1c: Explain and justify (both verbally and **in writing**) the rationale for your professional judgements and decisions when working with differences in perspectives from:

- individuals requiring services and their carers
- others within your own team and organization
- other professionals.

activity 7.4

Writing skills for study and social work practice

How could some of the writing skills that you use during your social work course help you to develop the specific writing skills referred to in these National Occupational Standards?

To get you started, you might consider that creating your own learning development plans and engaging with personal development planning (PDP) could help you to develop the kind of writing skills you will use in developing care plans (NOS 6.2).

summary of key points

- Writing skills are important for effective study and social work practice and crucially they are something that can be developed and improved.
- Feedback can, and should be, really helpful in terms of helping us to improve our writing skills.
- Academic essays need to contain specific elements and need to begin with an introduction, move on to the main body and finish with a conclusion.
- Other important types of academic writing include reflective writing, writing for presentations and the writing of projects and dissertations.
- The development of writing skills links directly with requirements for professional social work practice, as expressed through the National Occupational Standards.

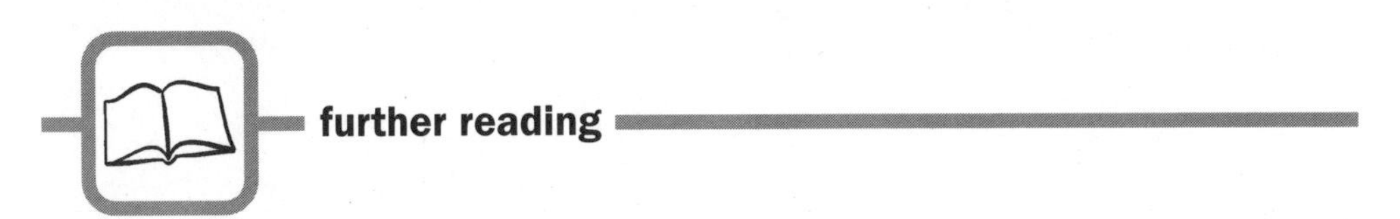

further reading

Creme, P. and Lea, M.R. (2008) *Writing at University: A guide for students*, 3rd edition. Maidenhead: Open University Press.

Greetham, B. (2001) *How to Write Better Essays*. Basingstoke: Palgrave Study Guides.

Healy, K. and Mulholland, J. (2007) *Writing Skills for Social Workers*. London: Sage.

Kennedy, D. (n.d.) *Essay writing: a guide for undergraduates*. Royal Literary Fund [online]. Available at: http://www.rlf.org.uk/fellowshipscheme/writing/index.cfm (accessed 16 December 2008)

Murray, N. and Hughes, G. (2008) *Writing Up Your University Assignments and Research Projects*. Maidenhead: Open University Press.
Redman, P. (2005) *Good Essay Writing: A social sciences guide*. London: Sage.
Rose, J. (2007) *The Mature Student's Guide to Writing*, 2nd edition. Basingstoke: Palgrave Macmillan.
Ward, A. and Wood, P. (n.d.) *Writing dissertations: a guide for graduates*. Royal Literary Fund [online]. Available at: http://www.rlf.org.uk/fellowshipscheme/writing/diswriting/intro.htm (accessed 16 December 2008)

8

Referencing Effectively

learning objectives

- To understand what referencing is and when you would need to use referencing in your academic work.
- To understand plagiarism and recognize how use of a correct referencing technique can help you to avoid plagiarizing.
- To recognize the difference between in-text references (citations) and reference lists.
- To be able to construct book, journal article and website references using the Harvard referencing style.

Referencing is a Learnable Skill

The good news is that it is possible to learn how to reference properly without investing too much precious time and effort. As with learning any practical skill, the more you use your referencing skills, the more accomplished you will become at producing academic references. There is nothing particularly difficult about referencing – it simply involves keeping a note of specific pieces of information about the sources that you use, and presenting these in a particular way when you come to include them in your essay or assignment.

Quick Definition: What is a reference?

- An acknowledgement that you have used the work or ideas (or exact words in the case of quotes) of others.
- References are usually to sources that have been published, broadcast, made available online or are in some other way available within the public domain.

Did You Know? Cultural differences in relation to referencing

- The UK education system values referencing as a way of respecting the individual contribution of others to the ever-expanding knowledge base.
- In other countries, there is a different approach to knowledge-sharing which does not place the same degree of emphasis or importance on referencing individual authors (Neville, 2007).

Some international students may find that there is a significant difference in expectations around referencing and associated academic practice in the UK. If you are in this position, you may find it useful to have a chat with your personal tutor about what the similarities and differences might be between the systems that you are used to, and the requirements of the UK system.

The Key to Successful Referencing

It is always a good idea to make sure you have a copy of your institution's referencing handbook (or equivalent guidance) when you produce academic writing. This allows you to:

- check which details you need to be including in a reference
- check which order this information needs to be presented in.

It really is as simple as that! Many social work degree courses will include a section on referencing in their course handbooks which will provide clear instructions as to how to reference and will usually provide examples so that you can see how it works in practice. At the very least, your institution should alert you to which referencing system they use. For many UK universities, the style of referencing used is known as the **Harvard Referencing System** although you should be aware that not all institutions use this system. The principles and examples of referencing that are included below are all based on the Harvard system.

Why are You Asked to Use Referencing?

Did You Know? Why reference?

1 It helps to demonstrate the range and breadth of your background reading. An essay containing 10 references is probably informed by a broader range of reading than one containing just a couple of references.
2 It shows that you have used academic sources to support your statements and arguments and are not just relying on unsupported, personal opinion.
3 It enables the reader to go back and inspect your original sources. They might want to do this if they think you have found an interesting new source or perhaps misinterpreted something.
4 It will be part of the marking criteria so some of your assignment or essay marks may come from your ability to reference accurately and consistently.
5 Finally, but most importantly, referencing helps to protect you against accusations of plagiarism or dishonesty.

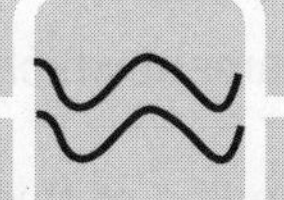

Box 8.1 reflection point

What is plagiarism?

- Plagiarism can be defined as 'a practice that involves knowingly taking and using another person's work and claiming it, directly or indirectly, as your own' (Neville, 2007: 28).
- Universities tend to view plagiarism as being a very serious matter as it undermines the honesty, integrity and quality of academic work.
- Students who are suspected of having engaged in plagiarism are usually required to attend a formal investigation meeting to discuss the allegations. If the plagiarism committee find that the student has indeed engaged in plagiarism, the consequences can be extremely serious.
- Often, it is quite easy for a marker to identify where a student has plagiarized in an academic assignment. Also, many institutions are requiring students to submit work through electronic plagiarism detection services such as 'TurnitinUK'.

As Postle (2007) notes, the Codes of Conduct (GSCC, 2002) require that social workers be 'honest and trustworthy' (Code 2.1). Clearly, demonstrating 'honesty' in the context of producing academic work is just as significant as behaving honestly in the practice environment where issues of professional integrity are concerned.

Referencing in Practice

When do you need to provide a reference?

One of the key aspects of learning how to reference properly is to recognize the occasions where you need to provide references in your academic work. You need to think about providing a reference:

- **whenever you refer to a particular theory or a particular argument or a specific viewpoint that has been put forward in a published form.** For example, if you are writing an assignment about anti-oppressive modes of social work practice and you want to mention the 'PCS Model', you should indicate that this has been developed in a book published in 1997 by Neil Thompson.

Example: **Referring to a specific social work approach**

You would like to develop a discussion of 'crisis theory' in an assignment which focuses on how practitioners carry out their work.

In this case, you would need to cite the fact that your understanding of this approach comes from **Jonathan Parker** and **Greta Bradleys** book ***Social Work Practice*** published in **2007**, 2nd edn, and provide a full reference to this work in your reference list.

- **whenever you draw on published statistics, specific examples drawn from 'real life' or actual case studies.** These are the types of information that you should be using to support your points and arguments but you must be careful to include a reference to the source of the information.

Example: **Using published statistical information**

You are writing an essay on aspects of social inequality in the United Kingdom and through your research you have found that on average someone with a degree qualification earns more than double the weekly income of those people who do not have any qualifications.

In this particular case, the statistic was included as part of a report called ***A Summary of Focus on Social Inequalities*** written by **Penny Babb** in **2005** and published by the **Office for National Statistics**. You would therefore need to include a citation to this publication at the appropriate point in your essay.

- **When using direct quotations.** Whenever you directly quote the words that someone has already written, you need to make this clear in your essay or assignment and also provide a reference to the original text that contained those words.

Example: **Using direct quotes**

In an essay discussing disability, you want to include the exact words written by **Anthony Giddens** on page 283 of his book ***Sociology***, where he discusses different models of disabilities:

'... defenders of the social model have argued that rather than denying everyday experiences of impairment, the *social* model merely seeks to focus attention on the social barriers to full participation in society that are raised against disabled people'.

- **When paraphrasing.** This is where you put someone else's original words into your own words. In other words, you re-phrase (or paraphrase) what has been said in a published piece of writing by finding your own choice of words in which to express it. Even though you are using your own words when you paraphrase, you still need to provide a reference to your original source material to indicate where the idea originates from.

Use of paraphrasing and direct quotes

Quick Tip: Paraphrase or direct quote?

- In general, it is better to paraphrase the words of others rather than include lots of direct quotes in your essays and assignments.
- The reason for this is that if you are using a lot of direct quotes (in other words, using a lot of material that is essentially someone else's way of expressing an idea or opinion), then clearly you are not demonstrating to the assessor that you actually understand the material yourself.

There may be occasions where you really struggle to put something into your own words. In situations like this, you may decide that it is best to use a direct quote but wherever you do, try to make sure that you *always* comment on the quoted material and indicate what is particularly useful or helpful about it.

activity 8.1

Check your understanding of when referencing is required

Read through the descriptions of various scenarios below and indicate whether you think the reader needs to use a reference by circling the 'tick', or if you think a reference is not required then circle a 'cross':

1. Amir has read something about social exclusion in a book on sociology by Antony Giddens. He has taken the gist of what was written but has put this into his own words (i.e. paraphrased it) in a sentence in his social policy assignment. ☑ ☒
2. Stef wants to refer to the fact that Tony Blair was the UK Prime Minister from 1997 until 2007 in his social sciences essay. ☑ ☒
3. Dina has read an article in the *British Journal of Social Work* and intends to use a direct quote from this in her 'Assessment, Planning and Evaluation' module assignment. ☑ ☒
4. Aisha is writing about her own experiences on a placement working with older people in her social work practice portfolio. ☑ ☒
5. Maryanne uses some statistics in her social welfare essay that were mentioned by a tutor in a recent lecture. ☑ ☒
6. Lauren is writing a conclusion to her assignment on evidence-based social work practice, in which she summarizes the main ideas that she has already discussed (and referenced) in the main body of her essay. Does she need to repeat the same references in her conclusion? ☑ ☒
7. Samuel has found a useful article on a website and has used some direct words and phrases, together with some paraphrasing (putting things into his own words), to write a paragraph in his law and human justice essay. ☑ ☒

When you have completed this activity, check your answers against those given at the end of this chapter in Box 8.2.

In-text references and reference lists

When you use references, you include the information in two different places within the essay or assignment:

1 In-text references (also called citation)
2 Reference list.

Did You Know? In-text reference (citation)

In-text referencing is the means by which you indicate when you have used a source in the main body of your essay.

For instance, if you paraphrase a section from a book, you need to indicate where the original material has come from by using an in-text reference in your sentence.

When using the Harvard referencing system, the in-text reference is usually made up of:

- the **author's surname** (first names or initials are not included)
- the **year of publication**
- for direct quotes, you also need to include the **page number** that the quote is taken from.

Have a look at the examples of in-text referencing below:

***Example:* Citing something that has been paraphrased from a book**

> The three main reasons why the majority of service users seek help from social workers are to receive help in maintaining their current quality of life, to bring about limited changes in their lives or, lastly, for help with managing more radical life change. (**Trevithick, 2005**)

***Example:* Citing a direct quote from a journal article**

Some examples in the literature emphasize the need to provide an equitable service which also acknowledges the specific needs and contexts of lesbians and gay men:

> We need each lesbian and gay man to be seen as a unique individual within her/his own context and an understanding that this will include her/his social and political current and historical context. For example, a lesbian foster carer needs the same support as all foster carers but she might also want to discuss the impact that a foster child's grandfather's homophobia is having on her own birth child. **(Cosis Brown, 2008: 270)**

What happens if there is no author's surname?

Occasionally, you may want to provide a reference to a publication where it is not clear as to who has authored the publication or document. This is not uncommon with some web-based resources where it is not clearly stated on the web page or web document who has authored the material. In this case, you would need to use the name of the organization that has published the material in your 'in-text' reference. For instance, if you wanted to make a reference to a report entitled 'Using digital media to access information and good practice for paid carers of older people' which was published by a group called the 'Interactive Technologies Research Group', rather than a named, individual author, your 'in-text reference' would be as shown below:

What to do if there is no author's name

Example of citation:

> Information sharing, training support, communication and record keeping are some of the ways in which using digital technology could help care workers working within residential care homes for the elderly. (**Interactive Technologies Research Group, 2006**)

What happens if there are three or more authors?

If you are providing an in-text reference to something that has been written by three or more authors, then you do not need to list each of the authors' surnames in the in-text reference. Instead, you can simply use the surname of the first author and then write **et al.**, which is an abbreviated Latin phrase, meaning 'and others'. However, when it comes to putting the full reference in your reference list, you must list all of the authors' names.

What happens if there are three or more authors?

Example of in-text reference (citation):

Some examples of service-user involvement in social work courses include service-user conversations. **(Elliott et al., 2005)**

Example of how this would look in your full reference list:

Elliott, T., Frazer, T., Garrand, D., Hickinbotham, J., Horton, V., Mann, J., Soper, S., Turner, J., Turner, M. and Whiteford, A. (2005) 'Practice learning and assessment on BSc (Hons) Social Work: "service user conversations"', *Social Work Education* 24(4): 451–66.

What happens if there is no date of publication?

When you are referencing books and journal articles, it should be easy to find out when the source was published. Books will include the date of publication along with other useful bits of information on the book's title page. This is usually found on the fourth page of the book and includes information about when and where the book was published and printed. Paper-based journals will usually indicate the year of publication on the front cover of the journal.

If you are accessing a journal article in an electronic format, then the year of publication will usually be clearly shown on the first page of the electronic journal article. However, other sources of information including some web pages, leaflets and reports may not always show a year of publication on them. In this case, instead of omitting a year of publication, you need to indicate that the year information was not available by including the words **no date** in your in-text reference (it can also be abbreviated to 'n.d.'). The following example shows this in practice:

What to do if there is no date of publication

Example of citation in an essay sentence:

NHS Choices **(n.d.)** have published a list of the main recognized symptoms of stress and social work students need to learn to recognize these in themselves and in others.

What happens if an author, or organization, has published two pieces of work in the same year and I want to refer to them both?

Example: For example, the Health and Safety Executive (HSE) have published two separate pieces of work in 2008, and you want to refer to both of them.

(Continued)

- If you just use (**HSE, 2008**) as your in-text reference, the reader is not going to know which of the two pieces of work published in 2008 this refers to.
- So, in this case, you would add letters of the alphabet to the year in order to distinguish between the two publications.
- For example, (**HSE, 2008a**) is clearly going to refer to a different source than (**HSE, 2008b**).

If you check the full reference list at the end of this book, you will see that there are in fact two references that correspond with each of these in-text references. You will see that HSE 2008a corresponds to a report called 'Working together to reduce stress at work' and HSE 2008b relates to a different report about self-reported workplace illness and injuries.

Reference Lists

Did You Know? Reference lists

- You need to include what are called **full references** at the end of your essay.
- These record more information about your sources and appear in an alphabetically ordered reference list.

Reference lists are not particularly difficult to put together as long as you have recorded all of the relevant information that you will need to include as you have gone along. If you find it difficult to get into the habit of remembering to take a record of the relevant details when you borrow a library book or access a journal article, you may find it useful to take a copy of the **Reference Record Sheets** that we have included at the end of this chapter in Figures 8.2, 8.3 and 8.4. These remind you of the relevant details that you should be making a note of as you refer to different sources.

Referencing books in your reference list

The following panel shows the important bits of information that you need to provide when referencing books in your reference list:

Table 8.1 Information needed for a book reference

Type	*Example*
Author's surname:	**Trevithick**
Author's initial(s):	**P**
Year book was published:	**2005**
Title of book:	**Social Work Skills**
Edition (if not first edition):	**2nd edition**
Place of publication:	**Maidenhead**
Publishing company:	**Open University Press**

When it comes to presenting this information in your reference list, you would present it in the following order:

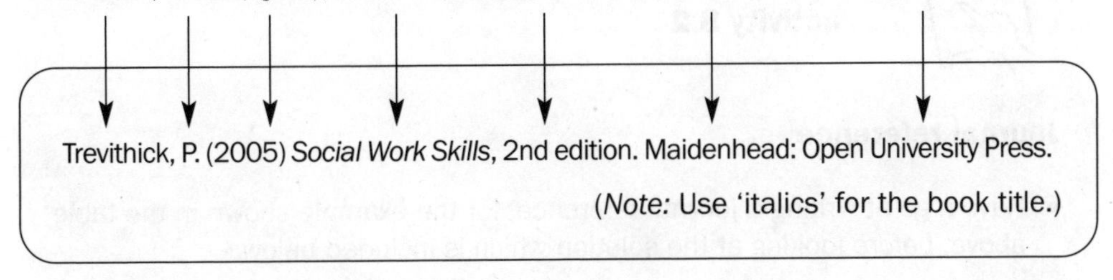

Referencing journal articles in your reference list

The process of referencing a journal article is very similar to that of referencing books, but due to the way that journals are published, there are some additional pieces of information that need to be included. Basically, journals are like academic 'magazines' in the sense that they are published on a regular basis (often four times per year) and consist of a number of articles, reviews and editorial pieces written by a number of different academics and practitioners.

Most journals are published in volumes and each volume contains a number of parts or issues. So if an academic journal is first published in January 2007 and is published four times per year, the first volume will normally consist of issues one to four. In January 2008, the second volume would begin and again would consist of four issues published throughout the year. For a journal article reference, you would also provide the page numbers that the journal article starts and finishes on.

This information is then put together in the following order to create a correctly formatted journal reference:

Author's surname, initials, (year), article title in single inverted commas, journal title in italics, volume no., issues no., page span.

Table 8.2 Information needed for a journal article reference

Type	*Example*
Authors' surname(s) and initial(s):	**Warner, J. and Gabe, J.**
Year of publication:	**2008**
Article title:	**Risk, mental disorder and social work practice: a gendered landscape**
Title of journal:	**British Journal of Social Work**
Volume number:	**38**
Part number:	**1**
Page span:	**117–34**

activity 8.2

Journal reference

- Have a go at writing a journal reference, for the example shown in the table above, *before* looking at the solution which is included below.

So, for the journal article details shown in the table above, the correct reference format would be:

Warner, J. and Gabe, J. (2008) 'Risk, mental disorder and social work practice: a gendered landscape', *British Journal of Social Work* 38(1): 117–134.

(*Note*: Use single speech (quotation) marks for the article title, and 'italics' for the journal title.)

Referencing websites and online resources

The information used when referencing websites and online resources is slightly different to that used for books and journal articles. This is partly due to the nature of how the World Wide Web works with its uniform resource locators (URLs, otherwise known as 'web addresses') and the fact that web pages may be updated or removed from one day to the next. Also, you may find that it is sometimes difficult to identify who has written a particular web page or document and also when the document was written.

Quick Tip: Web-based materials

When working with web-based material, you need to:

- **record the exact web address of the page** that you are referring to (allows the reader to visit the resource)
- **note the date on which you accessed the document** (identifies that the information was valid at the time that you accessed it).

Clearly, some web-based material is prone to ongoing alteration and even removal. However, in the case of something like online official reports, the content of these documents should not change once they have been published but their online location may well be altered if an organization decides to redesign or overhaul their website. The following shows the details required for a reference to a web page which is part of the Social Policy and Social Work (SWAP) website:

Table 8.3 Information needed for a website reference

Type	*Example*
Author's name OR editor's name OR organization's name:	**Young, P.**
Year written or last updated:	**2003**
Title of web page or document:	**What is the scholarship of learning and teaching?**
URL (web address):	**http://www.swap.ac.uk/research/introduction.asp**
Date you accessed document:	**12 February 2007**

Please take careful note of the way that this information needs to be presented when you write out your full reference:

Author/editor/organization name, (year), title in italics, [online]. Available at: <provide web address>, (date accessed).

activity 8.3

Website reference

- Have a go at writing a website reference, for the example shown in the table above, *before* looking at the solution which is included on the following page.

So, for the website details included in the table above, the correct reference format would be:

> Young, P. (2003) *What is the scholarship of learning and teaching?* [online]. Available at: http://www.swap.ac.uk/research/introduction.asp (accessed 12 February 2007)
>
> (*Note*: Use 'italics' for the web page title.)

The screen grab below shows how to identify the relevant information that is required for web references:

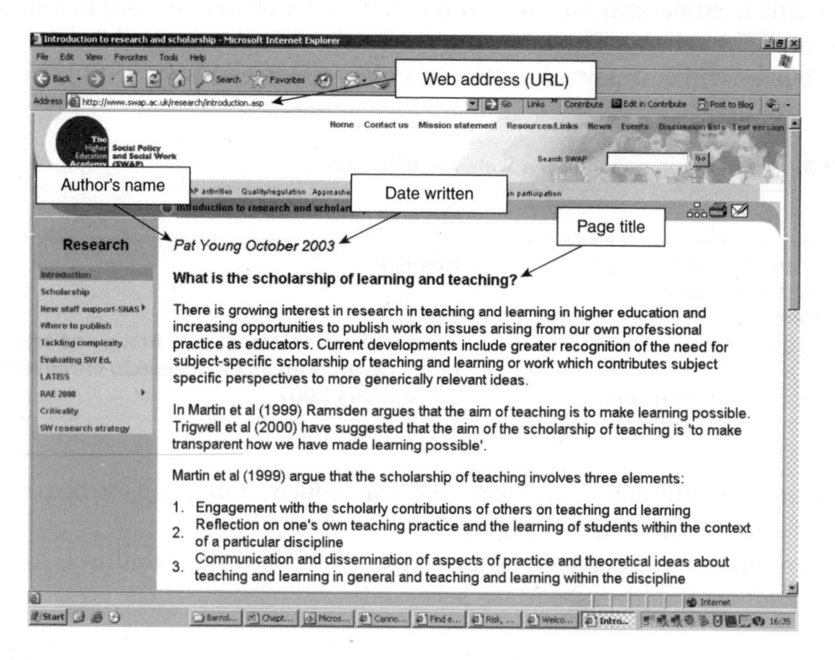

Figure 8.1 Screenshot from SWAP website (used with permission of SWAP)

Referencing other types of material

We have briefly focused on the Harvard referencing style for just three of the most frequently used types of information used by social work students. However, other types of material should be referenced including:

- newspaper articles
- television programmes

- films
- photographs and illustrations
- conference proceedings
- legal materials
- government publications.

There is insufficient space to go into the intricacies of referencing all of these types of material here but you should make sure that you seek advice from your institution about the referencing system that they use. Many university and college libraries will have paper-based or online guides to referencing and it is vital that you access this information before you begin your academic essays or assignments.

Quick Tip: Help with referencing

- If you find that you are struggling with referencing, it is definitely worth trying to enlist the help and support of a sympathetic colleague, lecturer, study skills tutor or librarian to help you to get it right.
- There is no point in ignoring the issue as it will only get picked up again and again in future assignments.
- Remember, it takes time and practice to learn how to reference accurately and consistently.

Referencing Exercises

- The following activities will be of most benefit to you if you know that your institution uses the Harvard Referencing System.
- If your institution uses another system, then it may be best to skip past this exercise to avoid confusing yourself.
- After you have completed these activities, compare your answers with those given in Boxes 8.2, 8.3 and 8.4 at the end of this chapter.

activity 8.4

Scenario 1 – Practice BOOK References

- You have been asked to write an essay which discusses service-user involvement in social work practice.

(Continued)

- You come across a book in your institution's library called *Social Work: An introduction to contemporary practice*, which contains a chapter on this topic.
- You take this book out on loan, read the chapter and decide to use a direct quote from it in your essay.
- Before you return the book to the library, you look at the title page and note that the book was published in Harlow by a publishing company called 'Pearson Education'.
- You also notice that the book was published in 2008 and has been written by four authors – Kate Wilson, Gillian Ruch, Mark Lymbery and Andrew Cooper.

1 The direct quote that you used was from page 414 of this book. What details would you need to include in your in-text reference?
2 Using the Harvard Referencing System, show how you would present this book as a full reference in your reference list at the end of the essay.

activity 8.5

Scenario 2 – Practice JOURNAL References

- You spend some time searching for journal articles that relate to the topic of your essay.
- You find an interesting article called 'Tightening the net: children, community and control', which makes some interesting arguments in relation to children and social policy.
- You decide to include a reference to this in a paragraph of your essay in which you discuss young people and issues of social exclusion.

Before you accessed the full text of this article, your institution's library catalogue displayed a screen of information about the journal article, which is included below:

Article title:	Tightening the net: children, community and control
Authors:	Adrian L. James; Allison James
Publication frequency:	4 issues per year
Published in:	British Journal of Sociology, Volume 52, Issue 2, June 2001, pages 211–28
Subject:	Social Sciences

1 If you had paraphrased a passage from this article in the main body of your essay, which details would need to be included in your in-text reference?
2 Pick out the relevant bits of information and show how you would present this journal article as a full reference in the reference list at the end of your essay.

activity 8.6

Scenario 3 – WEBSITE References

- You find a report focusing on issues of immigration and social cohesion on the Joseph Rowntree Foundation website, which you want to reference in an assignment.
- The report is:
    - o authored by Mary Hickman, Helen Crowley and Nick Mai
    - o called 'Immigration and social cohesion in the UK'
    - o published by the Joseph Rowntree Foundation in 2008
    - o available at this URL (web address):

http://www.jrf.org.uk/sites/files/jrf/2230-deprivation-cohesion-immigration.pdf

- For the purpose of this activity, imagine that you accessed this resource on 16 May 2009.

1 If you had paraphrased a passage from this report in the main body of your essay, which details would need to be included in your in-text reference?
2 Pick out the relevant bits of information and show how you would present this online report as a full reference in the reference list at the end of your essay.

Other Referencing Tips

Referencing a chapter from an edited book

You may want to provide a reference to a chapter that a particular author has written, which has been published in an edited collection. When it comes to providing an in-text citation, you would provide the chapter author's surname and the year of publication as usual e.g. (**Beresford, 2005**).

However, when you come to produce the full reference in your reference list, you would do it in a slightly different way to a standard book reference, as follows:

Surname (of chapter author), initial(s), (year), title of chapter, editor's initial, editor's surname (ed.) Book title in italics. Place of publication: publisher's name.

So, using the Beresford example shown above, the full reference would look like this:

Example of referencing a chapter from an edited book:

Beresford, P. (2005) 'Social approaches to madness and distress: user perspectives and user knowledges', in J. Tew (ed.) *Social Perspectives in Mental Health: Developing social models to understand work with mental distress*. London: Jessica Kingsley.

Secondary referencing

Did You Know? What is secondary referencing?

- This is where you read a book, journal article or some other type of publication in which the author refers to a piece of work, written by someone else, that you would like to make reference to in your assignment.
- It is called 'secondary referencing' because you are referencing a source that someone else has read and included in their work, rather than reading that source directly yourself.

Secondary referencing example: You may be doing an assignment on social workers and stress, and after reading Chapter 3 in this book, you want to use the reference to work by Lloyd et al. (2002) that we have included.

Technically, your lecturers would always tell you to try to go and find the original source and read that. So, in this example, they would expect you to:

- find the full Lloyd et al. reference in our reference list at the end of this book
- use this to track the article down so that you can read it for yourself.

One of the reasons for this is so that you can satisfy yourself that we have correctly interpreted and reported on Lloyd et al.'s findings. However, sometimes it may be difficult to get hold of an original text and if this is the case, you would need to use 'secondary referencing'.

How does secondary referencing work?

It is probably best to show this by using an example:

Secondary in-text referencing example:

If you were providing an **in-text reference** in your essay to the Lloyd et al. study that we have mentioned in this book, your reference would be (**Lloyd et al., 2005 cited in Stogdon and Kiteley, 2010**).

- Notice how you have basically linked two in-text references together with the words '**cited in**'?
- The work that you are referring to is always put first (e.g. in this case, the study by Lloyd et al.), followed by the work that you read about it in (e.g. in this case, the book you are currently reading!).

When it comes to producing your full reference in your reference list, you are again basically linking two full references together, as shown here:

Secondary referencing example:

Lloyd, C., King, R. and Chenoweth, L. (2002) 'Social work, stress and burnout: a review', *Journal of Mental Health* 11(3): 255–65. **Cited in:** Stogdon, C. and Kiteley, R. (2010) *Study Skills for Social Workers*. London: Sage.

Box 8.2 Answers to Activity 8.1

1 ☑, 2. ☒, 3. ☑, 4. ☒, 5. ☑, 6. ☒, 7. ☑

Box 8.3 Solution to Activity 8.4 (Book Reference)

1 (Wilson et al., 2008)
2 Wilson, K., Ruch, G., Lymbery, M. and Cooper, A. (2008) *Social Work: An introduction to contemporary practice*. Harlow: Pearson Education pp. 414.

Box 8.4 Solution to Activity 8.5 (Journal Reference)

1 (James and James, 2001).
2 James, A.L. and James, A. (2001) 'Tightening the net: children, community and control', *British Journal of Sociology* 52(2): 211–28.

Box 8.5 Solution to Activity 8.6 (Website Reference)

1 (Hickman et al., 2008).
2 Hickman, M., Crowley, H. and Mai, N. (2008) *Immigration and social cohesion in the UK*. Joseph Rowntree Foundation [online]. Available at: http://www.jrf.org.uk/sites/files/jrf/2230-deprivation-cohesion-immigration.pdf (accessed 16 May 2009).

summary of key points

- Referencing is about acknowledging the contribution that other people's work has made to your own work.
- A correct and accurate referencing technique adds to the academic quality and integrity of your work.
- Plagiarism is the attempt to pass off someone else's work as your own and is to be avoided. Good referencing technique can help you to do this.
- The Harvard Referencing System works by including a brief citation in the text and a full reference in the reference list which appears at the end of your piece of work.

further reading

Neville, C. (2007) *The Complete Guide to Referencing and Avoiding Plagiarism*. Maidenhead: Open University Press.

Pears, R. and Shields, G. (2008) *Cite Them Right: The essential referencing guide*, 7th edition. Newcastle upon Tyne: Pear Tree Books.

Author's surname and initial(s):	
Year of publication:	
Title of book:	
Place of publication:	
Name of publishing company:	
Comments:	

Author's surname and initial(s):	
Year of publication:	
Title of book:	
Place of publication:	
Name of publishing company:	
Comments:	

Author's surname and initial(s):	
Year of publication:	
Title of book:	
Place of publication:	
Name of publishing company:	
Comments:	

Figure 8.2 References record sheet for books

Note: Feel free to print off or photocopy as many of these as you need.

Author's surname and initial(s):	
Year of publication:	
Title of article:	
Title of journal:	
Volume number (if any):	
Part number (if any):	
Page numbers (first and last):	
Comments:	

Author's surname and initial(s):	
Year of publication:	
Title of article:	
Title of journal:	
Volume number (if any):	
Part number (if any):	
Page numbers (first and last):	
Comments:	

Author's surname and initial(s):	
Year of publication:	
Title of article:	
Title of journal:	
Volume number (if any):	
Part number (if any):	
Page numbers (first and last):	
Comments:	

Figure 8.3 Reference record sheet for journal articles

Note: Feel free to print off or photocopy as many of these as you need.

Author's surname and initial(s), or organisation that published resource:	
Year of publication (if available):	
Title of web resource:	
Web address:	
Date you accessed resource:	
Comments:	

Author's surname and initial(s), or organisation that published resource:	
Year of publication (if available):	
Title of web resource:	
Web address:	
Date you accessed resource:	
Comments:	

Author's surname and initial(s), or organisation that published resource:	
Year of publication (if available):	
Title of web resource:	
Web address:	
Date you accessed resource:	
Comments:	

Figure 8.4 References record sheet for web resources

Note: Feel free to print off or photocopy as many of these as you need.

9

Communication and Awareness Skills

learning objectives

- To understand why communication is so important to effective social work practice.
- To develop an understanding of the skills involved in communicating well.
- To consider the range of professional and study contexts in which communication skills are used.
- To develop an appreciation and awareness of the importance of listening.

Social work has communication at the very core of its skill base and the way that you develop your communication skills during your training will have significance for your future practice as a qualified worker GSCC (2002).

Service-users, Carers and Communication Skills

You may have already been aware of service-user involvement in the recruitment process that you went through, as many HEIs invite service-users to be part of the interview and selection process. You may find that service-users are also involved in the design and delivery of the course as well as the assessment process. Some universities use a student and service-user conversation approach (Elliott et al., 2005), and within our own institution, service-users are actively involved in interviewing potential students as well as helping them to develop effective interviewing and communication skills.

Box 9.1 reflection point

The benefits of student social workers working closely with service-users

- Service-users possess 'expert knowledge' and this can be accessed and used by a social worker who uses effective communication to build up rapport and trust.
- Social work practice involves the active participation and decision making of service-users and this requires clearly defined and efficient channels of communication.
- Working closely with service-users encourages you to understand how different approaches to thinking about communication (e.g. active listening, non-verbal) can be related to working with actual members of the community.
- You are better-equipped to relate to the experiences and perspectives of service-users and carers at an early stage of your course.

Research suggests that service-users strongly value this involvement in social work courses (Wenman, 2005: 38), particularly in relation to:

- playing a part in shaping future services
- raising awareness amongst students of the real, lived experiences of service-users
- encouraging and challenging students to think about provision of services.

Developing Your Confidence in Communicating

In the very first week of your course, you will probably be encouraged by tutors to begin to develop your communication in a verbal way and this usually involves some painful activity in which you will be asked to speak to the person next to you, exchange a few personal details and then you be asked to introduce your neighbour to the group. If you have not walked out at this stage, you will hopefully be given some explanation for the excruciatingly embarrassing experience. Your tutor will no doubt try to convince you that the course is focused on the opportunities for students to develop confidence in all aspects of communication which will involve talking to people that you have never met before. And also that this is good preparation for your future work as a social worker – in relation to social work practice, your tutors will have support on this from many others, such as Golightly (2008), Jaspers (2003) and the GSCC (2002). Dealing with your initial embarrassment and perhaps lack of confidence is probably one of the most challenging aspects of starting on a social work course.

Communication and Social Work

When social workers have initial contact with service-users and carers, they may have a limited amount of time to gather pertinent information in a situation which may be both urgent and serious in relation to the decisions that may affect the rights of service-users for a long period of time.

Box 9.2 reflection point

Communication and information gathering

The information that is gathered at this initial point of contact may well need to form the basis of future court hearings and formal reviews. The ability to demonstrate communication skills in an open and honest way is a crucial starting point for the information gathering that social workers need to do.

The Codes of Practice and Key Roles (GSCC, 2002) give social workers a clear mandate to communicate in a way which does not marginalize and which has a focus on preserving the autonomy of the service-user wherever risk permits. As a social work student, you will be required to demonstrate your communications skills at a number of points on the course.

Quick tip: Communicate well in practice by...

- asking relevant and pertinent questions about the practice that you have seen
- communicating appropriately with any service-users and colleagues that you might meet as part of this experience.

- If you are on a three-year course, it is likely that you will be required to show that you can communicate effectively when you go out into practice to shadow a qualified social worker.
- As part of the university-based work in your first year, it is likely that you be required to do a formal presentation which will be either an individual one or as part of a group, or both.
- The skills that you will be expected to develop will need to be in place in advance of your placements which will usually take place at later stages of the course.

Written and verbal communication skills

Your communication skills will include both **written** and **verbal** ones and you will have the opportunity to begin to develop these skills in the university as part of your preparation for practice:

- Your note-taking in lectures will be the start of the written skills.
- Your contribution to discussions and tutorials will be the starting point for your verbal and non-verbal skills.

Supporting the development of communication skills

Whether you are a work-based student or a university-based one, there will be a requirement for you to be signed off as fit to continue in your social work training before you go on assessed placement in a social work setting (GSCC, 2002). Your communication skills will be observed by either your line manager, mentor or tutor, who will usually write a report which will comment on your suitability to continue your training. If social workers are meeting service-users in situations when emotions are running high, it is important that the social workers are confident in their ability to communicate effectively to ensure that the information they gather is both relevant and accurate.

Ensuring Accuracy – Information Fit for Purpose

Social work relies on:

- information
- reflections
- observations

to inform the judgements that need to be made about practice including risk, intervention and assessment.

In order to ascertain if information is relevant and accurate, it is important for you to fully understand why you have been asked to gather the particular information. You will need to feel confident to ask why, and to do this you will need to be able to communicate effectively in a verbal way – if this feels like a chicken and egg situation, you are on the right track, e.g. to communicate effectively with service-users and carers, you first need to be able to communicate with your:

- tutor
- practice educator
- line manager or mentor.

Another important aspect of gathering accurate information is **checking if the information is correct.**

activity 9.1

Checking your grasp of information

1 Ask a friend, colleague or member of your family to tell you about their interests or hobby and try hard to listen to the details of what they tell you.
2 When they have finished, try feeding back to them as much of what they said as you can, and then ask them if you are on the right track.
3 What did you find most difficult or challenging about this activity? How might you use this to help you improve your communication skills?

By practising feeding back information you have heard regularly, you will enhance your capacity to work in an empowering way with service-users and carers when you are on your practice placement.

Listening

Listening in social work practice is fundamental to our understanding and effective work with service-users and colleagues. We will explore some of the ways that you can develop your listening skills to enhance both your academic and practise work.

It is useful to consider some of your existing skills in relation to listening to others as you will practise this skill in many aspects of your relationships.

activity 9.2

Listening and being listened to ...

Think about how you have developed your understanding of the importance of both listening and being listened to. In order to help you do this, identify a time when:

- you have had a positive experience of being listened to – for example, when you visited a doctor who gave you enough time to detail your health concerns
- you have listened carefully to a friend or colleague who was very upset about the ending of a relationship
- you have talked to your personal tutor about any worries you might have – for example, concerns about meeting deadlines for submission of work
- you have worked closely with a distressed child – for example, s/he may have talked to you about some serious issues of abuse.

The experience of **being listened to** often evokes a positive response in relation to our own self-esteem because:

- we feel valued if we are listened to when we are taken seriously
- the listener has given some time to hear what we have to say.

Listening to someone who talks about a very important issue for them can also make us feel valued because they will have chosen carefully the person to whom they want to share the information.

In looking at your own development of listening skills, it would be useful to think about your responses to the following questions.

Are you put off from listening by your previous experience of a person – or a person similar to the one you are not eager to listen to?

Studying in higher education will be a very different environment from school as you will be expected to rely much more on your own organization skills, so it is very important that you are able to listen to the information and assignment guidance given to you by your tutors. If you are returning to education after a gap, you may have an image of yourself as being someone who is not academic. If you had a negative experience of education in the past, it may well be worth having a focused tutorial with a tutor, in order to dispel some of your fears and anxieties.

How comfortable are you with silences?

Silences are often culturally specific and it may be that you are totally uncomfortable with extended silence in a conversation. As a social worker, you will need to enable someone to talk to you about things that are really painful and upsetting for them. When we are upset, we often need to speak at our own pace and think about how we can find a form of words to express exactly what we want to say. In this situation, we may need to pause and think and the person who is listening will need to be patient and comfortable with the silences. It is perhaps important to consider why you end a silence – is it because you are uncomfortable or is it because you want to say something to help the person make sense of their situation?

Are you happier speaking than listening?

Do friends and family tell you that you like the sound of your own voice and that it is often hard to get a word in edgeways – oh dear! This is not as dismal as it may seem at first as this may ring true with your own awareness of how you engage with people. Being overenthusiastic can lead to dominance in a conversation, and you may have a lot to say but it may also be pertinent to look at your own style of speaking. Do you compete in conversations so that you usually have the last word?

Think about how you listen to people when you first meet them

Are you interested in people when you meet them for the first time and do you genuinely want to engage in conversation with them? Do you interrupt people when they are still speaking – this often means that you will have stopped listening quite a while before you speak as you will be busy thinking about what you are going to say?

There is a real dilemma here as social workers need to be confident and comfortable with the use of discussion as a means of assessing and supporting people but they also need to demonstrate a serious concern for the accuracy of information. This accuracy is assured if we refer to the service-user as the expert in their own situation, so the importance of effective listening is reinforced as an important skill.

Active Listening

Box 9.3 reflection point

Your patterns of communication

- Consider the way that you listen to people who are close to you and who you have daily contact with.
- When you are having a conversation, be aware of how much time you spend talking and how much time you spend listening.

There are many routine conversations that take place almost automatically, such as:

- 'Have you got your dinner money?'
- 'What have you got on today?'

It may well be that to listen with 'half an ear' to these conversations is perfectly reasonable and adequate but the conversations that we have in social work are rarely safe unless we do give our full attention to the content.

There has been much written about the importance of **active listening** (Cornell University, 1993) and this is certainly a skill that will complement your understanding and application of the Key Roles, COP and Value Requirements (GSCC, 2002).

Did You Know? What is active listening?

Active listening is a way of giving our full attention to someone else when they are talking to us or telling us something. It requires us to:

- focus on the other person's behaviour and body language
- avoid introducing our own judgements or opinions.

when the speaker has finished, the active listener may then 'reflect back', or paraphrase, what has been heard, in order to check out their understanding of what was said.

The following exercise will give you the opportunity to understand how demanding serious, active listening can be but also how pleasant it is to be listened to in a genuine and uninterrupted way.

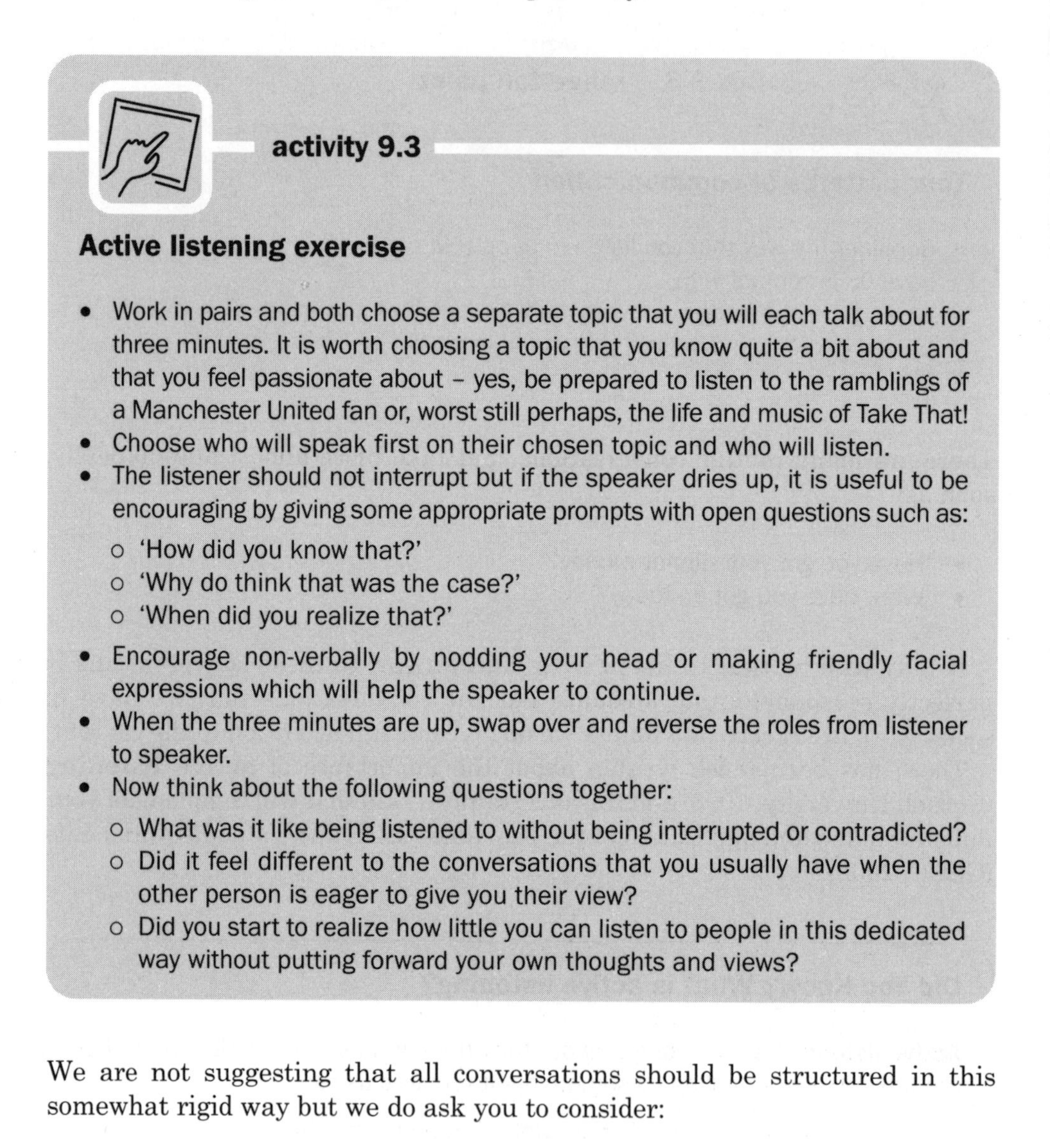

activity 9.3

Active listening exercise

- Work in pairs and both choose a separate topic that you will each talk about for three minutes. It is worth choosing a topic that you know quite a bit about and that you feel passionate about – yes, be prepared to listen to the ramblings of a Manchester United fan or, worst still perhaps, the life and music of Take That!
- Choose who will speak first on their chosen topic and who will listen.
- The listener should not interrupt but if the speaker dries up, it is useful to be encouraging by giving some appropriate prompts with open questions such as:
  - 'How did you know that?'
  - 'Why do think that was the case?'
  - 'When did you realize that?'
- Encourage non-verbally by nodding your head or making friendly facial expressions which will help the speaker to continue.
- When the three minutes are up, swap over and reverse the roles from listener to speaker.
- Now think about the following questions together:
  - What was it like being listened to without being interrupted or contradicted?
  - Did it feel different to the conversations that you usually have when the other person is eager to give you their view?
  - Did you start to realize how little you can listen to people in this dedicated way without putting forward your own thoughts and views?

We are not suggesting that all conversations should be structured in this somewhat rigid way but we do ask you to consider:

- the importance of gathering accurate information in a social work context
- the importance of being serious about listening in such a way that we can be confident about the accuracy of the information obtained
- the ways in which social work involves the discussion of complex thoughts and feelings which will inform decisions of great magnitude so it is doubly relevant that the skills of active listening are applied.

Verbal Communication

It is through conversation and dialogue that the relationships are formed in which social work practice takes place. If this is the case, then how do we differentiate between conversations between friends, and the 'friendly' conversation that social workers and service-users and carers have with each other (Koprowska, 2005)?

There are some wider issues here about the professional boundaries that need to exist in order to enable a relationship to be constructed whilst ensuring that a service is delivered in an appropriate way. If we look closely at the content of conversational exchanges, we will see both similarities and differences in relation to personal and professional dialogues.

Communication and Value Requirements

The Codes of Practice (GSCC, 2002) states clearly that social workers must demonstrate respect towards the service-users and carers who they are working with in a professional context. The need to speak and listen respectfully is embedded in the Value Requirements (GSCC, 2002) and is also generally true of relationships between people on a personal as well as professional level. However, social work conversations are often about the restriction or denial of liberty and the communication needs to be efficient in broaching these very serious aspects (Hayne, 2003).

In a personal interaction between friends, it would be an unusual situation where the discussion would focus on one person denying freedom to the other, so in this way the style and content would be incomparable with the professional communication. If we consider further how social workers talk to service-users and carers, we need to look at the assessment of risk and the consequences of this in relation to communication.

Box 9.4 reflection point

Potentially challenging or complex conversations

- How do social workers start the conversation in which they have to tell a service-user that their child has been referred to them because of a suspicious injury?
- Where do we begin to have the discussion about a very important and highly charged situation which for example could potentially lead to the child being subject to care proceedings?

Respect

The Codes of Practice give a clear mandate for **respect** to be demonstrated and genuinely felt, in any communication. As such, it sets the scene and gives guidance about politeness and sensitivity along with the recognition that the person may, understandably, be very upset at the point of contact with social workers. The demonstration of respect will incorporate some of the Value Requirements of professional practice and will draw upon the belief in openness and honesty in professional relationships.

Box 9.5 reflection point

Finding the right words

- Think about the words that might be used when we start a conversation that is potentially difficult.
- What do we say when we knock on the door?
- Which words do we choose when we have been required to visit a family when abuse has been alleged?
- Think about how you would want to be spoken to by the professional who had to visit you and your family when abuse had been alleged?

We would suggest that most people would want to have clear information about the purpose of the visit and as many details as possible. If we recognize that respect forms the basis of our communication, we have the guidance necessary to speak to service-users and carers in a way which preserves dignity and ensures fairness, regardless of the contentious context of the matter to be discussed. Your ability to identify relevant non-verbal messages will also form a key part of your safe practice as a social work student.

Non-verbal Communication – Observing Communication Through Behaviour

Words are clearly an important tool in relation to communicating with other people but do not necessarily convey the most meaning. In fact, Mehrabian (cited in Cornell University, 1993) says:

Meaning = 55% facial expression + 38% tone of voice + 7% words

As a social worker, a person will communicate with you through their behaviour and not necessarily just through words. For example, if you have made several appointments to meet with a service-user or carer and they have consistently not turned up, then there is potentially a very clear message for you in relation to their willingness to meet with you! Alternatively, you may have the wrong address, so it is always important to check the accuracy of basic information that is given to you when you are asked to contact someone. The accuracy of other information may be gleaned by observing the way that people react when they are using words and also the way that people convey their real feelings through mannerisms, tone of voice and body language.

activity 9.4

Assessing non-verbal signs

What kinds of messages would you 'hear' if you were having a conversation with someone and they behaved in the following ways:

1 Sat with arms tightly crossed and avoided eye contact?
2 Constantly checked their watch and fidgeted?
3 Gave regular eye contact and adopted an open posture?

Body language may give off a certain hostility, anxiety or resistance and this may be shown by behaviour such as folded arms, yawning (although the person may just be really tired), tapping the foot or shaking the leg (Cornell University, 1993).

It is important that non-verbal signs are not taken in isolation from the content of a discussion. It may be that anxiety is high because the discussion is focusing on a matter of real distress to the service-user. In the activity described above, it would be understandable to assume that:

- the person in situation 1 was acting defensively or did not welcome the conversation
- the person in situation 2 was either bored or late for an appointment
- the person in situation 3 was actively listening to you.

Box 9.6 reflection point

Consider your own body language

A way of interpreting the signs and signals of others is to begin by looking at your own messages that you give out non-verbally:

- Do you look at your watch a lot when you are in a hurry?
- Are you able to maintain appropriate eye contact when you are anxious or worried?
- Do you fidget when you are bored?
- What are the signs that you are anxious or worried?

It is important that you are able to reflect on the messages that you are sending out and see them in the context of your overall communication skills.

Eyes – the Mirrors of the Soul?

Appropriate use of eye contact

How do we use eye contact appropriately to communicate in an effective and culturally sensitive way?

- It may be that prolonged eye contact is regarded as a lack of respect and it is important to be clear where cultural norms would support this perspective.
- Prolonged eye contact could be a source of agitation to someone who is upset and it is therefore important to use direct eye contact as a positive indication of giving undivided attention but to be very aware of the possible misinterpretations (Onyett, 2003).

Conversely, avoidance of eye contact can communicate lack of interest or annoyance. Have you ever been at a reception desk and asked for information only to be ignored by the person on the other side who did not look at you? How did you respond to this?

Think about how you felt in situations similar to those described above, and how these feelings might be the same as a service-user or carer who receives similar treatment.

There will be many opportunities in your training for you to examine the learning needs that you may have in relation to communication. It is helpful to explore how you might identify some of these learning needs and to do this in relation to thinking about communicating with service-users. It is useful to consider whether you think that you should have a specific way of communicating with service-users that differs from your communications in other relationships that you have with people.

activity 9.5

Quick communication skills audit

So now come the really difficult questions to consider in relation to your communication learning needs:

- How do you communicate with your partner?
- How do you communicate with your colleagues?
- How do you communicate with your friends?

Try scoring your responses using the following scale:
Very well (10–9) | Well (8–7) | Sometimes good (6–5) | Not so good (4–3) | Poor (s/he sulks!) (1–2)

- If you are very brave, you might re-run the questions and ask how you score your communication skills when you are upset, stressed, tired, angry or very busy.
- For a really honest (but potentially painful) answer, you could ask a trusted friend to score you.

The results may sometimes be disheartening but will have a crucial significance in relation to your experience as a social worker if you can take them on board. Tiredness, lack of time, stress and distress are all factors which you will experience when you are working in practice, so how do we ensure that your communication skills will endure when they are tested in such challenging circumstances?

It is useful to look at some of the more formal settings in which we will be expected to demonstrate both written and verbal communication skills.

Presentations

It is a myth amongst students that your social work tutors have included individual and group presentations in order to act in a punitive and controlling way! They will find many other ways of doing this! Seriously, presentation skills will be an important part of your repertoire of communication and will not only be relevant during your training but throughout your practice following qualification. Social workers have to present their work in various ways, to differing audiences and are frequently required to speak in formal settings, such as in court or at a statutory review or tribunal.

Box 9.7 Putting together a successful presentation

☑	**Be prepared** – you will need to read about the subject and understand what you are going to present.
☑	**Be aware of the time limits** – there will be a specified time limit and your time management skills will come into their own here.
☑	**Decide how much information you want to include on the slide** and how much you will give as a supplementary handout.
☑	**Rehearse** in the room you will be using for your presentation and find a trusted but honest friend to hear your presentation.
☑	**Become familiar with the equipment** – make sure it is working and you know how to work it.
☑	**Introduce yourself** and give the source of the information, references, etc.
☑	**Do not read from the slides** without giving any further information.
☑	**Be clear about when you will invite questions** – do you want to be interrupted or will you take them at the end?
☑	Decide if you will **use lecture notes or index cards** and number them to match the slides.
☑	**Let your audience know when you have finished your presentation.**

During your presentation, you will be able to gauge some of the non-verbal messages that come from the audience and be prepared to change your style of delivery if people seem to be nodding off to sleep.

These formal opportunities for you to deliver presentations give you the platform to develop your confidence and style which, in turn, will contribute to your effectiveness and credibility as a rounded professional social work practitioner.

Awareness

To consider 'awareness' as a skill suggests that it can be seen as tangible and concrete and we would like you to think about how this might be. Awareness of your self in relation to the learning that you are accessing has a particular importance if we look at the learning opportunities which will be presented to you on your course. Whether it is formal group work or working with other students in a tutor group, you will be expected to identify some of the behaviours which facilitate communication in a group setting. Looking at how you present yourself in a group is the first step to understanding awareness as a skill to assist you in your development as a social worker (GSCC, 2002).

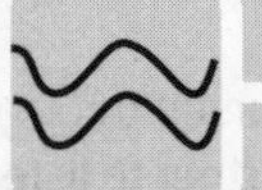

Box 9.8 reflection point

Self-awareness

It is useful to ask yourself the following questions:

- Do I enjoy meeting new people?
- Am I embarrassed when speaking to people for the first time?
- Do I think that everyone else on the course seems to know what they are talking about and I have not a clue?
- Do I struggle to have my say when there are more confident people in the group?
- Am I happier staying quiet in a group and letting other people speak?
- Have I had previous experiences in a group which have rocked my confidence?

Group settings

Awareness of the areas that you may need to address will become part of your overall development but it may be worth exploring just where your previous experiences have impacted upon your confidence in a group setting. This understanding will be important to your success in the student group and will be important to you when you are in your assessed practice. For example, if you are phased by a dominant voice in a group, this may have some serious results if you are in a team when you need to express your views but do not have the confidence to do so. A discussion of specific work may well include the exploration of some tentative thoughts which need to be considered with colleagues, and you need to have the confidence to be able to express your view or feed back on an observation which may have a significance that has not yet been recognized. Having the understanding that you lack confidence in particular settings may be the starting point of awareness. So what do you do about it now you have become aware?

Quick Tip: Building confidence for group interaction

- **Check that your own view of how you behave in a group is how others see you** – it may be that you are being overcritical and that you are seen quite differently by others.
- **Prepare for the group** – get your facts right! Having the information that you need will help to make you feel confident about the discussion.
- **Practise your performance** – choose a flattering mirror and talk yourself through your presentation or, better still, choose a long-suffering friend or partner to listen and give you some critical feedback – in this case, it might be useful to establish some ground rules so that you do not take it too personally.
- **Look at your mood** – When you are not confident, look at what else is affecting the way you are feeling and thinking – worries and stress about other aspects of our lives may impact on our working practice (Knapp and Daly, 2002). This could come from a serious concern about someone close or the fact that your car ran out of petrol on the way in.
- **Think about the understanding and knowledge that you have gained from your studies and how this might be useful in establishing your confidence and credibility in the group.**

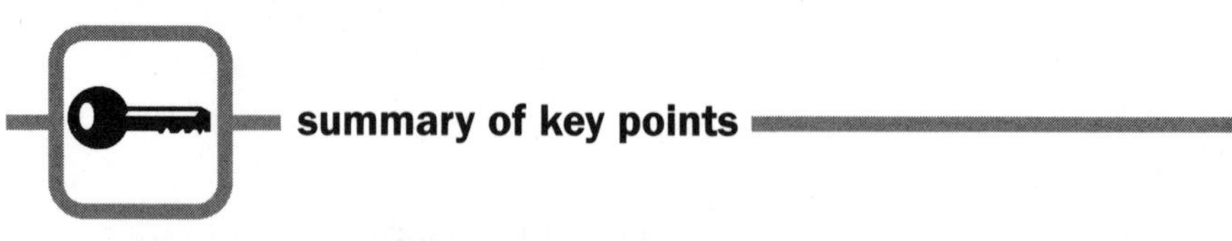

- We have explored some of the complexities of verbal, non-verbal and written communication skills.
- Listening skills, and in particular active listening, is key to becoming an effective communicator.

- The professional requirements for social work give a lead as to how we should construct dialogues with the people we work with in relation to both service-users and carers and colleagues.

useful resources

Why do we need confidentiality? (RLO-CETL learning resource)
Available at: http://www.ucel.ac.uk/rlos/confidentiality/index.html
The website provides an online tutorial focusing on the importance and significance of confidentiality in health and social care. It also includes the roles of social worker, a health visitor and a GP and is useful for Inter-Professional Learning (IPL).

further reading

Chivers, B. and Shoolbred, M. (2007) *A Student's Guide to Presentations* (Study Skills Series). London: Sage.
Donnelly, E. and Neville, L. (2008) *Communication and Interpersonal Skills*. Exeter: Reflect Press.
Koprowska, J. (2005) *Communication and Interpersonal Skills in Social Work*. Exeter: Learning Matters.
Trevithick, P. (2005) *Social Work Skills*, 2nd edition. Maidenhead: Open University Press. (especially Chapters 4 and 5).

10

Using Feedback Effectively

learning objectives

- To develop an understanding of the use of personal development plans.
- To understand the role and value of feedback.
- To appreciate the vital learning that can arise from feedback from service-users and carers.
- To develop an understanding of how you can deal with criticism in a productive way.

It is important to remember that the fact that you are studying on your social work course means that other people have assessed you to have the potential to develop and progress towards achieving the status of a qualified social worker. This assessment through the selection for the course is confirmation that the admissions tutors and, in the case of work-based students, the employers, have all agreed that you have met the necessary requirements to be enrolled on the course. It is important to remember this, as you may be feeling slightly less confident when you actually start the course – the recognition of your own strengths and abilities may be difficult to bring to mind when you are faced with the reality of the new challenges of studying in higher education.

You will not be expected to have all the knowledge in place when you start the course. Your university studies and placement will provide you with the necessary learning opportunities to gain this knowledge and understanding. Concepts of adult learning include the expectation that you as the student will take a level of responsibility for your own development. This will include being proactive in relation to accessing support and guidance, whether it be from your mentor, tutor, line manager or practice educator. A useful tool at the starting point may be the use of the Personal Development Plan (PDP). Drawing up the Personal Development Plan can be your introduction to receiving feedback from both your tutor and work-based mentor.

The Personal Development Plan

Did You Know? The Personal Development Plan (PDP)

Personal development planning describes the deliberate process of thinking about and reflecting upon your own:

- personal learning
- performance
- achievements.

PDP focuses on how you can utilize and develop these aspects of your development further, in order to help you achieve your personal, educational and professional goals and aspirations.

A Personal Development Plan is not only used whilst you are on your social work course, as it is currently used by many employers as a way to assess ongoing training and development needs in relation to post-qualifying practice. Whilst the idea of looking at your learning needs after qualification may seem a little premature, it is important to recognize that the more effectively you use this tool at the start of your training, the more useful it is likely to be for you in your ongoing career.

Identifying strengths and weaknesses

Initially, your tutor or mentor will ask you to identify your own strengths and weaknesses in relation to learning and this really forms the first part of your understanding of feedback because you will be asked to provide evidence for the claims that you make.

Example: Fraser identifies that he has a particular strength in the area of written communication. His tutor asks him to write a sample letter to demonstrate this strength and address the following situation.

'Write a letter to Mr and Mrs Smith saying that you have been asked to see them by the manager of the day nursery that their child attends because of concerns about the child's behaviour towards other children.'

Fraser is a student social worker and has known the Smiths for three weeks. The letter he drafts is assessed by his tutor and his mentor and they both agree that he has not demonstrated a particular strength in written communication because his letter reads:

> Dear Mr and Mrs Smith
>
> I hope that you are well?
>
> I would like to visit you at home next week and wondered if 2.30 on Wednesday would be convenient for you?
>
> Please will you let me know if you are able to see me at this time?
>
> Yours sincerely
>
> Fraser Murphy

- The feedback that Fraser receives includes concern that he has not communicated in writing in a suitable manner because he has not given any indication why he would like to see the Smiths.
- The feedback is especially challenging because it requires him to re-evaluate his own skill assessment.
- Feedback can be uncomfortable and a normal human response to this is to deny the accuracy of it and even blame the person who is giving the constructive feedback.
- Feedback should enable you to look closely at how you use your own strengths and abilities and also recognize that one of the important skills in your academic and practice learning will be your ability to utilize your sense of self.

How the PDP can help

The PDP can be useful if you are reluctant to accept the feedback because as part of it (the PDP), you will be asked to consider your learning to date and to examine the areas that you have found more accessible and those areas that you have struggled to understand. An important part of looking at your prior learning will be to consider how you have experienced feedback in the past and whether the criticism has been:

- **constructive**?
- perceived as a wholly **negative** experience?

As a student social worker, you will be developing your skills of processing information which is based on evidence and it is pertinent that any disagreement about the content of the feedback should be discussed in a way which is open, respectful and non-aggressive. This is not dissimilar to way that the Value Requirements and Code of Practice would suggest that social workers should conduct themselves (GSCC, 2002).

An active engagement with the process of the PDP will mean that you are being asked to give feedback to your tutor on your own abilities and also to invite feedback from your tutor/mentor as to how accurate they see your self-perception of your skills. This is not a straightforward or simple process as:

- it may be that your confidence is not at its highest
- you are at the early stages of getting to know your tutor
- you may have uncertainties about how the information about your learning will be used.

Box 10.1 reflection point

Managing the PDP process

It will be important for you to establish a clear understanding about how your PDP work is used, for example:

- How much of your PDP will be shared with your mentor or line manager if you are a work-based student?
- What are the time limits to realize the learning needs that have been identified?
- Who takes responsibility for the review of the progress and who will have access to the progress and at what stage will this be given?

The PDP is most useful if used as a working document which can be referred to and revisited as you progress on your course. As with most plans, it will no doubt need to be reconsidered and revised according to your progress and in the light of other circumstances that may need to be considered. A common hitch with work-based students is that the demands of your work in the agency take precedence over academic study and as such any plan may need to be redrawn and rescheduled (see Chapter 4 for more on work-based learning).

Making a start on your PDP

You will usually be asked to draw up your PDP with your personal tutor during the early stages of your course and it will comprise of:

- a comprehensive list of your learning needs
- a list of tasks that will show how you plan to achieve the necessary progress in the areas that you have identified
- an indication of how you might monitor and review your progress.

Example: Your PDP may look something like this:

- **Strengths** - good time keeping and the ability to meet deadlines.
- **Weaknesses** – easily distracted and this means that tasks take much longer than planned.
- **Tasks** – to develop a realistic timeframe for both the preparation and completion of work.

If you look at the detail of the tasks, it may be that you start to think about:

- how you organize your study time,
- why the distractions have interfered with your planned work,
- where you study,
- how often you are interrupted.

If you have taken over the dining room table in your home as the resting place for your academic books, do not be surprised when your train of thought is broken several times each day by hungry looks from the people who share that home.

So how will you access these opportunities for your own learning? One of the key building blocks for the whole range of your skill development is how well you are able to generate and respond to feedback. Consequently, this can become a very important part of your development in your journey towards becoming a qualified social worker.

Why Feed Back?

Asking 'why do tutors give feedback?' is a pertinent and relevant question. Tutors give a mark for a piece of work and you will be given guidance as to the meaning of the numerical mark or grade, so why do we need the written comments as well? Academic work may reach a specific mark but it is likely that the reasons as to why a piece of work has earned the given mark, or perhaps more importantly why it has not achieved a higher mark, are more complicated.

The written comments in the feedback you receive will form part of the 'explanation' of why the mark has been awarded. We would like to make a plea here on behalf of marking tutors, who are often criticized for giving a low mark. Generally speaking, because this is not an exact science, it is not the marker who decides the mark but it is the quality of the work which is the deciding factor. Seen from this viewpoint, the marker has a 'mechanistic' function which is determined by the assignment guidance and the marking framework.

Feedback is about future development

The general intention of feedback in relation to specific pieces of work is to:

- give guidance for future development
- encourage you to take on board the comments and use them to improve your standard of work.

Most academic work is now moderated both internally and externally so it is unlikely that only one marker will have looked at your work (or work of a similar grade in the overall sample). This means that there has been a serious effort to achieve consistency of marking. If you are genuinely unhappy or confused by the feedback or mark that you have received, it is important to discuss this with your tutor and to access the procedures for review that will be in place in your own institution.

Feedback may be difficult to accept

It is important to recognize that feedback (written description or marks/grades) may be difficult to accept – particularly if it is *critical without being constructive*. In this situation, further discussion with the person providing the feedback may be helpful and appropriate. However, it may also be that the feedback is *unpalatable but accurate* and contradicts the perception that we may have of our own work. There is a real connection here to developing understanding around this resistance to constructive criticism and the ability to reflect on your progress and development. Reflection is something that we will go on to discuss in Chapter 11 and, again, has a relevance to both academic and practice-based social work.

Feedback in practice-based work

Feedback has a significant relevance to both your academic and practice-based work throughout your social work course and afterwards in qualified practice. The feedback that you receive on your academic work will hopefully guide you to improve your overall standard of written work. This will ultimately enable you to reach a higher classification in your degree and to achieve the necessary levels of written work required for professional social work practice. In your assessed practice, you will receive regular feedback from both your practice educator and colleagues but, most importantly, from the service-users and carers who you have worked with during your placement.

Feedback from practice educators

The feedback from your practice educator will usually be based on the direct observations of your practice and they are often done in a planned way. This will give you the opportunity to prepare and, importantly, to ensure that service-users or carers consent to the work you are doing with them being observed by your assessor. A significant part of your development on your social work course will be influenced by both the quality of the feedback that you receive and crucially the willingness that you show to take on board the content.

Feedback and communication skills

In social work practice, there is a role for feedback that connects directly to the communication skills that we have identified earlier. One of the skills we discussed was the importance for social workers to listen to people in both careful and active ways and to be confident that they have heard the information that has been given to them. One way of ensuring that we have heard accurately is to feed back the information to either the service-user or colleague and to ask if we have heard correctly. Developing an ease with giving feedback in this very practical way can be instrumental in developing the skill of giving feedback in more complex areas.

Feedback on your Assignments

An important part of understanding your own learning is the feedback that you are given in response to work that you have completed. It is important not to underestimate the anxieties that can accompany the request for feedback. If the first assignment on your social work course is your first piece of academic writing since you left school 20 years ago, then you will no doubt be more than a little worried about your writing skills. Equally, if you have gone to university straight from having completed 'A' Levels, the leap from school to higher education may seem like a gigantic one. You may feel overwhelmed by the apparent freedom and lack of supervision compared to your experience in the sixth form.

The anticipation of the feedback on this first piece of work can be stressful and it is important that you take some control of this by planning a tutorial to coincide with the return of the work. Alternatively, it may be that the feedback you are going to receive is part of the assessment of your practice and in this case it is equally important for you to plan a meeting with your practice educator as soon as possible after the observation has taken place. The responsibility for planning and arranging these meetings will be a clear indication that you have taken responsibility for your own learning by accessing the feedback in a constructive way. It is useful to 'rewind the scene' here and start with the piece of work that you have been asked to complete and look at the assignment guidance that you have been given at the outset.

This guidance will give you details of the areas that you are expected to address in relation to a specific piece of work – for example, you may be asked to demonstrate evidence of knowledge and understanding in the following areas:

Table 10.1 Sample assignment guidance sheet

Learning Outcomes	*Met*	*Not met*
1 Understanding of GSCC (2002) COP		
2 Awareness of Value Requirements		
3 Ability to use grammar, punctuation and referencing throughout		
4 Ability to structure your work in a logical way		
Each of the areas will attract 25% of the total marks.		

The guidance may not always be as detailed but you will always receive some information on the expectation of the marking tutor in relation to the piece of work that you are being asked to submit. Looking at the assignment guidance should give you a plan for the piece of work and, as such, a context for understanding the feedback that you will receive.

If you think about the guidance sheet shown above and think of an assignment that:

- is beautifully structured with a clear introduction, main part and conclusion
- concentrates only on the Value Requirements
- misses out the GSCC (2002) COP

then immediately 25% of the marks have been lost!

Additionally, if you have not:

- proofread your work carefully
- ensured that all your references have been properly attributed to their sources

then you may have only accessed half of the marks in that area which could mean that another 15% of the total marks have been lost. It may be that although you have addressed the Value Requirements, your discussion is not complete so perhaps here you have missed some key points in the discussion which will mean that you have missed 10% of the total marks in that area. You are now looking at 50% for the overall piece of work purely on the basis of what you have and have not addressed in the guidance.

Feedback from Service-users and Carers

Feedback from service-users and carers will be an important part of the assessment of your practice and you will be encouraged to highlight the need for this at the very start of your placement. When you are introduced to service-users and carers as a 'student', they will immediately know that you are being assessed in your practice so the conversation about the need for feedback should be able to happen in a naturalistic way. It is important to include service-users and carers in this process and doing this will give you the opportunity to demonstrate that you are meeting the COP in relation to empowerment.

Useful feedback from challenging situations

Empowerment in relation to service-users and carers is one of the building blocks of effective social work practice and will play a significant part in your overall understanding and development (Beresford, 2005). There may be a temptation to only seek feedback from situations where you know that the work you have done has been welcomed but meaningful feedback will come from situations where there has been contention. On occasion, there may be disagreement about the outcome of an intervention. However, if a service-user or carer can say that they have been treated with respect and dignity, despite the contention, then this is very important and relevant feedback on your practice skills which can be evidenced in your practice portfolio.

There is a human temptation to seek compliments so when we ask for a view on how effective we have been, it may be very tempting to only ask service-users who you know are pleased with the way that you have been working with them. The contentious situations where people are in disagreement with you will provide a real test of your professional ability to communicate in difficult situations.

Feedback and developmental needs

Your practice portfolio is one of the most significant pieces of work that you will produce on your social work course as it will provide both you and your practice educator with some tangible evidence of your face-to-face work with service-users and carers. Hence, feedback from the very people that you are working with becomes a crucial source of evidence of your suitability to practise social work in a safe, accountable and effective way (GSCC, 2002).

Box 10.2 reflection point

Feedback and your developmental needs

The feedback that you receive from service-users and carers not only forms an important part of your learning but it will also give you an insight into your future developmental needs:

- Think about how you might seek feedback from someone who you have to visit to tell them that they are not eligible for a service.
- Think about how you might ask for feedback from a young person who has been removed from her parents on a Care Order which was issued by the Court and that has been made on your assessment and recommendation.

In the first example of visiting someone to tell them that they are not eligible for a service, it may be that you have to consider your approach regarding your openness and honesty about the availability of services. You have a professional duty to demonstrate the Value Requirements (GSCC, 2002), so will need to ensure that you are treating the person with dignity and respect. Indeed, it may be that you think that it is wholly appropriate that the person is not eligible for a service and that you have to manage some of this conflict that you feel individually in relation to the expressed need by the service-user. You will also be mindful of the resources and function of the agency that you represent. Regardless of your own views, it will be appropriate to give the service-user detailed information on their rights to challenge the way in which services are allocated. To ask for feedback on your intervention will be difficult and will again stretch your communication skills and ability to hold a discussion with the service-user who holds a very different view from your own. The timing of your request for feedback will also be important and will give you the opportunity to look at your planning skills.

Presenting the need for feedback to others

At the start of your placement, it is important to be very clear with all service-users, carers and other colleagues that you are in the agency for a limited period of time. As part of your introduction, you will be able to say that you are a student who is being assessed and as such will be required to gather as much feedback as possible to help you to develop and become a qualified social worker. If you have presented the need for feedback in this way at the start of your placement, then the people you are working with will expect to provide it when your involvement comes to an end.

Quick Tip: How do you collect or record feedback?

Ways of asking for feedback can include:

- written questionnaires
- requests for verbal comments where appropriate.

Things to consider:

- the age and understanding of the person you are asking for feedback from
- being clear about how you will use the information that has been given to you, demonstrating your adherence to maintaining confidentiality in relation to your portfolio contents.

This will be another opportunity for you to record your understanding of the professional Value Requirements (GSCC, 2002) that you will be following as an important part of your learning and development on placement.

Feedback from Colleagues

As a student social worker, you will work alongside a variety of different colleagues from many different professional backgrounds. The skills that we have considered in relation to enabling and receiving feedback from service-users and carers, will apply equally to the feedback from colleagues. Your ability to draw on the skills of communication, time management and planning will have a particular relevance in your receptiveness to feedback, and indeed your reflective skills will also be useful if you are to reflect on the feedback that has been offered to you as part of your placement experience.

In relation to the feedback from colleagues who you are working closely with, it is likely that at the start of your placement your practice educator will be very clear about the formal and informal feedback that will be expected. Teams in social work will very often view a student placement as a shared responsibility and members will play an active part in the overall assessment of the student's practice. It is very important that you are clear about the role of colleagues in relation to your progress from the start of your placement to enable you to respond appropriately when feedback is given either to you directly or to your practice educator.

Feedback from Peers

We are not referring here to the peers of the realm as it is unlikely that you will be working in the House of Lords as part of your social work course! The peers that we are referring to are other students who you may be working with to produce a shared piece of work as part of your social work course. It is common in higher education to encourage students to work together in a collaborative way and this has a particular relevance for social work courses. Social work operates in a multi- and inter-disciplinary context so the ability to communicate with service-users, carers and professionals from diverse backgrounds is an important requirement. To begin the process of working with other students in training sows the seeds for productive relationships in future practice. An important facet of these relationships is the opportunity to comment on each others, work either in the university or in the practice setting.

Group work and feedback

In the university, it is likely that you will be asked to take part in group presentations that are assessed by both your peers and your tutors. Part of this assessment will include the opportunity for you to receive feedback on your presentation which will focus on your content and style and your ability to work as part of a team. The feedback that you receive from your peers will be based on their experience of working with you as part of the team. It may be that there has been a disagreement and part of your effectiveness, both as a team member and collectively as a team, will be the main source of the feedback. The content of the feedback will no doubt focus on how/if the disagreements were resolved and the learning of both the individuals and the group that has occurred from this experience.

Areas that you may wish to focus on when looking at how you will feed back to each other:

- individual contributions to the group task
- communication within the group
- group cohesion
- completion of the task
- evaluation of the whole learning from the exercise.

Your response to the feedback that you receive from your peers may be representative of how you react to criticism in a more general way.

Dealing with Criticism

Did You Know? Criticism and feedback

Is there a difference between criticism and feedback?

- Very often, **feedback** is defined as *criticism which is constructive* and offers some guidance for future learning
- **Criticism** is more often felt to be destructive, lacking in support and generally seen in a negative context.

Your understanding of criticism, when it includes ideas and suggestions of how to do things differently can play a key part in the progress and success of your learning.

- But do the two feel any different when they are directed at you?
- How do you deal with criticism?

activity 10.1

Your experience of criticism

Think about your experiences of being criticized in the past and consider how your present responses may well have been influenced by these earlier messages. To help you to do this, note down your responses to the following questions:

- Do you feel that *you* rather than your *actions* are the subject of criticism?
- Is it possible to separate the action from the person and to see the criticism in a more objective way?

It may be helpful to look at the factors which influence your responses to criticism:

- Criticism, whether constructive or not, can be a very uncomfortable feeling and there is a real risk that a defensive response is the knee-jerk reaction.
- The temptation to 'shoot the messenger' and try to discredit the credibility of the person giving the criticism is a sure way of learning very little from criticism, other than to convince yourself that the way to deal with criticism is to criticize.

Box 10.3 reflection point

Dealing with criticism

Some things to consider:

- Criticism can be painful.
- It can make you feel angry, upset or frustrated.
- It can make you feel powerless.

So how do we deal with the above? To separate the feelings from the content is something that is fundamental if the criticism is to be used in a productive way and reflects some of the very basic tenets of social work theory and practice. The way that you are able to recognize how emotions can influence your response to criticism will be an important part of your professional development. Your tutor/mentor will support you in the process of identifying when your emotional reaction influences your capacity for objective thought, and this awareness will be further developed by your practice educator during your formal supervision as part of your assessed practice on your course.

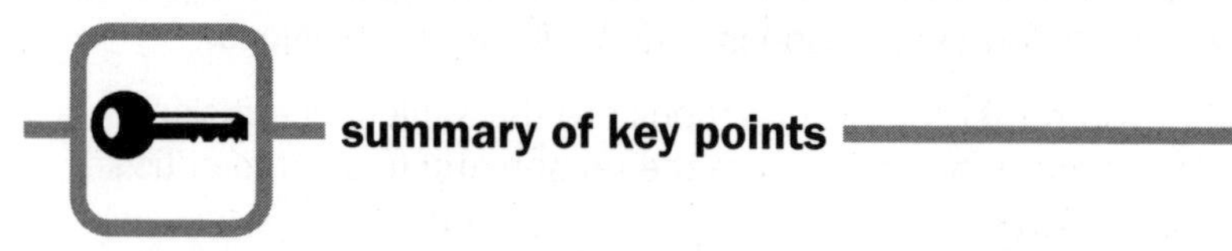

summary of key points

- Your openness and willingness to maximize the supervision process will help you to make sense of feedback and criticism.
- The feedback that you receive from colleagues, mentors, managers and, in particular, service-users and carers, will be an important learning resource in your ongoing professional development.
- The content of feedback can feed directly into identifying future personal development needs.
- This will be a building block for your future success and survival as a social worker.

further reading

Moss, B. (2007) *Communication Skills for Health and Social Care.* London: Sage. (See page 110 on 'Feedback – Giving and Receiving'.)

11

Reflection in Social Work

learning objectives

- To understand what reflection is, how it can be defined and to have an ability to apply a model of reflective practice to learning experiences.
- To understand the significance of developing your skills of reflection.
- To develop an awareness of how reflection links to professional values.
- To develop an awareness of how reflection links to the Codes of Practice.

As a new social work student, you may be completely puzzled by the concept of reflection. It may continue to be a source of puzzlement when you are no longer new. You may, of course, have experience in social work practice, which has required you to develop reflective skills to a sophisticated level in relation to looking thoughtfully at your own practice. Either way you are now being asked to develop your reflective skills in the role of student social worker.

Did You Know? What is reflection?

'Reflection is a process of reviewing an experience of practice in order to describe, analyse, evaluate and so inform learning about practice' (Reid, 1993: 306).

(Continued)

From this definition, we can broadly say that reflection involves:

- looking back on something that has happened
- thinking about the actual details of what took place and considering the evidence available to us
- weighing up what worked well and what was less successful
- using insight and understanding to get a better idea about our working practices
- identifying what we could do differently in the future to develop and improve our practice.

In previous reflections, you may have explored your thoughts and responses in depth but will not have been assessed on your ability to do this. However, now you will be preparing for this kind of assessment as a formal part of your qualifying training course. It is useful to consider reflection as a part of a continuum of understanding some of the basis tenets of social work:

COMMUNICATION-OBSERVATION-REFLECTION-JUDGEMENT-INTERVENTION-REVIEW-REFLECTION

Some thoughts that you may have at this stage:

- 'Why do we need to reflect?'
- 'What does reflection mean?'
- 'Why are we discussing reflection as part of study skills?'

The 'Why' and the 'What' of Reflection

Reflection in social work has been described as the opportunity to evaluate the decision-making process in social work practice with the specific intention of double checking the appropriateness of decisions and outcomes. This will sometimes lead to a change of decision which Munro (1996) identifies as a strength rather than a weakness. Schön (1991) comments on the importance of reflection when there is the potential for a conflict in the values that inform decision-making processes.

Box 11.1 reflection point

Reflection in social work

Social work operates in a world of complex relationships and situations.

- Many of the situations that you face as a social worker will challenge your own understanding of the world.
- It is the awareness of this understanding which will be a key to your effective practice.

Social work has a defined frame of reference in relation to the GSCC Codes of Practice, Value Requirements and Key Roles (GSCC, 2002), all of which address some of the ethics, beliefs and skill base for professional practice. This frame of reference will form the structure of your assessed practice as a student social worker. The connection of ethics to basic skills has a particularly complex structure as social work does not operate in a vacuum from the rest of society. It is this complexity that leads social work to embrace reflective practice.

Part of the understanding of the Value Requirements in social work is the recognition that your own personal values and beliefs may be in disagreement with them.

Box 11.2 reflection point

Professional requirements and personal values

If we consider the **professional requirement** to respect the choices of individuals, but have a **personal belief system** that restricts the opportunity for choice, as is the case in many organized religions which restrict the choices of women, then it is very important that we recognize the need to scrutinize our own interpretation of the framework, in order to be watchful of the influences that may negatively impact upon our decisions and assumptions in our day-to-day practice.

The need to reflect on personal values is only one part of the process of reflection throughout social work practice. As a student social worker, you will need to:

- demonstrate your ability to reflect as part of the evidence of your suitability to go on assessed practice
- write a reflective piece on your own values as part of your academic work on the course
- reflect on how the social work Value Requirements connect with the Codes of Practice.

A Tool for Reflection

We have identified the importance of reflection in social work practice, but how do we actually go about doing it? There are many models of reflection that have been developed and as you progress through your course, we would encourage you to explore the strengths and weaknesses of some of these. However, for now, we will stick with a fairly simple but effective model of reflection as shown below in Figure 11.1.

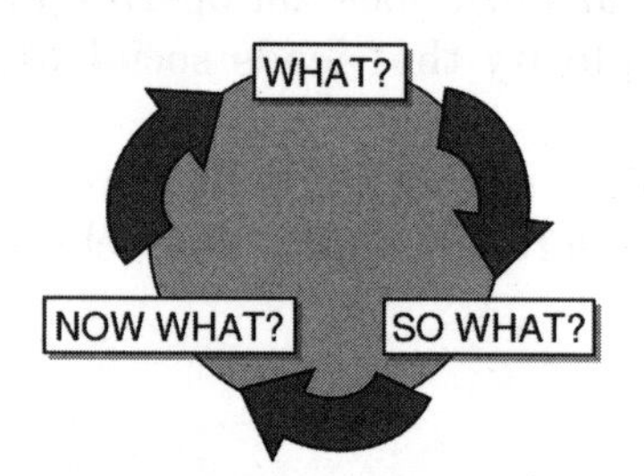

Figure 11.1 The 'what', 'so what' and 'now what' model of reflection (Borton, 1970)

With Borton's model of reflection, we move through three stages of thinking:

1 **WHAT?** – What is the incident, event or problem we need to think about?

Followed by:

2 **SO WHAT?** – So what was going through my mind as the situation unfolded? So what thoughts guided my actions, behaviour and responses to others? So what were the consequences of my thoughts and actions?

Followed by:

3 **NOW WHAT?** – Now what could I do differently in the future based on my understandings of what happened and how I responded?

This model will be useful to bear in mind as you complete some of the activities in this chapter.

The GSCC Codes of Practice (2002)

Did You Know? Codes of Practice

These Codes describe the standards of conduct that are expected from social care staff and as a social work student, you will be expected to follow them throughout the whole of your course.

As we have outlined earlier, your demonstration of understanding and application of the Codes of Practice (COP) will be assessed as part of the suitability criteria for you to go on assessed practice placements. It is helpful here to look in detail at some examples of the COP and to consider them in relation to your emerging skill of reflection.

1. Protect the rights and promote the interests of service-users and carers.

In order to protect the rights of the people we work with, it is important that we firstly know what the rights are and secondly appreciate how entitlement may be interpreted in a very subjective way as a result of the particular value base of the social worker.

Consider your response to the following activity:

activity 11.1

Reflection and social worker value bases

Len, who is 15, has been arrested on suspicion of assault on Evie, who is 79. She has been hospitalized as a result of the injuries. You are the key worker

(Continued)

in a residential unit where Len lives and you have been asked to go down to the police station to act as Appropriate Adult in the police interview.

Len has been arrested and not charged, or found guilty, so in English law we have a presumption of innocence until proven otherwise. However, you know that Len has three previous convictions for affray.

- You are on your way to the police station and thinking about the interview that awaits you, between Len and the interviewing police officer.
- What is going through your mind as you make your way there?
- Are you thinking about his previous convictions?
- Your uncle was assaulted three years ago by a teenage boy.

Do any of the above influence how you view the situation that you are entering?

Your ability to look at the information and consider your own reaction to it will enable you to measure the degree of impartiality that you are able to demonstrate. So it may be that you are very aware of the role of Appropriate Adult to monitor the rights of service-users whilst being interviewed by the police. You may also be confident that your prior knowledge will not influence how you deal with the situation. This confidence may have come from your capacity to consider how, as a social worker, you are influenced by prior knowledge and it is the ability to dwell on the information that you are processing which lowers the risk of you being negatively influenced in a way which compromises the rights of the service-user.

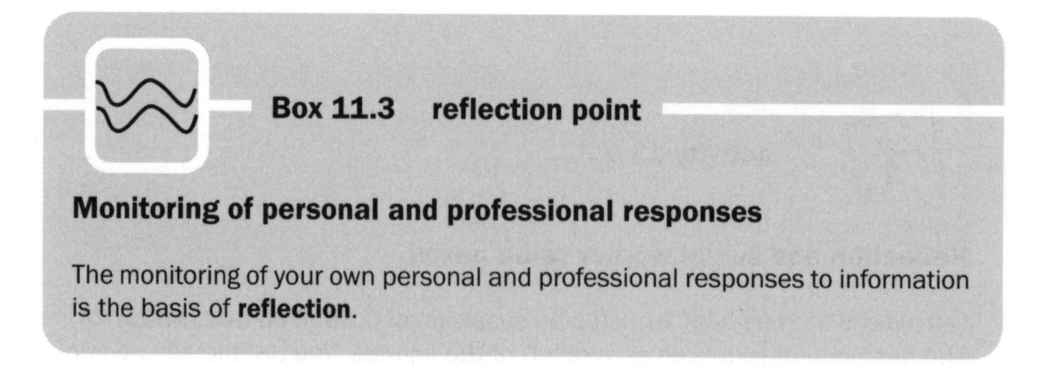

Box 11.3 reflection point

Monitoring of personal and professional responses

The monitoring of your own personal and professional responses to information is the basis of **reflection**.

Example: In the case described above, during supervision, you should have been given the opportunity to examine your own feelings when your uncle was assaulted. From this, you should have had the opportunity to explore how your response to that situation in your personal life could negatively influence your response to young people who have convictions for assault.

The understanding of the connection of your experiences to your practice is the key to **reflection**.

How does your reflection on your own values inform and assist your ability to 'protect the rights' of this particular service-user?

activity 11.2

Reflecting on your own values

Think about the following situation and examine how you really feel when you read the details for the first time and how your feelings might impact upon your ability to **reflect**.

Frank is 89 and is admitted to hospital with severe bruising to his arms and legs. He has a diagnosis of dementia and has been admitted several times to hospital because he has been found wandering alone on a busy road in the middle of the night.

He tells the doctor that he has fallen downstairs and that he is well looked after by his son and daughter-in-law who moved into his home to care for him. Frank has two grandchildren who attend a local private school. The doctor examines Frank and decides that she is concerned about the inconsistency of the injuries with the explanation and also is alarmed by his poor physical appearance. She has observed that he has an infestation of head lice and scabies.

- Did you think that Frank was being ill-treated?
- Were you most concerned with Frank or his family?

(Continued)

Think about your own beliefs about older people:

- Do you have relatives who are unable to look after themselves without support?
- How would your reflection on your own values and beliefs assist you in 'protecting the rights' of Frank?
- Let us explore your response if you have an older person living with you who is in a similar state – do you think that this experience would influence your response to Frank and to his relatives?
- If you are a carer for an older person, would you be more likely to consider the needs of the carers rather than Frank's?
- Did you start to think that perhaps Frank's family had moved in with him in order to benefit financially?

If you were now asked to assess Frank's situation:

- Do you think that your initial views would have an impact on your assessment?
- How would you measure any impact and would this be part of your reflection?

We have looked at the first COP (GSCC, 2002) and now let us consider the second in relation to developing your skills of reflection:

2. Strive to establish and maintain the trust and confidence of service-users and carers.

What are the skills you will use when you build the relationship and develop the trust and confidence of service-users and carers and, perhaps equally important, what do you need to reflect on in relation to your values to enable you to meet this particular COP?

- How does this COP connect to the professional values that you have to adhere to as a student social worker?
- How will you evaluate the effectiveness of these relationships?

The Value Requirements clearly state that social workers should have:

'... awareness of their own values, prejudices, ethical dilemmas and conflicts of interest and their implications for their practice' (GSCC, 2002).

If we consider this awareness in the context of reflection, we can explore the importance of understanding the make-up of a relationship in which there is often contention and disagreement. As a student social worker, it may be that you are faced with a situation that you find hard to understand and are completely opposed to the perspective that the service-user has decided upon. The values highlight that each service-user and carer can expect student social workers to show respect for, and the promotion of:

- each person as an individual
- independence and quality of life for individuals, whilst protecting them from harm
- dignity, privacy of individuals, families, carers, groups and communities.

In addition, students must also:

- recognize and facilitate each person's use of language and form of communication of their choice
- value, recognize and respect the diversity, expertise and experience of individuals, families, carers, groups and communities by communicating in an open, accurate and understandable way
- maintain the trust and confidence of individuals, families, carers, groups and communities by communicating in an open, accurate and understandable way
- understand and make use of strategies to challenge discrimination, disadvantage and other forms of inequality and injustice.

How do you as the student social worker develop a trusting relationship with someone who may have had a poor experience previously with social workers? The answer to this question is clear if we draw on examples from practice and consider the following case study.

Case study: Jenny

Jenny is 14 years old and has been referred to you by the education social worker who has worked with Jenny for three years. Jenny's dad, Bill, has motor neurone disease and is dependent on Jenny for all of his physical care and this has resulted in Jenny missing large chunks of time from school.

You are a student social worker, on a Young Carers Project, and have been asked to contact Jenny to see if she can be offered any support in her role as a young carer.

The education social worker has told you that Jenny and Bill received a visit in the past from a social worker who suggested that Bill went into residential nursing care on a permanent basis. Since that time, Jenny and Bill have refused to see anyone from social services.

activity 11.3

Reflection on Jenny's situation

Reflecting on how you can begin to build a relationship with Jenny which is based on trust, and gives her and Bill some confidence in you and the service that you can offer, answer the following:

1 What may you need to reflect upon before your first meeting with Jenny?
2 What would be the other areas that you think might impact upon Jenny's willingness to trust you?

When you have jotted down some ideas in response to these questions, self-assess them against the suggested answers included in Box 11.4 and Box 11.5 at the end of this chapter.

In returning to the question of why we reflect, it is important to consider how informative the process can be when we have to initially process information. Thinking about whether a particular piece of information is relevant to your social work practice is the beginning of reflecting upon how you might use the information to inform your response and look to both promoting independence whilst at the same time protecting from harm.

3. Promote the independence of service-users while protecting them as far as possible from danger or harm.

There is potential contradiction in this COP which on one level is encouraging the promotion of independent choice but on another level is clearly identifying the need to be engaged in safe practice which protects from harm and danger. The challenge for social work in situations which include assessment of risk is to maintain the right for people to have freedom of choice in areas that are relatively safe.

Reflecting on the nature of the risk can contribute to the overall assessment of danger and harm. It is pertinent to consider some of the risks that are encountered in everyday life, for example:

- You may choose to exceed the speed limit and run the risk of a prison sentence if you are involved in an accident whilst driving too fast – but how often would the risk be assessed in relation to the least serious outcome, i.e. it may be that you would be concerned about points on your licence but not about causing injury or death.

- Another aspect of daily risk is in relation to the hardy folk who choose to climb mountains which is a perfectly legal activity but with potentially life-threatening results. The risk is a considered one, which may be part of the attraction, but climbers who choose to take the risk are not criminalized unless they act in a reckless way which in turn puts others at risk.

Consider the role of reflection in relation to this third COP and think about how your practice could be made safer through the active use of your skills of reflection.

activity 11.4

Risk assessment reflection (i)

Think about the potential risk involved in leaving a 13-year-old boy in the house alone whilst you go to the local shop.

- The boy plays with matches and is seriously burned in the fire that he has accidentally started.
- You are the parent and you have left your son in this way on numerous occasions without any harm.
- He has recently started to baby-sit for a neighbour who has two small children and has done this without any problem at all.

Think about, and write down, what you think are the key issues here in relation to assessing the level of risk. There is a suggested answer to this activity in Box 11.6 at the end of this chapter.

The challenge for social work is to develop sufficient reflection to consider the dangers and harm and to then assess the level of risk that is posed by the behaviour. An important part of this assessment would be the close communication with the service-user involved to be able to talk about the reflections that you have and to use them to determine positions of risk.

4. Respect the rights of service-users while seeking to ensure their behaviour does not harm themselves or other people.

As a student social worker, there will be situations when you will need to stand by and watch someone make choices in their lifestyle which you know will lead to distressing outcomes.

activity 11.5

Risk assessment reflection (ii)

Imagine that you are working with a service-user who has a serious alcohol addiction and is unable to stop using despite the threat to their contact with their children.

- You have been asked to carry out a formal assessment which has been requested by the court as part of Care Proceedings.
- The risk assessment hinges on:
  - the alcohol use of the parents
  - their ability to care for their children when they are drinking.

What would your reflections be about the kinds of questions that would need to be answered? Write these down and then compare them with the suggested answer in Box 11.7 at the end of this chapter.

The questions you come up with (and those shown in the suggested answer) will inform your assessment but as you will see there is no textbook answer to the issues. It will be the specific details that your reflections will help you to interpret in terms of risk assessment. The parents may not be doing anything illegal in drinking excessively but their parenting ability when they use alcohol may mean that they cannot safely look after their children. Your ability to reflect on the specifics and to use your reflection to assist in the assessment of risk will be fundamental to your own safe practice.

5. Uphold public trust and confidence in social care services.

Social work operates in a very public arena and the scrutiny of social work practice is well documented, especially when things go badly wrong. The challenge to uphold the trust of the public may seem daunting to you as a student social worker. How will you undertake this responsibility and demonstrate that you are practising in accordance with this particular COP? The short answer is that you will not do this on your own and will need to be fully supported in your efforts to meet this challenge in your social work studies.

When you are working directly with a service-user, your ability to reflect with the person will go some way to upholding the individual's trust and confidence in your practice.

Reflection and Accountability

But what of the public as a whole and how has recent practice fared in relation to the public's perception of social work? High-profile child death cases have understandably been highly critical of certain practices in social work and it is a serious challenge for you as a student social worker to attempt to uphold trust and confidence in such a highly charged public arena. It may be that the wider public perception is of less significance to you as a student but your individual practice will have a certain level of public exposure.

In supervision, you will be encouraged to reflect upon how the impact of your individual practice is perceived by the service-users that you are working with and also to reflect on the consistency of your work across the whole range of your caseload. Is it reasonable to suggest that the way in which you work within the resources that you have can be measured for fairness and consistency? This reflection may lead you to consider other skills of time management. For instance, if you are spending grossly unequal amounts of time with one person to the detriment of your availability to another, then it would be an area for you to reflect upon and one where you would need to consider your allocation of time more evenly if appropriate.

Suggested Answers

Box 11.4 Suggested answer for Activity 11.3 (i)

Jenny has had a poor experience of social workers so it is likely that she may be suspicious of you and not inclined to trust you. Reflect on why this may be the case and think about how you would feel towards the social worker if you were Jenny and it was your dad who was being told he should go into care. Reflecting on how Jenny might be feeling towards social work and then discussing this openly with her will give you the opportunity to start in an open way and begin to build a base for an honest relationship which acknowledges the relevance of previous experiences.

Box 11.5 Suggested answer for Activity 11.3 (ii)

Jenny is missing school and there are serious repercussions if this were to continue, so it may be that you reflect upon how Jenny might want to conceal the amount of time that she needs to care for Bill. Alternatively, it may be that Jenny would rather be at school but is worried about Bill when she is away from him.

You and the education social worker represent a part of state authority which has to place Jenny's well-being as a top priority. If you think about how hard it may be for Jenny to be open and honest when the power imbalance is different and you do have access to the authority to impose her attendance at school, you may be able to establish trust through an open discussion of the reasons for your involvement. This will mean being very clear about what you can do and also what you cannot do, and agreeing to absence from school is one area that is impossible for you to condone or ignore. To have this clarity at the start of the relationship means that you will not have to disappoint Jenny at a later stage and as such is much more likely to build her confidence in your relationship with her.

Box 11.6 Suggested answer for Activity 11.4

Answer to Risk assessment reflection (i): Consider some of the issues here in relation to encouraging independence in, whilst protecting from harm and danger, a trustworthy 13-year-old boy who has never had problems in the past and shows maturity and independence in other areas.

- Was this a reasonable risk?
- Was this an accident that could have happened in spite of age?
- Should anyone be held responsible?
- What are the areas that you would reflect upon if the young person was already on the child protection register because of neglect by his parents when he was much younger?

Would you immediately think that this was unacceptable parenting?

Box 11.7 Suggested answer for Activity 11.5

Answer to Risk assessment reflection (ii):
Your reflections will most likely include:

- How old are the children?
- When does the alcohol use take place?
- How long have the parents used alcohol?
- Do the family have support with the care of their children?

summary of key points

- We have identified what reflection is and have considered Borton's 'what', 'so what' and 'now what' model of reflection.
- You have been invited to consider your own skills of reflection in relation to a number of exercises and activities.
- Reflective thinking skills link directly to the social work Codes of Practice and have an integral relationship to issues of professional accountability.

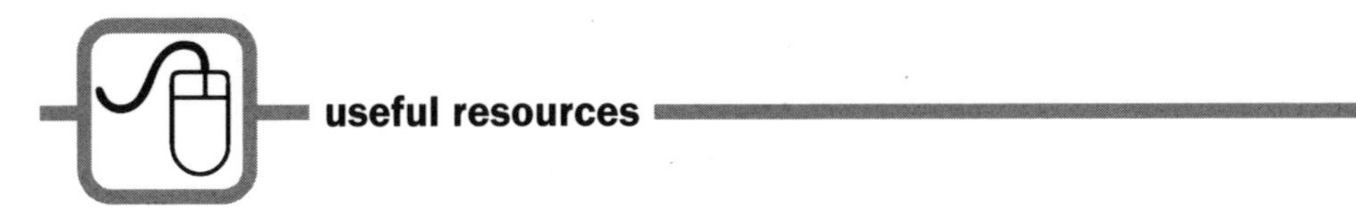

useful resources

Reflective Practice Learning Object
http://learnx.iriss.ac.uk/open_virtual_file_path/i06n253719t/flash/object.html

IRISS's learning object focuses on the concept of 'reflective practice' and includes some useful activities that are relevant for social work students.

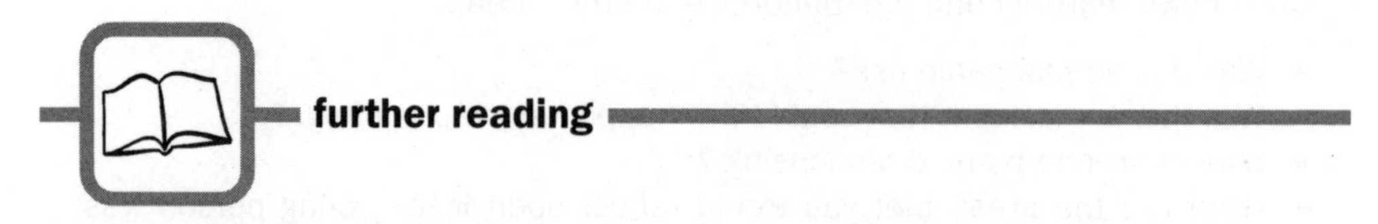

Jaspers, M. (2003) *Beginning Reflective Practice*. Cheltenham: Nelson Thornes.

Knott, C. and Scragg, T. (2007) *Reflective Practice in Social Work*. Exeter: Learning Matters.

Martyn, H. (2000) *Developing Reflective Practice*. Bristol: Policy Press.

Thompson, N. and Thompson, S. (2008) *The Social Work Companion*. Basingstoke: Palgrave Macmillan. (See 2.7 Reflective practice on p. 137.)

12

Developing Social Work Portfolios

learning objectives

- To understand the types of portfolios you are likely to produce as part of your course, including e-portfolios.
- To develop an awareness of the link between portfolio creation and the evidencing of continuous professional development.
- To consider the ways in which portfolios invite you to showcase your learning.
- To develop a greater understanding of the elements that make up core skills, practice and CPD portfolios.

Portfolios

During your social work course, it is highly likely that you will be required to complete at least two portfolios for the assessment of your practice and possibly a third to evidence your core skills in Continuing Professional Development (CPD). The CPD portfolio will be designed to help you to showcase your understanding of the personal and professional knowledge skills and values which are required of you in order to become a qualified social worker.

E-portfolios

E-portfolios offer you the chance to create 'digital' (or electronic) portfolios as opposed to hard-copy, paper-based documents. You may be asked to develop an electronic portfolio as part of your course of study, or in later years as part of your CPD activities. E-portfolios are currently used in a number of ways in social work courses, including:

- the collection of evidence to demonstrate the development of IT skills
- the demonstration of fitness for practice learning or for the production of practice portfolios (Sumpter, 2007).

Did You Know? Advantages of e-portfolios

Some of the advantages of e-portfolios for you, as a student, are that they are:

- **easy to edit**
- **accessible** – you can normally access them wherever you have access to the Internet
- **portable** – you can take them with you as they can be exported and imported into other systems
- **able to be viewed by others** – e.g. tutors, other students and those outside of the institution (e.g. potential employers)
- **flexible** – they allow you to work in a variety of media including digital images, audio and video files, as well as text
- **easily located** – they cannot be lost (unless due to data loss) or misplaced unlike paper-based portfolios

Many of the key principles underpinning the collection of evidence and the construction of portfolios will remain the same in the case of e-portfolios. If your institution is making use of e-portfolios, they will give you support, advice and guidance as to how to access and make the most effective use of them. Also, many of the skills discussed in Chapter 5: Learning Online are relevant to the use of e-portfolios.

Core Skills Portfolios

Did You Know? Core skills portfolios

Core skills portfolios are usually assessed as part of your suitability to go on assessed practice and may include:

- a **reflective overview** of your own learning during the first part of your course (Chapter 11)

- **evidence** that you have an awareness of the Key Roles, Value Requirements and the knowledge and skills associated with them (Chapters 4, 9 and 11)
- a **report from your tutor or line manager** which gives a clear recommendation about your suitability to be assessed in practice
- **feedback** from the social worker who has provided the opportunity for you to shadow their practice (Chapter 10)
- **your own reflections** on your experience of shadowing a qualified social worker (Chapter 11)
- some of the **computer and information technology (C & IT) work** that you have produced to show your progress in relation to your IT skills (Chapters 13 and 14)
- use of a **learning journal** – containing personal reflections and insights into your own learning (Chapters 2 and 11)

Let us take a look at these in more detail:

A reflective overview

Your course may use another name for this piece of work but it is very likely that you will be asked to produce some work in which you reflect on your own learning and development during the early stages of your course.

Why do a reflective overview?

Did You Know? Reflective overview

This piece of work will give the opportunity to:

- **focus** closely on the content of the modules that you are studying
- **reflect on** your own reaction to these new areas of understanding
- **think about** how you have responded to specific areas of knowledge that have challenged your view of the effectiveness of social work
- **critically examine** some of the more demanding experiences in your learning
- **consider** these in relation to areas that you may need to address when you identify your future learning needs

Shadowing

When you reflect on your learning, you will also need to consider the experience of shadowing a qualified social worker.

Did You Know? Shadowing a qualified social worker

- The opportunity to see a social worker in action is a requirement of the GSCC (2002).
- It enables you to have a snapshot of the role that you are training for.
- It gives the social worker that you are shadowing the opportunity to assess your initial suitability to continue to train as a social worker.

Not surprisingly, shadowing can be really stressful for you as a student social worker and preparation for this opportunity will be very important. Here, you will be able to draw on your skills of:

- effective communication (Chapter 9)
- stress management (Chapter 3).

The qualified social worker you shadow will write a short report on her/his observations of you, and this will highlight both your strengths and areas for development that you may have been demonstrating during your period of shadowing.

In reflecting on your learning, you will have the opportunity to:

- demonstrate your openness to take on new learning
- show how you have responded to feedback.

activity 12.1

You and your shadow!

Before you undertake your 'shadowing' opportunity, put together a learning development plan to help you prepare and get the most learning out of the experience.

- What could you do to help you to prepare?
- What kinds of self-development activities or exercises could you do to help you to gain confidence in your:
  - communication skills
  - time management
  - demonstration of your willingness to learn
  - openness to feedback and willingness to act upon it?
- Use the blank learning development plan in Figure 2.2 (Chapter 2) to help you with this activity.

Key requirements

You will not be expected to have a full understanding of the key requirements in the first part of your course but you will be asked to show that you have basic awareness of their existence. You will also be asked to evidence that you appreciate the legal and professional context of the regulation of social work as a professional activity (Thompson, 2009).

Your course will have made some preliminary checks about your suitability through an Enhanced Criminal Records check but the monitoring of your own values and beliefs will take place through both academic work and your conduct towards students and staff. This is a powerful area and you will be expected to look critically at some of the more complicated aspects of values from perspectives of risk, on the one hand, to liberty on the other.

Box 12.1 reflection point

Risk vs liberty?

Social workers operate at the interface of state regulation in relation to individual freedom so it is important that an understanding of this complex level of responsibility is cultivated on an informed and carefully considered base (Adams, 2002).

- Can you think of any examples from your own experience, or through cases reported in the media, where this complex level of responsibility is illustrated?
- What kinds of things help robust decision making in cases which are not straightforward?

A report from your tutor or line manager

If you are on an employment- or work-based course, it is usual for the recommendation to come from your line manager regarding your suitability to progress to assessed practice.

Did You Know? Assessing suitability for practice

It is only recently that it has been possible to assess a social work student's suitability to continue on the course before going into assessed practice (GSCC, 2002).

(Continued)

- Your initial understanding of the **values, knowledge and skills** necessary for social work practice will be assessed before you go on placement.
- This guards against a student going on placement who has clearly demonstrated, perhaps through their behaviour in the university, that they are unsuitable to be in the social work profession.
- It avoids exposing service-users and carers to student social workers who are regarded as unsuitable for assessment in practice.

Did You Know? What goes into a tutor or line manager's report?

The report should comment accurately on your:

- timekeeping
- ability to meet deadlines
- general understanding
- application of Key Roles and Value Requirements.

The Continuous Professional Development (CPD) Portfolio

The CPD portfolio will:

- draw on the learning that has occurred from all the modules that you will have studied
- will usually focus on preparation for the assessment of your professional practice.

In order to be supported to go into this assessment, you will need to show that the learning you have experienced has given you a basic understanding of the social work role in the broadest sense. To do this, you will need to have developed a confidence in the specific areas of:

- communication
- knowledge, values and skills
- key roles.

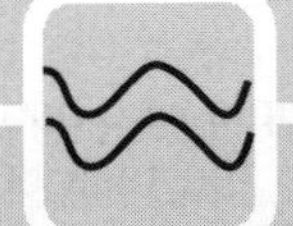

Box 12.2 reflection point

Presenting portfolios

- How are you going to **introduce the reader to your portfolio**?
- Will you give **a profile of your personal details in relation to your experiences in social work before and during** your time on your social work course? (This may be very useful in the context of the experience of shadowing a qualified social worker.)
- **Have you been asked to identify other personal details** around race, ethnicity, class, gender, disability, etc.? How do you think they impact upon your work in this portfolio?
- Have you **cross-referenced** the reader to the different parts of the portfolio which collectively strengthen the evidence of your learning?

Introducing your portfolio

The introduction in your portfolio will set the scene for the reader in relation to the context of your piece of work. As with any assessed piece of work, it is useful and relevant to demonstrate your learning and progression by clearly showing the point at which you began. Your introduction will also be the place where you demonstrate your intention to address the learning outcomes for the module:

> ***Example:*** 'In this portfolio I will evidence my organizational skills in relation to my time management as seen in the Personal Development Plan in Section ...'

Drawing on personal experiences

You may be asked to include a detailed account of your relevant experiences and this can perhaps be thoughtfully developed along the following lines:

> ***Example:*** 'Before starting on this social work degree I have worked as a volunteer in a youth justice setting which gave me some understanding of the importance

(Continued)

of effective communication. Part of my role was to talk to young people who had been given a community sentence and to help them to engage in the task of developing understanding around their offending behaviour.

Often the young people found talking to volunteers and staff very difficult and I learnt that the most effective communication was established through shared tasks in a non-threatening setting – I was really surprised at the conversation that emerged when helping a young person make the tea and coffee for the group! This understanding was developed further when I shadowed a qualified social worker in the first year of the course.

I was attached to a social worker in an older people's team who was working with service-users who had a diagnosis of dementia. The social worker talked to me about the importance of listening carefully and demonstrated this when he was listening to a service-user who was very upset. He emphasized the importance of listening in a respectful way and the connection with effective communication skills.'

Drawing upon your own experiences from your personal and work life, from before and during the course, will provide a clear context to your development in your CPD portfolio. The personal experiences that are relevant to the evidence in this portfolio may include, for example:

Example: 'My understanding about the importance of careful listening first began as a child when I visited my great aunt who lives in a care home because of her dementia. I can remember my mother carefully checking that she had understood my great aunt by repeating her words. At the time I thought that my mother had not heard properly but now I realize that she was making sure she had heard exactly what my great aunt was saying.'

In this way, you will be connecting your practice experiences with your personal ones and be in an informed position to explore how the two areas are interlinked.

Reflecting on issues of identity

If you are asked as part of your CPD portfolio to reflect on issues of your own identity, it is important that you fully understand why you are being asked to do this – for example, you may be asked to consider some of the power differentials that relate to race and ethnicity (Trevithick, 2005).

Box 12.3 reflection point

Experience, identity and practice

There may be specific experiences that you have had which will impact on your practice. For example:

- If you have dealt with racism or discrimination on a personal level, you may have specific understanding of how this might impact on your work with people who have similar experiences.
- It might be appropriate for you draw on this to evidence your learning about the impact of oppression in relation to professional social work practice.
- Your experience may have a relevance to discussions with your practice educator who may or may not have similar experiences depending on their own profile.
- It may be that you have experienced racism or discrimination within an organizational setting and it is useful to consider these experiences in relation to the new practice setting in which you are being assessed.

The CPD portfolio will require:

- a clear examination of your own understanding of professional social work values
- a clear examination of how your personal beliefs and values complement the professional social work ones.

The use of cross-referencing

We have looked at the importance of referencing in relation to your academic work (Chapter 8) and a further aspect of this is your ability to cross-reference your work.

Did You Know? Cross-referencing sources of evidence

Demonstration of your learning can be reinforced by cross-referencing more than one example of 'evidence' in the portfolio.

(Continued)

Example: You produce a reflective statement in which you:

- clearly discuss how you have looked at your own values in relation to social work values
- go on to highlight some of the theoretical understandings that you have explored as part of an assignment on values.

By completing the second part of this piece of work, you will be corroborating the first part of your evidence of learning in this area.

This emphasizes the importance of drawing on more than one source of evidence to support your academic work. Assessments which are based on observations from more than one source have a credibility which underpins effective practice (Thompson, 2009).

It is useful to draw upon areas of social work practice which have been scrutinized in the public arena and to look at the recommendations that have been made regarding the importance of evidence-based decisions (Trevithick, 2005). Developing your cross-referencing at the start of your course establishes the building blocks for both strong academic work and safe practice in the future.

- Cross-referencing is about pointing your reader in the direction of some relevant information or evidence that you have included in your portfolio.
- It follows the same principles as standard referencing. You are basically aiming to support what you are saying by providing some evidence to back it up.
- In portfolio work, you are more likely to make reference to your own experiences or pieces of evidence about your practice, rather than academic textbooks.
- We have demonstrated the principle of cross-referencing in this book, where we refer you to other chapters that deal with related topics.

Quick Tip: How to do cross-referencing

Use the word 'LINK' to help you remember what to do when cross-referencing:

L – **Look** for connections between ideas, reflections and evidence ... *then:*
I – **Insert** references at appropriate points in portfolio writing ... *which include:*
N – **Numbers** (page/chapter numbers for sources of evidence) ... *then finally:*
K – **Keep copies** of sources of evidence, for inclusion in your appendices

Example: 'I can sometimes have a tendency to be very shy when I meet new people. However, when I completed my shadowing of a qualified social worker I consciously worked on things like asking relevant questions and talking informally to service-users. I was pleased and encouraged to see that the feedback from the social worker I shadowed described me as being confident and a good communicator' **(see p. 14: Feedback from Social Worker Shadowing)**.

Practice Portfolios

The whole purpose of assessment in practice is to ensure that you have been given the appropriate learning opportunities to be able to clearly evidence your abilities as a safe and competent social worker.

Box 12.4 reflection point

Safety, competence and trust

It is important that social workers are able to convey their safeness in practice to service-users, carers and others in order to establish relationships and credibility and be able to then go on to work effectively (Beresford, 2005).

The legal requirements for the assessment of practice are clearly stated (GSCC, 2002). The obligatory 200 days in assessed practice for social work students is a non-negotiable, legal requirement. The evidence of your assessed practice is usually contained in the practice portfolio in which you will have the opportunity to demonstrate your understanding and application of:

- the **Key Roles**, which include the National Occupational Standards for social work
- the **Value Requirements** for social work practice.

The two areas above will cover significant aspects of your practice but you will also need to identify and evidence your understanding and application of appropriate social work theories.

Did You Know? Practice portfolio contents

The practice portfolio may include the following contents (but it is important to look at the specific requirements of your course and follow guidance from your tutors):

1 The placement agreement
2 The evidence grid
3 The learning journal
4 Direct observations
5 Feedback from service-users and carers
6 Feedback from colleagues
7 Work records
8 Academic work
9 The Practice Educator's report

The Placement Agreement

This is an important part of your portfolio as it will usually be the first piece of work that you complete for it. The agreement will also give you a clear guide to the type of work that you will undertake during your assessed practice. The knowledge and skills that you will be expected to demonstrate will also be discussed with your practice educator and tutor when you meet to draw up your agreement.

Quick Tip: Skills involved in drawing up the agreement

- Usually, you will take notes of the discussion so your **listening skills** will be important here.
- You will need to **summarize the information** as it will not be practical to record every word of the actual discussion.
- You will need to pay special attention to **accuracy** and ensure that the information that you record is a **true account** of the discussion.
- You will need to **think about information fairly quickly** and decide on the importance and relevance of it.

Specific learning requirements and placements

You may have an assessed learning need which has resulted in the recommendation that you make an audio recording of your lectures and this will need to be addressed at the earliest stage within your placement setting. The agreement meeting is usually the first meeting you will have together with your tutor and practice educator. Highlighting the specific needs at this early stage will mean that resources can be put in place to ensure that you have a fair chance of equal treatment from the start of the placement. It may also be that whilst you are applying your listening skills, you are also sifting through the information in order to prioritize and précis the content of the discussion. You may feel a little overwhelmed by these tasks and your pre-meeting preparation will be of enormous benefit to you. For instance, it is good planning to have a discussion with your tutor to gain clarity on the expectations of your role in the meeting and also to seek guidance on the time frame that you will be working to in relation to the completion of the agreement.

It will probably be fine for you to produce a draft of the agreement after the meeting so that you can discuss it with both your practice educator and tutor before finalizing it. It should then be signed by all parties in the early stages of the placement. This will then give you:

- clarity about the expectations of you
- details of the induction programme
- some detail about the practicalities of the setting.

Did You Know? Placement agreements

Placement agreements should include details of:

- the arrangements around **insurance**
- the arrangements for **expenses**
- the agency protocol regarding **safe working practices**.

Most importantly, they should outline:

- the **work that you are going to undertake**
- the **arrangements for your supervision**.

The importance of supervision is well established at all levels of social work but the relevance for you as a student social worker cannot be overemphasized.

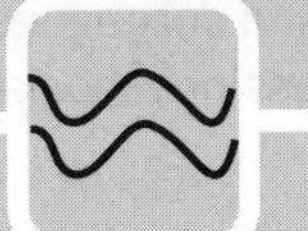

Box 12.5 reflection point

Safe practice and supervision

The safe practice that we discussed earlier has a particular connection to supervision and the commitment to supervision that you establish at this stage in your career will be of real significance when you become a qualified social worker.

The evidence grid

Evidence grids are often used to help you to organize and show how things link together in your portfolio in a clear and systematic way. It may be that your course uses an alternative format to a grid but however you are asked to produce the information, it is important that you can clearly demonstrate to the reader that you have met the portfolio requirements.

Did You Know? Evidence grids

An evidence grid:

- shows at a glance that you have provided evidence in all the necessary areas for assessment
- can be a helpful aid when you are creating your portfolio as you can use it to highlight any gaps that you spot as you go along
- can be discussed with your practice educator who will be able to identify the necessary learning opportunities for you to address each learning criteria.

The learning journal

This will be a vehicle for you to convey the whole gamut of thoughts, feelings, observations and understanding that you will experience during your practice placement through reflective writing.

Did You Know? Learning journal contents

In the journal, you will be asked to:

- write about the experiences that you have on placement
- identify and reflect on your thoughts, feelings and understanding of the situations that you have been involved in with service-users, carers and colleagues
- look at these in relation to both your own learning and the professional social work requirements (GSCC, 2002).

This professional context positions the journal in a very different place to a diary, which may be written as a record of personal thoughts and feelings, but not written with the explicit intention of being read and assessed by others.

Let us think about the kind of situation that you might want to write about in your learning journal:

Case study: **Learning Journal Incident**

You have just started your final placement in an Initial Response Team in the Children and Family Services Department of a Local Authority. You have been on a joint visit with a social worker who is a senior practitioner in the team. The social worker had been asked to visit by the GP because she was concerned about the family. The parents had visited the GP and said that they could no longer cope with their two children – twin boys aged 14 who attend a special school because of their specific behavioural needs.

When you visited with the social worker, you observed that the children were constantly swearing and spitting at the parents and seemed to ignore any attempts by the parents to get them to settle down. The social worker listened to the parents and discovered that they felt the children's behaviour had deteriorated since they had moved to their new school. They said they had previously worked closely with the Education Social Worker and the Educational Psychologist. The social worker suggested that he contact the Education Social Worker and Psychologist to determine if any further support was available and would ask them to see the family again. The parents said they would prefer for the children to be taken into care to give them a rest but the social worker said that this was not an option at this point in time.

On the car journey back to the office, you asked the social worker why he had not removed the children as they were obviously in need of urgent protection. He was quite amused by your response and said that you might have a very different view of protection when you had spent more time in the Initial Response Team. He added that if he were to remove all children from similar situations, he would be removing about 150 in that area alone!

You feel patronized and angry at the response from the social worker and you also feel worried about his decision-making skills and think that the family has been left in a dangerous situation.

Some points which may be useful to consider are:

- Can you reflect on the above and consider how your feelings may influence your assessment of the situation and the social worker's response?
- How much knowledge do you have about the role of social workers in the Initial Response Team?
- Perhaps you already have previous experience of working in this area of practice which has influenced your reaction?
- Can you identify the skills that were used by the social worker?
- Can you voice your reaction in a way that does not apportion blame but does focus on the areas of learning that may be relevant for you?
- Have you thought about how you respond to feedback when it is critical of you?
- Now consider the connection between your learning and the Value Requirements, Key Roles and Code of Practice.

activity 12.2

Recording this case in your learning journal

So, now have a go at writing this up, as if it were an entry in your learning journal:

Learning Journal Entry:

Direct observations

Did You Know? Direct observations

- It is a GSCC (2002) requirement for you to be observed on at least **three** occasions during each placement.
- An important part of your portfolio will be the record of the **direct observations of your practice**.
- Two of the observations will need to be done by your practice educator.
- One can be done by another colleague with the agreement of your practice educator.
- The requirement is for *at least* three and it may well be that your practice educator decides to do 33 or more!

Note:

In some placement settings, e.g. a residential facility, it may be that you are working alongside your practice educator and that your practice will be observed in a naturalistic and routine way. In this setting, your practice educator observations will be nearer the 33 figure!

Skills for learning from direct observations

Box 12.6 reflection point

Preparing for direct observations

- The arrangements for the direct observation will require some time-management and planning skills on your part as you will need to coordinate your contact with the service-user with the availability of your practice educator.
- It is likely that your practice educator will ask you to prepare for the direct observation by identifying the aims and objectives of your contact with the service-user, e.g. why are you seeing the service-user?
    - Has the purpose of the visit been made clear to the service-user?
    - What are the areas of your learning that it would be helpful for your practice educator to focus on?
    - This preparation will draw upon both your professional understanding of social work interventions and your skills of reflection on your own learning needs.
- Seeking permission from the service-user and clearly explaining the purpose of the direct observation will give the opportunity to demonstrate both your verbal and non-verbal communication skills. The written account of the observation will enable you to showcase your written communication skills.
- Your demonstration of your understanding of the Value Requirements, Key Roles and Codes of Practice will enable you to gain confidence in the role that you are expected to play within the team.

Work Records

It may be that you are not required to give samples of work records in your portfolio but you will undoubtedly be required to produce work records as part of your placement.

IT skills and work records

In many social work settings, the recording of work will be done on computer on very specific agency systems. Your induction to the placement should include an introduction to these systems and your access will usually be organized by your practice educator.

The IT skills that you will need to record your work appropriately within the placement setting will have been established through the IT aspects of your social work course (see Chapters 13 and 14).

Writing skills and work records

Your written work will need to demonstrate your skills in sentence construction, grammar and spelling. It may be that you have an identified specific learning need which is supported with a software package which will need to be installed in the agency at the start of your placement. This is something that you need to be proactive about at the placement agreement meeting with your practice educator and tutor.

The ability to write accurate and fluent reports is a fundamental skill in safe social work practice and failures in this area have been reported in the enquiries into tragic circumstances in practice (Trevithick, 2005).

Listening and comprehension

The making of the work record will draw upon your skills of both listening and understanding in relation to the information that is being given to you. It will also draw on your skills of sifting information and prioritizing to establish the significance of the details of the content.

Read through the following information and identify what you think are the most relevant points.

Case study: Joe

Joe is 15 years old and has been missing from a Young People's Unit for the last three days. He has a passionate love of music and one day plans to be a music producer. In the past, he has gone missing for days at a time and has returned without giving any explanation. He is an insulin-dependent diabetic and is chaotic in his diet so frequently has to be admitted to hospital to be stabilized.

He has three brothers and two sisters and has stayed in contact with them in spite of being separated from them since he came into care. His brothers and sisters live 40 miles away and he has only seen them in the presence of his social worker. He is a West Ham United supporter and is keen to take up a work experience opportunity with the club's Youth Team. The work experience placement is due to start in two days' time. Joe has been at the Young People's Unit for the last four years and the staff at the unit have reported that he has recently seemed to be very settled and looking forward to his work experience and planning his future. He has been reported as a missing person to the police.

activity 12.3

Putting together your work record

Write down some brief responses to the following questions:

- What are your first thoughts when you read this information?
- Do you know what is expected of you by the placement agency when you make a work record?
- Are there specific requirements in relation to the statutory nature of the work?
- Do you think that there are parts of this information that are more important than others?
- How would you record the information in order of risk?
- How important is the accuracy of the times?

Being clear about exactly what needs to be part of a work record connects very closely to clarity about the role that you have as a student social worker. It follows that if you are unsure about the work that you are doing, then inevitably you will be unsure about the record that you need to make. Rather than speculate here about the relevance of the information in relation to Joe, it may be that the kinds of questions shown above would form the basis of your supervision with your practice educator.

Academic work

You will be required to include samples of your academic work in your practice portfolio. Always make sure that you keep copies of your essays and assignments safe, and that you carefully file away any feedback that you receive on them.

The practice educator's report

Your practice educator will gather the evidence to make a recommendation when assessing your practice. Your skills in presenting the work that you have done and your understanding of the professional requirements will influence the quality of the evidence.

- Your practice educator will look at your ability to communicate with her/him as a template of your communication skills generally, and this will be picked up in the report. You do not have to like everyone you work with but you do need to establish a good working relationship which ensures that clear and effective communication channels are not hindered by personal likes and dislikes.
- Your practice educator will undoubtedly have a 'cat flap' of opportunity rather than a window in which to write your report.
- You will need to strictly adhere to the agreed deadlines for the submission of work needed in order for the report to be written, and this will draw upon your time-management skills (Chapter 3).

Example: You may have childcare problems personally because of a training day for teachers at your child's school but to ask for special allowances for this may rankle with your practice educator who has a child in the same situation but has made plans to cover the childcare.

We are not suggesting here that all situations can be planned for and sickness and other unpredictable events will occur. However, to make a crisis out of a situation about which you have had plenty of notice may lead to your practice educator questioning your time-management and planning skills.

summary of key points

- The social work portfolios that you will be required to complete during your time on your course include:
  - e-portfolios
  - core skills portfolios
  - CPD portfolios
  - practice portfolios.
- The specific skills required to produce effective portfolios include:
  - cross-referencing
  - learning from direct observation
  - reflective writing in learning journals
  - organization and use of evidence grids.

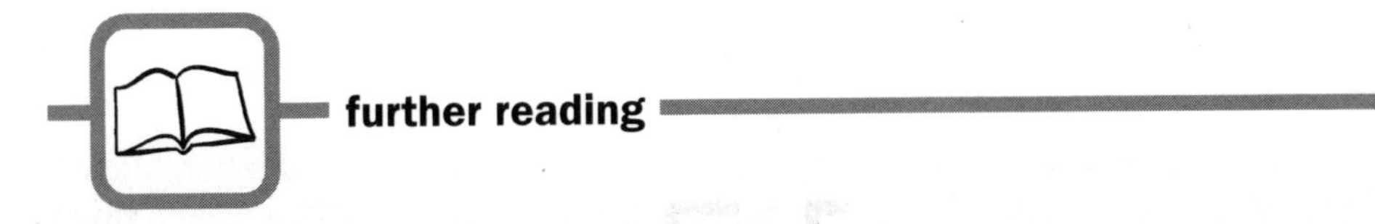

further reading

Walker, H. (2008) *Studying for Your Social Work Degree*. Exeter: Learning Matters.

13

Computing Principles and Concepts

learning objectives

- To understand some of the concepts and principles underlying the use of computers within the context of social work study and professional practice, including:
  - basic concepts of IT
  - using electronic communications effectively and appropriately
  - managing files
  - assistive technologies
  - health and safety issues
  - data protection issues.

Social Work and Computing Skills

Whilst you will not be expected to become a computing expert by the time you finish your course in social work, it is useful to think about how you might use your time as a student, and in placement, to develop and build upon your existing computing skills.

Box 13.1 reflection point

ICT Skills and Social Work

Some students struggle to see the relevance of ICT skills to a profession which is fundamentally about communicating and interacting with people. The reason that the GSCC insists that students are able to demonstrate competencies in using computers is reflective of the widespread use of IT systems within professional social work environments. This includes:

- the inputting and storing of electronic files and records
- searching electronic databases for evidence-based research
- communicating with other colleagues and agencies using email
- presenting professional-looking reports and documents
- assisting with time-management processes

enabling social workers to have a greater input into discussions around the development of services and systems (Waldman, 2007).

You may already have well-developed ICT skills and if you are in this position, you should try to focus on how you can use these transferable ICT skills within the context of social work practice (Holt and Rafferty, 2005).

Do computers change the nature of social work practice?

Some social work academics have suggested that the greater use of ICT systems, especially databases, is having a profound impact on the nature of social work practice. Parton (2008), in particular, argues that social work is moving from a narrative perspective to a 'database way of thinking and operating' (p. 253). He notes that the current emphasis on recording, processing and managing information through databases systematizes the collection of data and marginalizes social workers' discretion which means that 'knowledge that cannot be squeezed into the required format disappears or gets lost' (p. 262). This kind of research alerts us to the fact that the use of ICT within professional practice is never a 'neutral' activity, but always carries certain models of knowledge creation with it. It also illustrates the need to develop a critical perspective in relation to the uses of ICTs.

The Basic Concepts of IT

Having a general overview of the main elements that make up a computer system:

- helps to develop your confidence, as the computer is no longer a 'mysterious box' which seems to have a life and will of its own
- helps to develop your basic vocabulary of computing terms which you can use when talking to IT technicians about any problems you may be having with computer equipment in the workplace.

Table 13.1 Basic concepts of ICT – quick Q & A

Question	*Answer*
What is a computer?	A tool which allows the user to perform calculations, and to then store the results of these calculations. This principle underlies all of the tasks we do with a computer, from word processing to manipulating digital images.
What is 'hardware'?	The physical parts that make up the computer system (e.g. the monitor, the tower or processing unit, the keyboard, the mouse, etc.).
What is 'software'?	The instructions or programs that make the computer operate in a certain way or allow the user to perform specific tasks (e.g. word processing, sending emails, browsing the web).
What are the main parts of a computer?	1 **Central Processing Unit (CPU)** – this could be called the 'brains' of the computer. 2 **Memory** – two types of which are ***Random Access Memory (RAM)*** and ***Read-Only Memory (ROM).*** 3 **Hard disk** – a permanent storage drive (usually very large in modern computers). 4 **Removable storage drives** – e.g. DVD/CD-ROM drive.
What is Random Access Memory (RAM)?	The computer's temporary memory which can randomly access any piece of data (hence the name). Anything that is temporarily stored in RAM will be lost when the computer is shut down.
What is Read-Only Memory (ROM)?	This contains low-level programmes that the computer needs in order to start (boot up). This type of memory can only be read and not written to or written over.
What does the computer's hard disk do?	It is the disk space that is used to save documents, files, folders, programs and other data.
What is a 'peripheral'?	A device which can be added, or connected, to a computer which extends its functionality. Examples of peripherals include printers, scanners and web cams.
What is the 'operating system' (sometimes called 'system software')?	The software used to control the computer, communicate with peripheral devices (such as printers) and process inputs (e.g. keyboard stroke) and outputs (e.g. print-out).
What are 'applications' (sometimes called application software)?	Programs which allow you to perform specific tasks or 'applications'. Examples include Microsoft Word or 'Writer' which is part of Open Office – both can be used for word processing.

Table 13.1 ***(Continued)***

Question	*Answer*
What types of license are there for software?	1 **Licensed** – you need to purchase a license from the company who manufactures the software. 2 **Shareware** – you can try the software out for free for a trial period, but then you need to purchase a license. 3 **Freeware** – you can install and use the software for free. 4 **Open Source** – the software is developed by a community of computer programmers rather than a commercial company. Can be installed, downloaded and modified for free. Examples include 'Open Office'.
What is a computer network?	Basically, a number of computers that are connected and can usually share data, applications and peripherals.

Maintaining computer equipment

The following table provides a summary of 'dos' and 'do nots' in relation to computing hardware:

Box 13.2 Taking care of computing hardware

- Computing equipment can get very warm, so you need to keep it in a well-ventilated space.
- You must keep computer hardware dry – be careful with drinks and try to avoid placing them on the same desk that your computing equipment is on.
- Dust is another enemy of computing equipment, and can ultimately damage the internal workings of computers – make sure your equipment does not become dusty.
- Always shut down a computer using the 'Shut-down' option on the 'Start' menu. Closing a computer down whilst it is in the middle of processing data or completing some other kind of process can result in problems.
- Always eject disks, USB sticks and other storage devices properly to avoid losing data or corrupting your files. If you are not sure, how to do this, ask your department's IT technician or your institution's student IT helpdesk.

Managing Files Effectively

If a computer is connected to a network (such as the computers that you will use within your institution), then you may find that you are able to access a number of **networked drives**. You may find that your institution allocates you some personal student storage space on one of their networked, institutional drives.

Table 13.2 What are files, folders and drives?

Files	A computer's basic unit of information storage. Examples of files include: • word-processed documents • spreadsheets • databases • digital photographs • mp3 audio tracks
Folders	Containers which can be created in order to store files and other folders. A folder which is contained inside another folder is known as a sub-folder.
Drives	Physical storage devices which store files and folders. The main drive that sits inside of your computer is normally known as the C: drive, but it is not uncommon for computers to have more than one internal drive these days.

The application (or program) that is most often used for basic file management tasks is called **Windows Explorer** (if you use a Macintosh computer, the equivalent software is called 'Finder').

File extensions

Whenever you name or save a file (for example, a Word document), Windows automatically attaches the appropriate file extension:

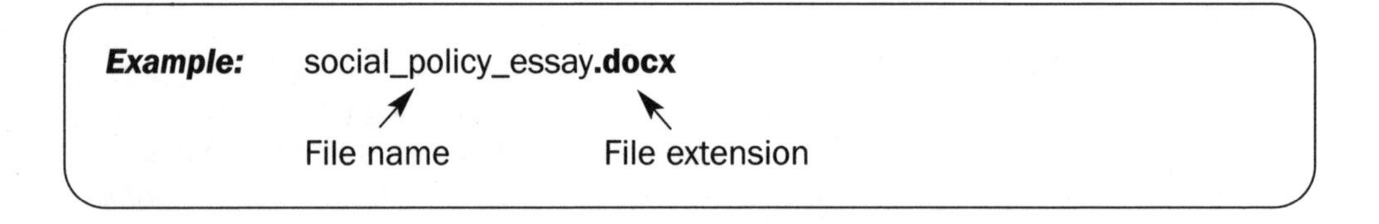

The file extension can help you to identify the type of information contained in a file. In the example shown above, we can tell from the file extension .docx that 'social_policy_essay' is a word-processed document that was created using Microsoft Word 2007.

Table 13.3 Other common file extensions

Type of file	*File extension*
Microsoft Word 2007 document	.docx
Microsoft PowerPoint 2007 presentation	.pptx
Microsoft Excel 2007 spreadsheet	.xlsx
Plain text file	.txt
Rich text format	.rtf
Web page (hyper-text format language)	.html OR .htm
JPEG image file	.jpeg OR .jpg
Portable Document Format	.pdf

Table 13.4 File sizes

Unit of file size	*Equals*
1 Byte (B)	8 bits
1 Kilobyte (KB)	1024 Bytes (B)
1 Megabyte (MB)	1024 Kilobytes (KB)
1 Gigabyte (GB)	1024 Megabytes (MB)
1 Terrabyte (TB)	1024 Gigabytes (GB)

File sizes

All files have a particular size and this is measured in bytes. Bytes can be expressed in different units, including:

- bytes
- kilobytes
- megabytes
- gigabytes
- terrabytes

It is useful to develop a sense of how big a file is in order to know how much space it will occupy on your hard disk or removable storage device. For instance, most Word documents tend to be quite small in size, but video files can be several gigabytes.

File size is a particularly important consideration when it comes to sending email attachments to other people – you should try to avoid sending them something that is so big that it fills up their mailbox (unless you have discussed it with them prior to sending it).

Keyboard shortcuts

It is common to use icons and pull-down menu options in order to carry out tasks and commands when we are using a piece of computer software. However, many common tasks can also be performed by typing particular combinations of keys on the keyboard – these are known as **keyboard shortcuts**.

Did You Know? Keyboard shortcuts:

- can often be quicker then spending time selecting a tab on the ribbon and searching for the correct icon
- can be useful for people who use assistive technologies such as screen-reading software. For example, a blind or visually impaired computer-user may not be able to see pull-down menus or visual icons on screen, but they can use keyboard shortcuts in order to operate the computer.

Table 13.5 Commonly used keyboard shortcuts

Task	*Keyboard shortcut*
Open an existing file	CTRL + o
Open a new file	CTRL + n
Save the current file	CTRL + s
Copy a selected item to the clipboard	CTRL + c
Cut a selected item to the clipboard	CTRL + x
Print the current file	CTRL + p
Paste an item from the clipboard	CTRL + v
Undo the last action	CTRL + z

To use a keyboard shortcut, press the first key and keep it depressed whilst you press down the second key. The common key combinations are shown in Table 13.5.

There is also an accessibility feature called **sticky keys** which allows people with limited mobility, or who find it difficult to hold two or more keys down at the same time, to utilize keyboard shortcuts.

Did You Know? Microsoft accessibility features

You can get help and support about accessing Microsoft accessibility features, such as 'sticky keys', 'screen magnification' and 'screen reading' through the Microsoft Accessibility micro-site which is available at: http://www.microsoft.com/enable/default.aspx

Using Databases to Access Information

What are databases?

Databases allow raw data to be stored and retrieved. For example, some of your own personal information will have been recorded on your institution's student records database when you enrolled on your course. This will have included basic contact information, your date of birth and your previous educational experience. It will also include details of any disability you may have declared and details of your ethnic origin and may also include information about your socio-economic status.

How are databases used in social work practice?

Databases are used extensively in health and social care environments and one of their key uses is in the storage and retrieval of clients' or service-users' details.

When important information is stored in databases, it enables the database-user to:

- **search** the database to see what kind of data is already known and recorded about a particular individual, item or service (e.g. details that have already been recorded in relation to a particular service-user) – this is known as searching or **querying** the database.
- **add and amend** existing database entries (e.g. a service-user may change their address and this would need to be updated on a service-user database).
- **collect together** specific data from a particular database and bring it all together in one document. This is known as running a **report**. For instance, information about a particular service-user could be collected together in the process of preparing a 'care plan' report.

Did You Know? Using databases in social work practice

- The databases you use when in practice will vary depending on the local authority that you are employed by.
- The main principles of using databases will be the same for any system although screens, menus and options may look different.
- Commonly used databases include CRIS, SWIFT and CareFirst (Gregor, 2006).

Database Fundamentals

Data and information

The 'stuff' that is added to databases is referred to as data.

Did You Know? Data

- 'Data' can take the form of:
    - text
    - numbers
    - images
    - sounds and video
- Raw data can become useful information when we know what it refers to and can draw some meaning from it.

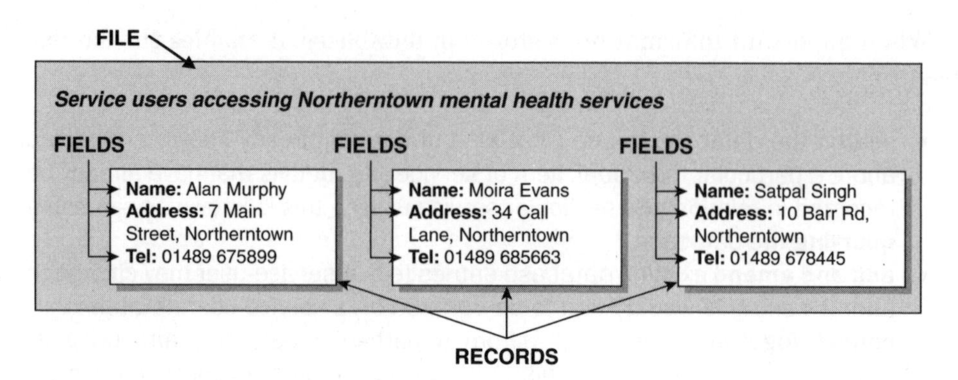

Figure 13.1 Fields, records and files in databases

The following is an example of raw data which probably does not mean much to us in its current form:

> *Example of data:* Kiteley, MA1/06, 3169

However, if we say: 'Mr **Kiteley** is a lecturer who is based in the **M**ilton **A**nnexe building, in room **1/06**, and can be reached on telephone extension **3169**', we can start to understand the kind of data that is being recorded, and how this data is being organized.

Fields, records and files

Databases are typically made up of fields, records and files. In Figure 13.1 we have a database of service-users who access local mental health services.

- This database **file** contains a number of **records** about individual service-users.
- Each service-user **record** is made up of several **fields** (i.e. 'name', 'address', 'tel'), which are common to each record.

Working with databases and inputting data

Most databases that you will come into contact with during your social work course, and in professional practice, will already have been set up and organized ready for you to use. You will most usually be:

- adding, editing or possibly deleting data
- searching the database for information
- pulling off information in the form of reports.

Programs such as Microsoft Access can be used to create your own databases and this comes as part of the Microsoft Office software. An alternative, free database application is **Base** which is part of the Open Office open-source office suite.

Academic databases

The following are examples of databases which contain research resources in relation to social work and the social sciences. Read the brief descriptions of resources 1 and 2, shown below, in order to get a sense of what each one does, and then use the web addresses shown in order to access them.

Example: 1. Social Care Online (SCIE) – http://www.scie-socialcareonline.org.uk

This is a free, online database containing a wide range of social care information for students and professionals, including:

- reports
- research briefings
- journal articles
- links to relevant government websites.

Example: 2. Intute: Social Sciences – http://www.intute.ac.uk/socialsciences

This is another free, online database which brings together subject-specific resources for use within education and research. The **social sciences** section allows you to search for a range of hand-picked, quality-assessed resources or to use key headings (e.g. 'social welfare') to focus in on materials relating to key topics.

activity 13.1

Using professional and academic databases

Imagine that you have been asked to look into how aspects of social exclusion affect young people in the United Kingdom.

PART 1:

1 Access the **SCIE** website.
2 Use the Intermediate search facility to carry out a free text search for '**young people**' AND '**social exclusion**' – how many results are returned?

(Continued)

3 Repeat the search but this time select the 'Full text only?' box, so that only results offering full-text access are returned. How many results are returned this time?
4 Try accessing some of the resources listed.

PART 2:

1 Access the '**Intute: Social Sciences**' website.
2 Carry out a basic search on '**young people**' and '**social exclusion**' – how many results are returned?
3 If you scroll down and browse through your results, you will notice that some of them focus on non-UK research, including some American studies.
4 Repeat the search by going to the '**Advanced Search**' screen. Use the same search terms but this time set the '**Country of Origin**' to United Kingdom – how many results are returned?
5 If you have completed the advanced search successfully, you should find you have less results, and that those that are shown originate from the UK.

QUICK TIP: Advanced searching

Whenever you use databases and search engines, try to get into the habit of using the '**Advanced Search**' option.

- This will help to give you more control over the relevance of the results that are returned – which will mean less time is wasted for you.
- Most advanced search pages will contain a 'help' link which will provide guidance on how to get the most out of advanced searching.

activity 13.2

Other useful databases

The following subscription-only, database services are normally accessed through one of your institution's library web pages and you will probably need to enter a username and password in order to access them:

- **ASSIA** (Applied Social Sciences Index and Abstracts)
- **CareKnowledge** (http://www.careknowledge.com)
- **CSA (Social Services Abstracts).**

1 Contact your department's academic librarian in order to find out if you have access to these resources and how you would access them.
2 Are there other specialized databases that your institution subscribes to which would be useful for social work?

Computing and Assistive Technologies

Not all computer-users make use of a keyboard, mouse or even read text from a monitor. For instance:

- some disabled people may not have the physical dexterity required in order to precisely position a cursor using a mouse or may not be able to use a keyboard
- some blind or visually impaired people may not be able to see what is happening on a computer screen
- deaf people may find that they require assistance when accessing audio-visual resources.

If you have a disability yourself, or know of someone who is disabled, you may use specific software or hardware to assist you with your computer use. As a social worker, it is important to be aware that there is a range of assistive technologies that some disabled people (colleagues, service-users, carers) may use.

Table 13.6 Some examples of assistive technology

Technology	*Use*	*Used by*
Screen-readers	Reads textual content of screen out for blind or visually impaired users	Some blind or visually impaired people
Screen magnification	Allows the user to magnify a portion of the screen	Some blind or visually impaired people
Alternative input devices	Provide alternatives to mice or keyboards including tracker balls.	Some physically disabled people

activity 13.3

Assistive technologies audit

There are a number of assistive technologies which are now offered as part of most computer operating systems:

1. Investigate what kinds of assistive technology are available on the computers that you use at your institution, at work or at home.
2. Use a search engine to do some research about the kinds of assistive technologies that are available for disabled people and make a list of any you were not previously aware of.

Most local authorities have taken steps to ensure that their websites are accessible to disabled people, and this has in large part been thanks to the Disability Discrimination Act (1995) and bodies such as the Web Accessibility Initiative (WAI). However, despite the legal requirement to make information accessible, some service-users who use assistive technologies may still find that online services or information are not *always* user-friendly or easily accessed.

Dyslexia and assistive technologies

In 1999, a survey of UK higher education students suggested that, on average, 2.6% of students had some form of dyslexia (Singleton, 1999).

Did You Know? Defining dyslexia

The **British Dyslexia Association** (2007) defines dyslexia as:

'... a specific learning difficulty which mainly affects the development of literacy and language related skills'.

The condition is typically characterized by difficulties with:

- phonological processing (dealing with sounds of language)
- working memory
- the rapid naming of things

- the speed at which things can be processed
- the disparity in strength of some cognitive skills in comparison to the individual's other cognitive abilities.

Source: BDA, 2007.

Dyslexia can impact on individuals in different ways, but may mean that extra help or support is needed with reading and writing. Specific assistive technologies such as **ReadWrite Gold** and **Kurzweil 3000** include scanning and screen-reading functions which can read back text to a student. If you are dyslexic, this could be helpful in the process of writing your own essays and assignments, but could also be useful when tackling reading assignments.

Useful Resource: Assistance for disabled students

- If you have a disability, you would be encouraged to discuss this with your institution's **Disability Support Officer** to find out about the full range of services and support that you are entitled to receive.
- Many disabled students will be eligible for some financial assistance from the **Disabled Student Allowance** (DSA).
- Many institutions include **specialist assistive software packages** on their standard student computing desktop which could be of use to you. They should also be able to provide support in helping you to get started with any new software product.
- The JISC **TechDis** service aims to support accessibility and inclusion in UK higher and further education, and has some really useful online resources for students and HE/FE staff (see **http://www.techdis.ac.uk**).

Computing in Social Work Practice Settings

In some practice areas, you may find that computing resources are currently limited (Holt and Rafferty, 2005: 5), but there is increasing interest in making greater use of ICTs across the social care sector. For example, the Interactive Technologies Research Group (2006) has researched the use of digital technology to enable paid carers of older people to access information and share good practice.

activity 13.4

ICT Audit in practice learning settings (taken from Holt and Rafferty, 2005)

To gain a better appreciation of how ICT skills are applied to the real, everyday business of social work practice, conduct an ICT audit (a review) in your practice or work-based learning setting.

For instance:

- What kinds of software are used for what kinds of tasks?
- How does availability of ICT systems impact on your colleagues' workflow?
- Do the ICTs that are in use appear to assist your colleagues in providing an effective service to service-users and carers?
  - What works well?
  - What could work better?

VDU use and health and safety issues

Visual display unit (VDU), visual display technology (VDT) and display screen equipment (DSE) all refer to the use of a screen or monitor, usually forming part of a computer set-up. As VDUs have come to be used more frequently, and more heavily, in many areas of contemporary working life, including social work, there has been increased concern around ensuring that this sustained computer use does not negatively impact on people's health. The use of VDU equipment in itself will not necessarily cause you any health problems – it all comes down to *how* the equipment is used.

Did You Know? Health and Safety (DSE) Regulations

All employers have a legal responsibility under the **Health and Safety (Display Screen Equipment) Regulations (1992)** to ensure that any risks to employees' health, resulting from the use of VDUs, are minimized by ensuring that both workplaces and work tasks are appropriate and well designed.

It is important that you and your employer are aware of these regulations and that they are addressed during your induction into any new social work employment environment. There is not space within this book to go into the exact requirements for well-designed VDUs, but guidance and information can be found online.

> **Useful Resource: Display Screen Equipment Regulations**
>
> For an overview of the Display Screen Equipment Regulations (Health and Safety Executive), see **http://www.hse.gov.uk/msd/dse/guidance.htm**

Some of the general principles of well-designed VDUs are:

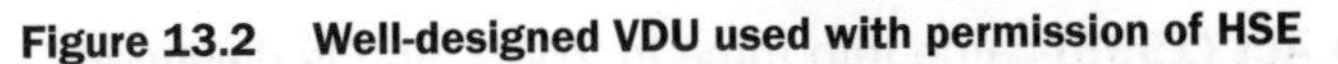

Figure 13.2 Well-designed VDU used with permission of HSE

- You should be provided with a fully adjustable office chair.
- There should be enough space on your desk for your keyboard, mouse and other resources such as documents and document holders.
- You should be able to adjust the angle of your monitor to avoid glare and find a position that is comfortable to use.
- The lighting in your office or environment should be suitable for VDU working.
- There should be sufficient space under your desk or workstation for you to be able to move your legs freely.
- The keyboard and mouse should be positioned in a suitable position so as not to induce arm or wrist strain, from over-stretching or failure to support the wrists and arms.

> **Did You Know?**
>
> Despite the fact that it is generally recognized that constant, prolonged use of VDUs can lead to musculo-skeletal conditions, such as **repetitive strain injury (RSI)** and possibly **carpal tunnel syndrome**, there is no legal limit as to how long employees can be expected to work at a VDU.

However, it is sensible to:

☑ Take regular breaks, even if this is just for a few minutes in each hour.
☑ Get up and move around so that your body has a chance to stretch.
☑ Avoid sitting in the same position for hours at a time.

You may even want to regularly perform some gentle stretching exercises.

What are the other main health and safety problems that can arise due to the use of computing equipment?

- **eye strain** resulting from extended 'staring' at the monitor
- generalized **muscle strain**, perhaps resulting from an inadequate working space
- untidy and loose cables which present a potential **trip hazard**
- people climbing up onto rotating office chairs and **falling** – this is potentially very dangerous and should obviously be avoided.

Data Protection Issues

Did You Know? The Data Protection Act

- The **Data Protection Act (1998)** came into force in 2000, and is designed to protect the use of personal data by businesses and organizations.
- It is clearly significant for social workers who record, process and access personal information about service-users on a routine basis, using computerized databases.

Some of the key points of the Data Protection Act relate to how data is collected, maintained and stored.

Box 13.3 Some key aspects of the Data Protection Act

- Data must be used only for the purpose for which it was originally collected.
- Data must not be given to a third party without the consent of the individual to whom the data refers. There are some exceptions to this, including the detection or prevention of crime.
- Data must only be kept for as long as it is needed and must be kept up to date.
- Any person is entitled to access a copy of the data that is held about them and can request that changes be made if the information is incorrect.
- Organizations must ensure that there are technical and organizational measures in place in order to safeguard the privacy of personal information.

One of the technical measures that might be used to safeguard information is the use of **firewalls** which are designed to prevent hackers or 'intruders' from accessing restricted areas of an organization's computing network. Also, data that is sent from one organization to another via electronic data exchange should be securely **encrypted** (put into a secret code) to prevent this data from being intercepted by a third party. Organizational aspects of maintaining compliance with the Data Protection Act relate more to educating employees about how they use systems in order to ensure that data is kept secure.

Did You Know? What can you do to ensure data protection?

- Do not leave computers available for others to access when you leave them unattended in areas accessible by the public.
- Use password protection or logout of your computer when you have finished using it.
- Keep usernames and passwords private and secure.
- Save your work regularly – you never know when there might be a sudden power cut or your computer may 'crash' (in other words, it freezes up and needs to be re-booted).

Quick Tip: Passwords

- The most secure passwords are a combination of letters and numbers. For example, 'arch63455' is more secure than 'jane'.
- Obvious passwords such as first names or surnames should be avoided.
- Changing passwords regularly helps to maintain security.

Several high-profile cases that have made the news headlines in recent years relate to the loss of personal data which has been held on laptop computers, CDs, memory sticks or other forms of transportable memory device. Most organizations will have strict guidelines relating to the transfer of data, often involving the use of specialist couriers, so avoid sending anything like this through the regular postal service. Also, be careful about the kinds of information you save to any personal storage device which you regularly carry between your home and your workplace. It is so easy to lose CDs and particularly small memory sticks!

activity 13.5

Serious reported data losses

Try entering the following phrases into a search engine (choose to search UK only):

- child benefits records loss
- NHS memory stick found in street
- NHS records lost
- MoD laptops lost
- prison officer data loss.

You should find several news reports that highlight very serious examples of data loss in recent years. Try to answer the following questions:

- What are the consequences of these data losses?
- What steps could have been taken to prevent these incidents from occurring?

summary of key points

- It is helpful to have a basic grasp of computing terminology and the key elements that make up computing systems.
- Principles of managing files, including file sizes and file types, help us to manage digital resources more effectively.
- Having an awareness of the underlying principles of databases is useful for understanding how they are used in professional practice and in academic contexts.
- Assistive technologies can be extremely useful for some disabled computer-users.
- The key health and safety principles in relation to VDU use within institutional and work-based settings come from the Health and Safety (Display Screen Equipment) Regulations (1992).
- If you use computers in the workplace, you have a responsibility to protect the data of others, as stated in the Data Protection Act (1998).

useful resources

OpenOffice.org – 'the free and open productivity suite'
Available at: http://www.openoffice.org
This website contains information about the Open Office open-source software and also the facility to freely download the Open Office software (versions are available for Windows, Linux, Solaris and Macintosh platforms).

Centre for Human Service Technology (CHST)
Available at: http://www.chst.soton.ac.uk/
CHST's focus is on the use of technologies within social welfare education. The website provides a series of links to project documents, reports and other publications.

further reading

Gregor, C. (2006) *Practical Computing Skills for Social Work*. Exeter: Learning Matters. (Chapters 1–4 and 7 in particular relate to the content of this chapter.)

14

Computing Skills Workshop

learning objectives

- To develop an understanding, and practical experience of, the kinds of features in word-processing software that can help with preparing academic assignments.
- To develop an understanding, and practical experience of, presentation software to create basic presentations, and an overview of how to control them in presentation mode.
- To develop an understanding, and practical experience of, spreadsheet software to create simple spreadsheets, perform calculations using basic formulae and create simple bar charts.

Whilst most of the chapters in this book are 'stand-alone' and can be dipped in and out of as you see fit, we would strongly recommend that you have read Chapter 13 before beginning to work through this skills workshop. The previous chapter develops your understanding of basic computing concepts and terminology which will help to underpin your learning in this chapter.

Help Options and Online Resources

Box 14.1 Accessing 'Help' in Microsoft Office® 2007 programs

To access the help facility in any of the Microsoft Office® 2007 programs, either:

- click the **Help** icon

  OR

- press the **F1** key on the keyboard.

This will bring up a help window. You can then choose from a list of help topics and sub-categories or you can choose to search the help pages by typing relevant words into the search box and clicking the 'Search' icon.

The help option can be extremely useful in assisting you to get a better understanding of the software. For instance, you may know that you want to move a chunk of text in a little way from the left-hand margin, in order to show that you have taken a direct quote from a book or journal article. However, you may not be aware that Word® refers to this as *indenting*. The key to getting the most out of the help facility is to try various options if you do not find what you want straight away. Also, try asking a friend, colleague or family member if they know how a particular task is most commonly described or referred to.

Box 14.2 Increasing font sizes for greater accessibility

You can increase the size of the font in the Microsoft Office® 2007 help menus by clicking the **Change Font Size** icon and selecting the desired font size. This may be particularly helpful for some students with visual impairments.

Features in Microsoft Office® 2007

This chapter focuses on the use of Microsoft Office® 2007, which has introduced some fairly radical changes to the software. Many of the features described will be transferable to earlier versions of Microsoft Office®, but you may need to look in slightly different places in order to access some of the commands. Make use of the 'Help' function if you get lost or confused.

Some features in Microsoft Office® 2007 are completely new and do not exist in previous versions, including:

Quick Access Toolbar

This is a compact toolbar which contains icons that represent the commonly performed tasks such as **Save**, **Undo**, **Redo** or **Print**.

Undo has changed – as well as being able to undo the very last thing that you did, it also now gives you a drop-down menu which allows you to undo multiple elements in your 'actions' history. This is helpful if you realize that you do not necessarily want to undo the last thing you did, but in fact want to undo the last five tasks that you completed!

The Ribbon

The Ribbon is a new feature in Microsoft Office® 2007 which organizes options and commands into categories which are known as **contextual tabs** (or simply 'tabs'). Selecting one of the tabs brings up a selection of commands/options which are associated with that tab. The Ribbon replaces the old, pull-down menu style of accessing commands in Microsoft Office®.

> ***Example:*** If you want to make any sort of changes to the **Page Layout** of a Word® 2007 document, such as altering whether the document was in landscape or portrait format, you go to the Ribbon and select the **Page Layout tab** to display its associated commands and options.

Once you have become more familiar with how the tabs and commands are organized, you should begin to feel more comfortable with Office 2007.

Screen tips

There are built-in 'screen tips' (basically labels) which help if you cannot remember what a particular icon does – activate them by moving your cursor over the icon that you are interested in.

Live preview

'Live preview' allows you to see the consequences of making a change (hence 'preview') before you actually commit to making it.

> ***Example:*** Highlight a section of text in a Word® document and move your cursor down the list of font styles. 'Live preview' displays what the text would look like if you went ahead and made your selection.

Word Processing

As a student, and professional social worker, there are numerous occasions when you will need to use word-processing software including:

- working on essays, assignments and portfolio documents
- typing letters, memorandums or other correspondence
- producing reports
- completing forms associated with appraisal, supervision or other employment processes.

This brief overview will focus on the use of the Microsoft Word® software, as it is probably the most commonly used word-processing software on the market. If you have bought your own PC or laptop, you will probably find that it came installed with either Microsoft Office® (or Microsoft Works®, which is basically a slimmed-down, 'lightweight' version of Microsoft Office®). There are other word-processing applications that are available and you may have come across free, open-source software called Open Office which includes 'Writer'. This works along similar lines to Microsoft Word® (although Word® 2007 *looks* very different).

We are using Microsoft Word® 2007 in the following examples, but the principles will be relevant to any word-processing package. However, if you are using another package, you might have to access options in a slightly different way.

> **Quick Tip: Help on the web!**
>
> - The **World Wide Web (WWW)** is a great source of free guides and tutorials for many types of common software applications.
> - If you are using Microsoft Office®, try searching for **Microsoft Word tutorials**, or check out the range of free tutorials on the Microsoft website.

Inserting and deleting text

Inserting text into a document

1 Open up a new blank document in Word®.
2 The flashing cursor indicates where your text will appear.
3 Start to type and your text will appear on-screen.

Deleting text

1 Highlight or select the bit of text you want to **delete**.
2 Press the **Delete** key on the keyboard.

Alternatively, you can position your cursor directly to the right-hand side of the word or words you want to delete, and then keep pressing the **Back space** key until you have finished deleting.

Moving and copying text

One of the great advantages of word-processing work is that it is incredibly easy to make changes to your document, including moving text around.

Moving text

1. Select (highlight) the chunk of text that you want to move.
2. Use the mouse to click and drag this section to a new place in your document.

You can also highlight text and use the **Cut** and **Paste** commands to move text.

Copying and pasting text

1. Select (highlight) the chunk of text to be copied
2. Use the **Copy** command, to copy
3. Reposition the cursor and select the paste command.

Altering font style and size

Word® allows you to select from a wide range of font styles and font sizes.

- For academic essays and assignments, it is preferable to use simple **font styles** (most institutions insist that students use either **Times New Roman** or **Arial**).
- **Font size** is usually set to **12pt**.

If you are a student with a specific learning difficulty or disability, you may find it easier to work with a different font style and size – let your personal tutor know so that he or she can notify colleagues (with your consent).

Box 14.3 Altering font style in Word® 2007

1. Click the **Home** tab on the Ribbon.
2. Select the text that you want to change in your document (either click and select with your mouse or select all).
3. Click on the font list pull-down menu, to reveal a list of available font styles.
4. Click to select the font style you want to use.

Box 14.4 To alter font size in a Word® 2007 document

1. Select the **Home** tab on the Ribbon (if it is not already selected).
2. Select the text that you want to change in your document (either click and select with your mouse or select all).
3. Click on the font size pull-down list and select a number (e.g. 12pt) in order to set the font size.

Changing line spacing

The default (factory-set) setting for line spacing in Word® documents is set to 'single-line' spacing. Most institutions will ask you to hand in assignments that are **double-line** spaced. This has the effect of creating a blank line in between each line of your document which makes it much easier for tutors to add comments to your work when they are marking it.

Box 14.5 To adjust line spacing of a document in Word® 2007

1. Select the **Home** tab if not already selected.
2. Make sure that all of the text in your document is selected (select all).
3. Select the **line spacing icon** which gives you a pull-down list of different line spacing options. 1.0 corresponds to single-line spacing, **2.0 equals double-line spacing** and so on.
4. Select the appropriate option.

Word counts

Tutors usually set a particular word limit for academic assignments. For instance, you may be required to write a 4000-word assignment on a contemporary social policy issue. It is usually acceptable to go **10% over** (e.g. 4400) or be **10% under** (e.g. 3600). You will normally be asked to indicate your assignment word length by putting a word count figure at the end of it (and also possibly on assignment submission sheets).

Box 14.6 Obtaining a word count in Word® 2007

1. Select the **Review** tab if not already selected.
2. Select the **Word Count** icon.

(Continued)

3 A new **Word Count** window will appear which provides a number of statistics for your document, including the number of words.

Also note that:

- you would not normally include your 'reference list' in a word count
- you should include any quotes that you have used in your assignment.

Using bullet points

It can sometimes be useful to create lists of bullet points in a Word document but they are more usually found in reports or presentations, rather than academic essays or assignments.

Box 14.7 Creating a bullet-pointed list in Word® 2007

1 Make sure that the **Home** tab is selected.
2 Position your cursor in your document at the point at which you wish to begin your bullet point list.
3 Select the **Bullet point** icon.
4 Type in your first bullet point, then press the **Enter** key to move down to the next bullet point in your list.

Numbering pages

It is important to get into the habit of numbering all of the pages in your assignments as outlined here:

Box 14.8 Inserting page numbers in Word® 2007

1 Make sure that the **Insert** tab is selected.
2 Select the **Page Number** icon.
3 An option menu will appear giving you the choice of where to position the page number within your document. It is usual to set this to be at the 'bottom of the page' and either centred or right-aligned.

4 Word® will add the page number to the footer area of the document. Select 'Close Header and Footer' to return to the main document.

Spell checking

Word® includes a spell-checking feature which can be used to help you to identify any possible spelling errors. However, the spell-checking facility can never really replace thorough proofreading of your work.

Word® will automatically try to pick up any spelling errors as you are typing by putting a red, squiggly line under any word which it does not recognize. In some cases, this might be because:

- you have made a genuine spelling error
- you have used a name or specialized term which is not in Word's® dictionary.

Right-clicking with your mouse on any word underlined in red will give you a number of possible 'corrections'. You can choose to select the correct word if it is shown amongst the available options, or simply select 'ignore' and Word® will not make any changes.

Box 14.9 Spell checking

To run the spell-check facility on your entire document:

1 Select the **Review** tab.
2 Select the **Spelling & Grammar** option.
3 The **Spelling & Grammar** window will appear and will show any words which it picks up as potential spelling errors in red.

NB: Check that the 'Spelling and Grammar' checker is set to English (UK) as sometimes it can be set to English (US).

Headers and footers

Headers and footers are bits of information that you want to have displayed at the top (header) or bottom (footer) of the pages of your document. Typically, they may contain your name, the title of your course and the page number.

Box 14.10 Adding 'headers' and 'footers' to a Word® 2007 document

1. Select the **Insert** tab.
2. Select the **Header or Footer** icon.
3. Select the relevant option from the pull-down menu.
4. Type text into the appropriate header or footer portion of the page.
5. To get back to the main document, select 'Close Header and Footer'.

activity 14.1

A word-processing exercise

1. Open up a new word-processing document and put the title **ICT Skills Audit** at the top of the page. Centre this title and make sure that the font style is set to **Arial** and bold and that the font size is set to 16pt.
2. Create a header with your name in it.
3. Create a new subheading called **Word-processing skills** in Arial, 14pt. Then write a few sentences in Arial 12pt which consider your word-processing skills in relation to the following prompts:
   - What kinds of existing skills do you have in this area?
   - How might you develop your skills further whilst you study social work?
   - How will these skills be used within professional social work practice?
4. Next, create a new subheading called **Presentation software skills** and do the same as you did above. When you have finished this, repeat the process for the following:
   - Spreadsheet skills.
   - Email and Internet skills.
   - Database skills.
5. Insert page numbers.
6. Select all of the text in your document and set the line-spacing to 2.0 (double-line spaced).
7. Run the spell-checker facility and correct any spelling errors that you pick up.
8. Obtain a word count and add the phrase **Word Count** at the very end of your document and type in the relevant number.

9 Select your section on 'Email and Internet skills' and move this whole section so that it appears after the main document title.
10 Save this document with the file name **ICT Audit**.

Presentation Software

Most social work courses will require you to give either an individual or group presentation (or even both) at some point in your academic career. There will also be times in your professional role as a social worker where you will need to present information to colleagues, service-users, carers or other professionals.

This section describes how you can use Microsoft PowerPoint® 2007 software in order to enhance the delivery of your presentation. There are other pieces of software that will allow you to create similar electronic presentations such as 'Impress' which is part of the 'Open Office' open-source, office suite. Also, 'Google Docs' gives you the facility to create presentations and is free to use.

Microsoft PowerPoint® basically allows you to create slides which can contain:

- text
- images
- charts
- graphs
- video
- sound effects

If you have not delivered a PowerPoint® presentation before, you will almost certainly have been on the receiving end of one, as it is commonly used by teachers and lecturers.

What is a PowerPoint® presentation typically made up of?

A basic PowerPoint® presentation consists of a number of slides in which a combination of text and images are displayed. PowerPoint® tends to assume that most people are going to want to use bullet points on their slides. However, there are a number of different ways in which you can format your slides to accommodate different combinations of information.

You can change the visual appearance of the slides yourself by changing:

- text size, style and colours
- background slide colours and designs

or you can use a menu of pre-set slide designs which take care of all the visual design elements for you.

PowerPoint® allows you to create animation on your slides – for instance, a bullet point can glide in from the right-hand side of the screen, or appear and then fade away. It is also possible to apply custom animation to elements such as images, charts, graphs and other visual elements.

Did You Know? Learning about PowerPoint®

When you are learning to use PowerPoint®, there are two main processes you need to know about and these are:

1. Authoring your presentation – learning how to create, set up and visually enhance your slides.
2. Delivering your presentation – learning how to put the presentation into full-screen delivery mode, and controlling the presentation as you deliver it to your audience.

Part 1: Authoring your PowerPoint® Presentation

This brief guide is based on Microsoft Office PowerPoint® 2007 which looks quite different to previous versions of PowerPoint®.

Starting PowerPoint®

Box 14.11 Opening up PowerPoint® 2007

1. Select the computer's **Start** menu.
2. Select **Programs**.
3. Select **Microsoft Office®** in the programs menu.
4. As you move your cursor over this, a sub-menu should appear which includes **Microsoft Office PowerPoint®**.

Creating a new presentation

When you first open PowerPoint®, you will see:

- a new, blank 'title slide' for you to begin working on,
- the ribbon containing different tabs including 'Home', 'Insert', 'Design', etc.

Each Ribbon tab gives you access to different commands, which allow you to do various different things to your presentation.

The title slide

A 'title slide' simply allows you to create a main title and subtitle for your presentation. You might want to use your own name as the 'subtitle' for a presentation.

Box 14.12 Adding a title to the title slide

1 Click anywhere on the words **Click to add title**.
2 Type in a title of your choice.
3 To add a subtitle to your slide, click anywhere on the words **Click to add subtitle**.

Adding a new slide to your presentation

After you have created your title slide, you will want to begin adding more slides to your presentation.

Box 14.13 Creating new slides in PowerPoint® 2007

1 Make sure the **Home** tab is still selected on the Ribbon and then click on the **New Slide** icon.
(Note: If you click on the slide icon part of this button, PowerPoint® will automatically give you a new slide with the 'Title and Content' layout. If you click on the words 'New Slide', you will have the chance to choose a different layout from a range of options.)
2 Your new slide gives you the facility to add a title towards the top of the slide (**Click to add title**) and then you can begin to add bullet points (**Click to add text**).
3 After each bullet point, simply press the **Enter** key and the cursor will move down to the next line, allowing you to create your next bullet point.

Using clip art and images

Images or 'clip art' (Microsoft Office's® own collection of imagery and illustrations) can help to bring a bit of visual interest to your slides.

Box 14.14 Inserting clip art onto a slide in PowerPoint® 2007

1 Select the **Insert** tab on the Ribbon and then select the **Clip Art** button.
2 The **Clip Art Pane** appears on the right of the screen. This provides a **search** box – type in a word which best describes what kind of clip art you are searching for, e.g. 'computer' if you are looking for images relating to computing.
3 Next, click on the **Go** button. PowerPoint® will search through its library of clips and display any containing the keyword 'computer' (or whatever search word you used).
4 Scroll through the pictures to find one you like, then click on it to insert it into your slide.
5 The image appears right in the centre of your slide. Click in the centre of it and then drag it (using the mouse) to the position you would like it to appear in.

Using design templates

Design templates enable you to change the visual appearance of all the slides in your presentation. They alter font styles, colours and slide backgrounds.

Box 14.15 Using design templates in PowerPoint® 2007

1 Select the **Design** tab on the Ribbon and a selection of slide 'themes' will appear, in the form of small 'thumbnail' images.
2 To view any of these themes, simply move your cursor over the thumbnail image – Microsoft Office's® 'live preview' lets you see the result immediately.
3 Click on your preferred theme icon to apply it to your slides.
4 The theme will be applied to existing slides and any new slides that you create.

Part 2: Delivering Your Presentation

Delivering and controlling the presentation

When you have finished putting together the content for your PowerPoint® presentation, there will come a time when you wish to deliver the presentation to an audience using PowerPoint's® 'full-screen' mode.

Box 14.16 Putting the presentation into full-screen presentation mode

- Press the **F5** key on your keyboard.

  OR

- Select the **Slideshow** tab, then either the **From Beginning** or **From Current Slide** option.

Box 14.17 Moving from one slide to the next

All of the following options allow you to move on from one slide to the next:

- Press the **down arrow** key on the keyboard.
- Click the **mouse.**
- Press the **spacebar** on the keyboard.
- Press the **Enter** button on the keyboard.
- Press the letter **N** (for **N**ext) on the keyboard.

If you need to move the presentation back to the previous slide, any of the following options will allow you to do this:

- Press the **up arrow** key.
- Press the **backspace** key.
- Press the letter **P** (for **P**revious).

Box 14.18 Exiting full-screen presentation mode in PowerPoint® 2007

- If you need to exit from 'slide show' mode at any point in the presentation, you can do this by simply pressing the **Esc** key.
- When your presentation comes to an end, PowerPoint® will show a black screen after your final slide and will instruct you to **Click to Exit**.

PowerPoint® printing options (including handout mode)

Box 14.19 Printing options in PowerPoint® 2007

Select the **Office Button** and then choose the **Print** option. This will bring up a Print dialog box which gives you various different choices and options:

- The **Print what** pull-down menu allows you to print out **handouts** rather than full-slides – this is useful if you are intending to produce handouts for your audience. The 'handout' option allows you to specify the number of slides that appear on each page.
- The **Color/grayscale** option allows you to specify whether you print in colour, grayscale or pure black and white.

Using speaker's notes

Speaker's notes:

- are designed to prompt you to talk about, or do, certain things at key points in the presentation (they are like PowerPoint's® version of prompt cards)
- are NOT displayed on-screen when you deliver your presentation – they are purely for the speaker's benefit
- can be printed out so that you can take them in to your presentation.

Box 14.20 Printing out 'speaker's notes' in PowerPoint® 2007

To print out a version of your presentation which includes speaker's notes, select: **Office Button**, then **Print** and then change the **Print what** option to **Notes Pages**.

Box 14.21 Dos and don'ts of using PowerPoint® successfully

***DO* (OR AT LEAST TRY TO):**

☑ Make sure you are confident controlling your PowerPoint presentation (e.g. putting your presentation into full-screen mode, moving slides backwards and forwards, etc.).

- ☑ Ensure your font colour has enough contrast in comparison to the background colour of your slide.
- ☑ Use bullet points rather than long paragraphs of text which can be difficult for an audience to read.
- ☑ Make appropriate and effective use of graphics, charts, tables and diagrams in order to best communicate your point.
- ☑ Be cautious when applying animation or sound effects – sometimes 'less is more'.

***DO NOT* (OR TRY NOT TO):**

- ☒ Simply read from your slides. Bullet points can help you to talk naturally around your topic and your audience will feel like you are really addressing them, rather than simply reading from a script. If you are really nervous about losing your thread, have a script prepared as a back-up – but always try to present the material rather than read it if possible.
- ☒ Think that flashy graphics and animation will compensate for a lack of content – always remember that the purpose of a presentation is to communicate a theme or topic to an audience.
- ☒ Wander about in front of the data projection screen as you are talking, as it can be distracting and prevent your audience from being able to see your slides.
- ☒ Look behind you at the data projection screen as you deliver the presentation. Instead, use prompt cards, prepare a set of speaker's notes in PowerPoint or simply glance down occasionally at the computer monitor (which will normally be in front of you). This will help to keep you focused on your audience and to maintain eye contact.
- ☒ Cram too much information on one slide – break things down into digestible chunks.

activity 14.2

A presentation exercise

1 Open up your presentation software and create a title slide with the main title of **Ingredients for Successful Presentations**.

a Add your own name as the subtitle.

2 Create a new slide and give it a title of **Presentation Planning**.

(Continued)

Add three or four bullet points which summarize what you think is most important in relation to presentation planning (you may need to use your imagination if you have not delivered a presentation before).

3 Create another new slide and give it a title of **Presentation Design**.

Add three or four bullet points which summarize what you think are the main issues in relation to presentation design (HINT: Think of colour contrast, fussiness of slide design, size of text, use of images, etc.).

4 Create another new slide and give it a title of **Presentation Delivery**.

Add three or four bullet points which summarize what you think are the main issues in relation to how the presentation is delivered to an audience (HINT: Think about loudness of voice, pace of delivery, eye contact, controlling of nerves, etc.).

5 Create a final slide called **Summary**.

Add three or four bullet points which summarize the previous three slides.

6 Experiment with changing the slide background colour and text colours, or if using PowerPoint®, try applying one of the **design templates**.
7 Experiment with adding basic animation to the text on your slides.
8 Find three images, or pieces of clip art, to represent *planning*, *design* and *delivery* and add to the appropriate slide (taking care not to obscure or cover the bullet points).
9 Save your presentation with the file name **PresentationSuccess**.
10 Put your presentation into 'full-screen' mode and practise moving backwards and forwards through all five of your slides.

Using Spreadsheets

Did You Know? What are spreadsheets?

Spreadsheets allow people to:

- record information (often numeric but can also be text) in a grid-like document called a 'sheet'
- use formulae to perform calculations
- produce charts and graphs based on spreadsheet data.

They are more sophisticated than calculators since they can allow the user to keep adding or amending the spreadsheet.

Spreadsheets are often used to:

- help manage and keep track of budgets (e.g. a departmental or project budget)
- record statistical information (e.g. How many users does a particular service have? What is the ethnic or gender breakdown of service-users?) or any other situation where text and numbers need to be recorded.

Did You Know? The use of spreadsheets in social work and social care

You are likely to find spreadsheets being used by colleagues in managerial roles in order to keep track of organizational and departmental budgets.

For instance, the manager of a care home for older people would be expected to maintain records which record income against expenditure. Spreadsheets are useful because they let the user break things down into different categories. For example:

- staffing costs
- utility costs
- building maintenance
- catering costs

and so on.

This section focuses on the use of Microsoft Excel® 2007 for creating spreadsheets and graphs/charts. There is other software that will allow you to create spreadsheets in a similar way, and this includes **Calc** which is part of the Open Office open-source, office suite and **Google Docs** which is a free, online service.

All of the processes discussed below are available in earlier versions of Excel® – you might need to look in a slightly different place to find some of them, but the 'Help' facility should be useful in trying to locate them.

Opening Excel®

Box 14.22 Opening up Microsoft Excel®

To open up Microsoft Excel®:

1. Select the **Start** menu.
2. Select **Programs**.
3. Select **Microsoft Office**®.
4. A sub-menu should appear which includes **Microsoft Office Excel**®.

Creating a basic spreadsheet

When you first open Excel®, you will find:

- a new, blank 'spreadsheet' for you to begin working on
- the ribbon (towards the top of the screen) organized into different tabs including 'Home', 'Insert', 'Page Layout' and 'Formulas' (each tab gives access to different commands which allow you to do various things to your spreadsheets).

Columns, rows and cells

Spreadsheets are made up of **columns** and **rows** which contain small rectangular boxes which are known as **cells**.

- Each **column** is named after a **letter of the alphabet**, starting with 'A'.
- Each **row** is named with a **number,** starting with the number '1'.

Cell references

Every 'cell' has its own unique grid reference (or cell reference) which is made up of the column letter and the row number. For instance, the top-left cell in your spreadsheet is cell **A1**. Cells are used to contain the various bits of data that make up your spreadsheet.

Entering data into a cell

To enter data into a cell, simply:

- select a cell (either using your mouse and cursor, or using the arrow keys on your keyboard)
- start to type in the contents.

Using basic formulae in Excel®

Once you have entered numerical data into your spreadsheet, it is possible to use a range of Excel® formulae in order to perform calculations (adding, subtracting, multiplying and dividing, etc.) with your data. The advantage of this is that you can get Excel® to perform these processes on a virtually unlimited range of data very quickly.

To use formulae, you first need to click in a cell where you want the result of your formula to appear. Table 14.1 below summarizes the main types of formulae that you would use in a spreadsheet. Note that **all formulae start with the 'equals' sign**.

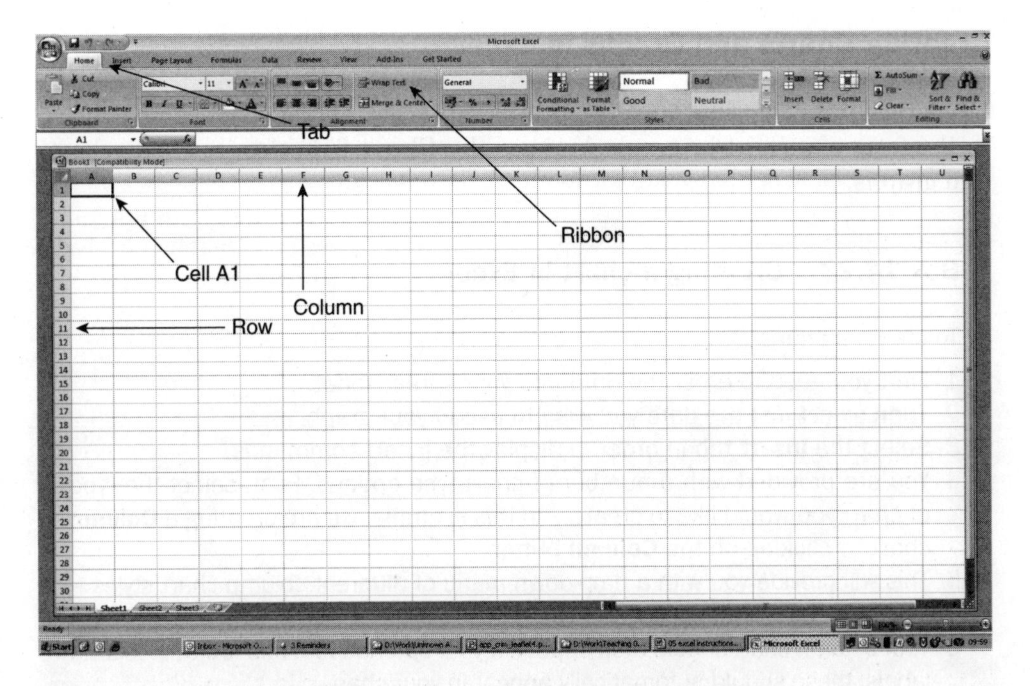

Figure 14.1 An example of an Excel Chart showing the position of titles

Table 14.1 Excel Formulae

Type of calculation	*Example of formula*	*What exactly would this formula do?*
Addition	=A5+A6	Add the value in cell A5 to that in A6
Subtraction	=A5–A6	Take the value of cell A6 away from that in A5
Division	=A5/A6	Divide the value in cell A5 by that in A6
Multiplication	=A5*A6	Multiply the value in cell A5 by the value in A6

When adding up a **range of cells**, you can use the **SUM** function. For instance, if you wanted to add the cells in Column A, from Row 2–12, you could use the formula:

> *Example of SUM formula:*
>
> =SUM(A2:A12)
>
> *Note:* The start and end cell references are separated by the use of a colon (:), and they are contained within brackets.

The **AutoSum** function also allows you to add a range of cells.

Creating Charts and Graphs in Excel®

Numerical data that has been input into an Excel® spreadsheet can be shown in the form of a chart or graph. You use the **Chart function** to create charts and graphs.

Box 14.23 Creating a chart in Excel®

To create a chart:

1. First you need to enter the data into your spreadsheet.
2. Then select just the data you wish to use in your graph.
3. Select the **Insert** tab in order to display the Insert commands.
4. You are provided with a number of chart-type options. First, select the type of chart you would like to create – in this example, we are creating a **Column** chart by clicking on the **Column** button.
5. This will provide you with a drop-down menu of different column chart styles – select an appropriate style.
6. Your column chart should then appear. If your spreadsheet has row and column labels, these should automatically appear in your chart.

Chart and axis titles

All charts and graphs need a **Chart Title** and **Axis Titles** – these are really important bits of information as they enable anyone who looks at the chart to:

- interpret what kind of information is being displayed
- understand the specific type of data that is being shown along the 'x' and 'y' axes.

Box 14.24 Labelling Excel® charts

1. Look for the **Chart Tools** section on the ribbon.
2. Select the **Layout** option.
3. Click on the **Chart Title** button and you will be given a range of options about how and where you want your chart title to appear. Select which of these options you think is most appropriate for your particular chart and enter your choice of title into the title box.
4. You also need to label the horizontal axis (often also referred to as the **x axis**) and the vertical axis (often referred to as the **y axis**).

When you create a new chart, it is normally positioned somewhere on your existing spreadsheet. You can choose to place your chart on its own separate 'page' (or sheet) if you wish.

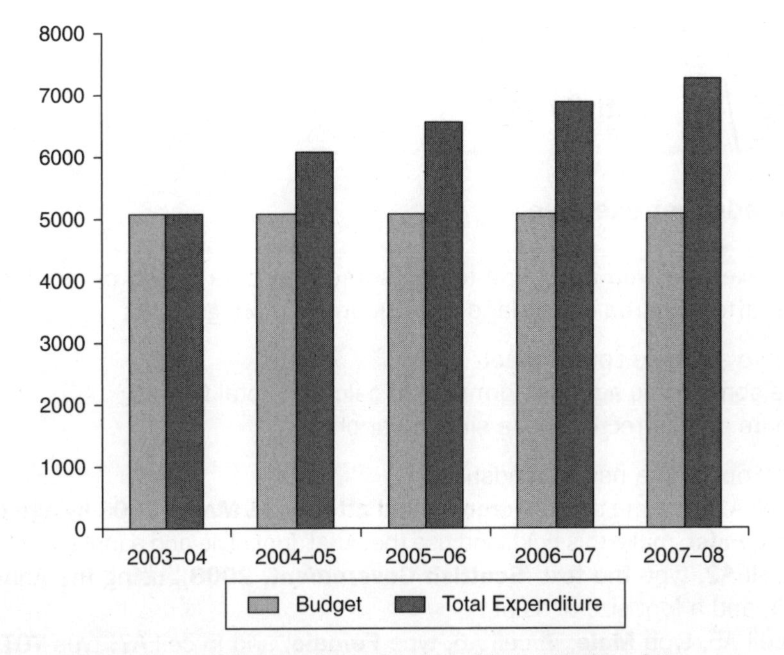

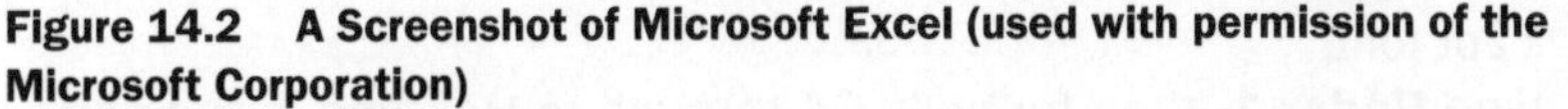

Figure 14.2 A Screenshot of Microsoft Excel (used with permission of the Microsoft Corporation)

Box 14.25 Changing the chart location

To change the location of your chart:

1. 'Right-click' with your mouse on the blank background area of the chart.
2. This will bring up a menu of options – you need to select the **Move Chart** option.
3. To position your chart on a new page (sheet), select the **New sheet** option, and then click **OK**.
4. The chart will now appear on its own sheet.

Box 14.26 Copying and pasting Excel® charts into Word

You can copy Excel® charts into Word documents which can be useful for assignments and reports:

1. Right-click with your mouse in the blank background area of the chart and select **Copy** from the menu that appears (or select **Home** tab then 'Copy').
2. Then go to your Word document and position the cursor in the location where you want your chart to appear.
3. Right-click with your cursor and select 'Paste' (or select **Home** tab then Paste).

activity 14.3

A spreadsheet exercise

In this exercise, you are going to use some real data based on numbers of looked-after children in Scotland (2008), and you are going to:

- create a simple spreadsheet
- use some basic addition formulae to calculate total figures
- create and correctly label a simple bar chart.

1. First, open up a new spreadsheet.
2. In cell A1, type the title **Children looked after at 31 March 2008 by age group and gender**, make this bold, and use the 'Arial' font style and a font size of 14pt.
3. In cell A2, type the text (**Scottish Government, 2008**), using the Arial font style and a font size of 12pt.
4. In cell A5, type **Male**; in cell A6, type **Female**; and in cell A7, type **TOTAL** in bold, Arial, 12pt font.
5. In cell B4, type **Under 1**, then for cells C4 through to H4, type in the age categories shown below in bold, Arial, 12pt font. In cell I4, type the word **TOTAL**. Select cells B4 through to I4 and right-align their contents.
6. Next, type in the numbers of looked-after children in each category as shown in the diagram below. So, for cell B5, you would type in **175**; for cell C5, it would be **1334** and so on. Use Arial, 12pt font – do not use bold for these figures.
7. Go back to row 3 and select the cells B3 through to H3. Merge and centre these cells (there is a button on the **Home** tab that allows you to do this). Then, in this new merged cell, type in **Age at 31 March 2008** in bold, Arial, 12pt font.

	A	B	C	D	E	F	G	H	I
1	**Children looked after at 31 March 2008 by age group and gender**								
2	(Scottish Government, 2008)								
3		Age at 31 March 2008							
4		Under 1	1 to 4	5 to 11	12 to 15	16 to 17	18	19 to 21	TOTAL
5	Male	175	1334	2872	2783	918	93	77	
6	Female	151	1251	2383	2074	687	36	52	
7	TOTAL								

8 Select cell **B7** and enter a formula which will allow you to add together the male and female figures for the **Under 1** age group – to give you a total number of children in this category (you could use AutoSum to do this, but it is useful to get familiar with how to put basic formulae together).
9 You do not need to type this formula in each of the columns – once you have calculated the total for column B, you can simply copy this formula across to the other columns, up until (and including) column H. If you are not sure how to do this, consult Excel's® help section and search for **copy a formula**.
10 Select cell I5 and type in a formula which will allow you to add up the range of figures from B5 through to H5. Use a **sum** formula, as described earlier in this chapter. This will give you the total number of male looked-after children, across all age groups. Copy this formula down to cell I6 in order to obtain the total number of female looked-after children, then copy the formula down to cell I7 in order to calculate the total number of looked-after children (i.e. both male and female, and across all age ranges) for Scotland.
11 Next, you are going to create a simple bar chart in order to show these figures in a visual form. Start in cell A4 and make a selection that extends to cell H6, select the **Insert** tab and then select the **column chart icon** and use a simple 2D column chart style. Give your chart a meaningful title and label the **x** and **y** axes appropriately.
12 Save your spreadsheet with the filename **Child Data**.

summary of key points

- Word-processing software, such as Microsoft Word®, is used to produce academic assignments, essays and reports. There are various features which enable students to do common formatting things easily, such as altering line spacing and obtaining word counts.
- Presentation software, such as Microsoft PowerPoint®, enables you to create presentation slides quickly and easily. There are two stages to using PowerPoint®:

  1 Authoring mode.
  2 Presentation mode.

- Spreadsheet software, such as Microsoft Excel®, is used to create spreadsheets, perform calculations using formulae and create bar charts.
- Practical exercises gave you the opportunity to put these skills into practice and to test your knowledge and understanding.

useful resources

OpenOffice.org – 'the free and open productivity suite'
Available at: http://www.openoffice.org
This website contains information about the Open Office open-source software and also the facility to freely download the Open Office software (versions are available for Windows, Linux, Solaris and Macintosh platforms).

further reading

Chivers, B. and Shoolbred, M. (2007) *A Student's Guide to Presentations* (Study Skills Series). London: Sage.

Clarke, A. (2005) *IT Skills for Successful Study*. Basingstoke: Palgrave Macmillan. (Note that this is only useful if you are using Microsoft Office XP® or earlier.)

Gregor, C. (2006) *Practical Computing Skills for Social Work*. Exeter: Learning Matters. (Chapters 5, 6 and 8 in particular relate to the content of this chapter.)

Appendix 1: Online resources for social workers and students

The authors do not take any responsibility for the content of these websites.

> British Association of Social Workers
http://www.basw.co.uk/
This is the website for the largest association within the UK representing social work and social workers. It provides a range of help, support and advice for newly qualified and established social workers.

> General Social Care Council (GSCC)
http://www.gscc.org.uk/Home/
GSCC's role is to regulate the training and conduct of social workers. The website contains useful resources and key documents, including the Codes of Practice for Social Care Workers and Employers.

> National Children's Bureau
http://www.ncb.org.uk/
The NCB seeks to improve the lives of children and young people and works with a number of partner agencies in pursuit of this. The website contains information on a vast range of issues affecting children and young people including youth justice, health issues and the prevention of social exclusion.

> Student involvement in SWAP
http://www.swap.ac.uk/aboutswap/website/student.html
SWAP is the Higher Education Academy's subject centre for social policy and social work. The website contains a range of resources about how social work students can become involved in SWAP.

Glossary of Terms

Abstract This is the part of a journal article or research report/dissertation, which summarizes the work in its entirety. It provides an overview of the question or issue the article is addressing, the approach that has been taken to the research and the main findings.

Anti-discriminatory practice This aims to combat unequal treatment and dismantle the barriers that can prevent people from being able to access services.

Appropriate adult This describes the role of an adult who accompanies young people (aged below 17), and other vulnerable adults when they are detained in custody.

Citation You use citation (or in-text references) to make a brief reference to a source in the main body of your essay. This can then be used by the reader to look up the full reference to that piece of work which should appear in your reference list. A citation will normally consist of the author's surname (or organization's name if there is no named author) and the year of publication. Additionally, you would provide a page number if providing a citation for a direct quote.

COP/Codes of Practice for Social Care Workers and Employers These codes describe the standards of conduct and practice expected of social care workers and their employers. Service-users, carers and other stakeholders are encouraged to refer to the codes of practice so that they have an awareness and understanding of the standards that have been set for the profession.

Discrimination This refers to unequal treatment directed towards individuals, or groups of people, on the grounds of their race, sexual orientation, gender, age, class or disability.

DoH The Department of Health is the government department which provides health and social care policy, guidance and publications for the NHS and social care profession.

Evidence-based practice This refers to practice which is informed by available research evidence and published expertise.

Flash Drive/USB Drive or Stick/Pen Drive/Memory Stick A data storage device which connects to a computer or other device using a USB port. The storage capacity of flash drives and related devices can range from 64 MB through to several GB.

Formative assessment This is an assessment which focuses on developing student learning. The results of formative assessment focus mainly on developmental feedback, and does not normally count towards formal academic credit.

GSCC The General Social Care Council is the body which registers social care workers in the UK and regulates their conduct and training.

Harvard Referencing System This is the name of a popular referencing system used by many UK higher education institutions. It consists of a brief citation in the main body of your work (author surname, year of publication) which relate to a list of full references which appear at the end of the piece of work.

Higher Education (HE) This is the non-compulsory, post-secondary education which is typically offered by universities, institutes of higher education and some colleges.

ICT Information and Communication Technology refers to the range of digital technologies that can be used to record, store, retrieve and exchange data and information.

IPL Inter-professional Learning refers to the process where participants from different professional disciplines (often health and social care related) are able to learn together, share expertise and gain an insight into different values and knowledge bases.

Literature (or 'the literature') This refers to the broad range of published, academic material.

Literature review This is a summary of the work that has been published on a particular topic.

Literature search This simply describes the process of searching the whole spectrum of academic sources for information, or research material, which is related to your research question or topic.

NOS National Occupational Standards. These provide a statement of the minimum skills, abilities and knowledge required to demonstrate competency in a professional role. There is a specific set of NOS for social work.

Paraphrasing This is where you summarize someone else's words, thoughts or ideas in your own words. You still need to provide a citation to the original source material when you use paraphrasing in your assignments.

Plagiarism This is the act of presenting someone else's work as if it were your own.

QAA The Quality Assurance Agency.

Reference list This is the list of full references, containing specific details about your sources, which is included at the end of assignments, essays and other pieces of academic work. The reference list is displayed in alphabetical order.

Referencing This is a process which acknowledges that you have used someone else's work in the course of producing your own piece of work.

Research methodology This is the approach, methods and strategies employed in collecting data and carrying out the research process.

Service-user Within the context of health and social care, this refers to a person who makes use of a particular service.

Social exclusion The Government defines social exclusion as involving the lack or denial of resources, rights, goods and services, and the inability to participate in the normal relationships and activities available to the majority of people in society.

Summative assessment This is an assessment which is formally marked (or graded), and assesses the level of learning at a particular point in time. Summative assessment usually contributes towards academic credits.

VLE A Virtual Learning Environment is an online learning environment which may incorporate a number of different types of learning resource (lecture notes, additional reading, multimedia learning packages), communication tools (discussion boards, email, chat tools) and learning management tools.

Work-based learning (WBL) This is formal learning which takes place within the context of work settings.

References

Adams, R. (2002) 'Social work process', in M.R. Adams, L. Damindli and M. Payne (eds) *Social Work Themes, Issues and Critical Debates*, 2nd edition. Basingstoke: Palgrave MacMillan.

Asthana, A. (2008) 'Social workers buckling under stress burden', *The Observer*, 15 June.

Babb, P. (2005) *A summary of focus on social inequalities.* Office for National Statistics. [online]. Available at: http://www.statistics.gov.uk/articles/nojournal/FOSI_summary_article.pdf [accessed 4 January 2009]

Beresford, P. (2005) 'Social approaches to madness and distress: user perspectives and user knowledges', in J. Tew (ed.) *Social Perspectives in Mental Health: Developing social models to understand work with mental distress.* London: Jessica Kingsley.

Beverley, A. and Worsley, A. (2007) *Learning and Teaching in Social Work Practice.* Basingstoke: Palgrave.

Bhopal, R. (2004) 'Glossary of terms relating to ethnicity and race: for reflection and debate', *Journal of Epidemiology and Community Health*, 58: 441–5.

Biggs, J. (1999) *Teaching for Quality Learning at University.* Buckingham: SRHE.

Borton, T. (1970) *Reach, Teach and Touch.* London: McGraw Hill.

British Dyslexia Association (BDA) (2007) *Dyslexia research information* [online]. Available at: http://www.bdadyslexia.org.uk/research.html [accessed 21 January 2009]

Brotherton, G. and Parker, S. (eds) (2009) *Work-based Learning and Practice Placement: A textbook for health and social care students.* Exeter: Reflect Press.

Burns, T. and Sinfield, S. (2008) *Essential Study Skills: The complete guide to success at university.* London: Sage.

Chivers, B. and Shoolbred, M. (2007) *A Student's Guide to Presentations* (Study Skills Series) London: Sage.

Clarke, A. (2005) *IT Skills for Successful Study.* Basingstoke: Palgrave Macmillan.

Clarke, A. (2008) *E-learning Skills.* Basingstoke: Palgrave Macmillan.

Clegg, B. (2008) *Studying Creatively.* London: Routledge.

Coffield, F., Moseley, D., Hall, E. and Ecclestone, K. (2004) *Should we be using learning styles? What research has to say to practice.* London: Learning and Skills Development Agency [online]. Available at: http://www.lsda.org.uk/files/PDF/1540.pdf [accessed 15 December 2008]

Cornell University (1993) *Therapeutic Crisis Intervention.* New York: Cornell University.

Cosis Brown, H. (2008) 'Social work and sexuality, working with lesbians and gay men: what remains the same and what is different?', *Practice* 20(4): 265 – 75.

Cottrell, S. (2003) *The Study Skills Handbook*, 2nd edition. Basingstoke: Palgrave Macmillan.

Cottrell, S. (2005) *Critical Thinking Skills.* Basingstoke: Palgrave Macmillan.

Creme, P. and Lea, M.R. (2008) *Writing at University: A guide for students*, 3rd edition. Maidenhead: Open University Press.

Cryer, P. (2006) *The Research Student's Guide to Success*, 3rd edition. Maidenhead: Open University Press.

DoH (2002) *Requirements for social work training*. Department of Health [online]. Available at: http://www.dh.gov.uk/prod_consum_dh/groups/dh_digitalassets/@dh/@en/documents/digitalasset/dh_4060262.pdf [accessed 14 April 2008]

Dolowitz, D., Buckler, S. and Sweeney, F. (2008) *Researching Online*. Basingstoke: Palgrave Macmillan.

Donnelly, E. and Neville, L. (2008) *Communication and Interpersonal Skills*. Exeter: Reflect Press.

Durrant, A., Rhodes, G. and Young, D. (2009) *University-level Work Based Learning*. Hendon: Middlesex University Press.

Eicher, J. (1987) *Making the Message Clear*. Santa Cruz: Grinder, DeLozier and Associates.

Elliott, T., Frazer, T., Garrand, D., Hickinbotham, J., Horton, V., Mann, J., Soper, S., Turner, J., Turner, M. and Whiteford, A. (2005) 'Practice learning and assessment on BSc (Hons) Social Work: "Service user conversations"', *Social Work Education* 24(4): 451–66.

Entwhistle, N. (1988) *Styles of Learning*. Edinburgh: David Fulton.

Fanthome, C. (2005) *The Student Life Handbook*. Basingstoke: Palgrave Macmillan.

Fink, A. (1998) *Conducting Research Literature Reviews*. London: Sage.

General Social Care Council (GSCC) (2002) *Codes of Practice for Social Care Workers and Employers*. London: GSCC.

Giddens, A. (2005) *Sociology*, 5th edition. Cambridge: Polity.

Greener, M. (2002) *The Which? Guide to Managing Stress*. London: Which? Ltd.

Greetham, B. (2001) *How to Write Better Essays*. Basingstoke: Palgrave Macmillan.

Gregor, C. (2006) *Practical Computer Skills for Social Work*. Exeter: Learning Matters.

Golightly, M. (2008) *Social Work and Mental Health*, 3rd edition. Exeter: Learning Matters.

Hargreaves, S. (2007) *Study Skills for Dyslexic Students* (Study Skills Series). London: Sage.

Hart, C. (1998) *Doing a Literature Review*. London: Sage.

Hayne, Y. (2003) 'Experiencing psychiatric client perspective on being mentally ill', *Journal of Psychiatric and Mental Health Nursing* 10: 722–9.

Healy, K. and Mulholland, J. (2007) *Writing Skills for Social Workers*. London: Sage.

Hickman, M., Crowley, H. and Mai, N. (2008) *Immigration and Social Cohesion in the UK*. Joseph Rowntree Foundation [online]. Available at: http://www.jrf.org.uk/sites/files/jrf/2230-deprivation-cohesion-immigration.pdf [accessed 06 January 2009]

Holt, J. and Rafferty, J. (2005) *Building skills into the curriculum: A guide to meeting the requirement for social work degree students to achieve information and communication technology skills*. SWAP [online]. Available at: http://www.swap.ac.uk/docs/SWAPECDL.pdf [accessed 12 January 2008]

Honey, P. and Mumford, A. (1982) *Manual of Learning Styles*. Maidenhead: Peter Honey Publications.

Hoult, E. (2006) *Learning Support for Mature Students*. (Study Skills Series) London: Sage.

HSE (2008a) *Working together to reduce stress at work* [online]. Available at: http://www.hse.gov.uk/pubns/indg424.pdf [accessed 17 October 2008]

HSE (2008b) *Self-reported work-related illness and workplace injuries in 2006/07: Results from the Labour Force Survey* [online]. Available at: http://www.hse.gov.uk/statistics/lfs/lfs0607.pdf [accessed 18 October 2008]

Interactive Technologies Research Group (2006) *Using digital media to access information and good practice for paid carers of older people*. SCIE [online]. Available at: http://www.scie.org.uk/publications/reports/report15.pdf [accessed 23 January 2008]

James, A.L. and James, A. (2001) 'Tightening the net: children, community and control', *British Journal of Sociology* 52 (2): 211–28.

Jaspers, M. (2003) *Beginning Reflective Practice*. Cheltenham: Nelson Thornes.

Kennedy, D. (n.d.) *Essay writing: a guide for undergraduates*. Royal Literary Fund [online]. Available at: http://www.rlf.org.uk/fellowshipscheme/writing/index.cfm [accessed 16 December 2008]

Knapp, M. and Daly, J.A. (2002) *Handbook of Interpersonal Communication*. London: Sage.

Knott, C. and Scragg, T. (2007) *Reflective Practice in Social Work*. Exeter: Learning Matters.

Knowles, M., Holton, E.F. and Swanson, R.A. (2005) *The Adult Learner*, 6th edition. London: Elsevier.

Kolb, D. (1984) *Experiential Learning: Experience as the source of learning and development*. London: Prentice Hall.

Koprowska, J. (2005) *Communication and Interpersonal Skills in Social Work*. Exeter: Learning Matters.

Levin, P. (2007a) *Conquer Study Stress*. Maidenhead: Open University Press.

Levin, P. (2007b) *Skilful Time Management*. Maidenhead: Open University Press.

Lloyd, C., King, R. and Chenoweth, L. (2002) 'Social work, stress and burnout: a review', *Journal of Mental Health* 11(3): 255–65.

Marton, F. and Säljö, R. (1976) 'On qualitative differences in learning – 1: outcome and process', *British Journal of Educational Psychology* 46: 4–11.

Martyn, H. (2000) *Developing Reflective Practice*. Bristol: Policy Press.

Mayes, T. and de Freitas, S. (2004) *Review of e-learning theories, frameworks and models. JISC e-Learning Models Desk Study* [online]. Available at: http://www.jisc.ac.uk/uploaded_documents/Stage%202%20Learning%20Models%20(Version%201).pdf [accessed 17 July 2008]

McMillan, K. and Weyers, J. (2006) *The Smarter Student*. Harlow: Pearson Education.

Metcalfe, M. (2006) *Reading Critically at University*. (Study Skills Series) London: Sage.

Methodology.co.uk – The Research Methods Resource Centre [online]. Available at: http://www.methodology.co.uk/ [accessed 15 October 2008]

Moon, J. (2006) *Learning Journals: A handbook for reflective practice and professional development*. Abingdon: Routledge.

Moon, J. (2007) *A Handbook of Reflective and Experiential Learning: Theory and practice*. London: RoutledgeFalmer.

Moran, C.C. and Hughes, L.P. (2006) 'Coping with stress: social work students and humour', *Social Work Education* 25(5): 501–17.

Moss, B. (2007) *Communication Skills for Health and Social Care*. London: Sage.

Munro, E. (1996) 'Avoidable and unavoidable mistakes in child protection work', *British Journal of Social Work* 42(3): 288 – 98.

Murray, N. and Hughes, G. (2008) *Writing Up Your University Assignments and Research Projects*. Maidenhead: Open University Press.

Neville, C. (2007) *The Complete Guide to Referencing and Avoiding Plagiarism*. Maidenhead: Open University Press.

NHS Choices (n.d.) *Symptoms of stress* [online]. Available at: http://www.nhs.uk/Conditions/Stress/Pages/Symptoms.aspx?url=Pages/what-is-it.aspx [accessed 24 January 2009]

Onyett, S. (2003) *Team Working in Mental Health*. Basingstoke: Palgrave MacMillan.

Parker, J. (2004) *Effective Practice Learning in Social Work*. Exeter: Learning Matters.

Parker, J. and Bradley, G. (2007) *Social Work Practice*, 2nd edition. Exeter: Learning Matters.

Parton, N. (2008) 'Changes in the form of knowledge in social work: from the "social" to the "informational"?', *British Journal of Social Work*, 38: 253–69.

Pears, R. and Shields, G. (2008) *Cite Them Right: The essential referencing guide*, 7th edition. Newcastle upon Tyne: Pear Tree Books.

Petty, G. (2004) *Teaching Today*. Cheltenham: Nelson Thornes.
Petty, G. (2006) *Evidence-based Teaching*. Cheltenham: Nelson Thornes.
Postle, K. (2007) *It couldn't happen here . . . A workshop to discuss detection and deterrence of plagiarism in social work students' assessed work*. SWAP Report [online]. Available at: http://www.swap.ac.uk/docs/projects/KarenPostle_plagiarism.pdf [accessed 12 November 2008]
Ramsden, P. (1992) *Learning to Teach in Higher Education*. London: Routledge.
Redman, P. (2005) *Good Essay Writing: A Social sciences guide*. London: Sage.
Reid, B. (1993) '"But we're doing it already": exploring a response to the concept of reflective practice in order to improve its facilitation', *Nurse Education Today* 13: 305–9.
Reynolds, M. (1997) 'Learning styles: a critique', *Management Learning* 28(2): 115–33.
Ridley, D. (2008) *The Literature Review – A Step-by-Step Guide for Students*. London: Sage.
Robinson, F.P. (1970) *Effective Study*, 4th edition. New York: Harper & Row.
Rose, J. (2007) *The Mature Student's Guide to Writing*, 2nd edition. Basingstoke: Palgrave Macmillan.
Rugg, G., Gerrard, S. and Hooper, S. (2008) *The Stress-free Guide to Studying at University*. (Study Skills Series) London: Sage.
Santy, J. and Smith, L. (2007) *Being an E-learner in Health and Social Care*. Abingdon: Routledge.
Schön, D. (1991) *The Reflective Practitioner: How professionals think in action*. Aldershot: Arena.
The Scottish Government (2008) *Children Looked After Statistics 2007–08* [online]. Available at: http://www.scotland.gov.uk/Publications/2008/11/25103230/0 [accessed 3 January 2009]
Shardlow, S. and Doel, M. (2005) *Modern Social Work Practice: Teaching and learning in practice settings*. Aldershot: Ashgate Publishing.
Shaw, C. and Palattayil, G. (2008) 'Issues of alcohol misuse among older people: attitudes and experiences of social work practitioners', *Practice – Social Work in Action* 20(3): 181–93.
Singleton, C.H. (Chair) (1999) *Dyslexia in Higher Education: Policy, Provision and Practice – Report of the National Working Party on Dyslexia in Higher Education*. University of Hull: National Working Party on Dyslexia in Higher Education.
Sumpter, A. (2007) *Uses of e-portfolios to develop reflection and assessment on social work degree programmes*. SWAP [online]. Available at: http://www.swap.ac.uk/docs/eltep_help sheet3.pdf [accessed 4 August 2008]
SWAP (2007) *The social work degree: preparing to succeed* – SWAP Guide 3 [online]. Available at: http://www.swap.ac.uk/docs/swapguide_3.pdf [accessed 3 October 2008]
Thompson, N. (1997) *Anti-discriminatory Practice*, 2nd edition. Basingstoke: Macmillan.
Thompson, N. (2009) *Practising Social Work*. Basingstoke: Palgrave MacMillan.
Thompson, N. and Thompson, S. (2008) *The Social Work Companion*. Basingstoke: Palgrave Macmillan.
TOPPS UK Partnership (2002) *The National Occupational Standards for Social Work*. Skills for Care [online]. Available at: http://www.skillsforcare.org.uk/developing_skills/National_Occupational_Standards/social_work.aspx [accessed 13 February 2008]
Trevithick, P. (2005) *Social Work Skills*, 2nd edition. Maidenhead: Open University Press.
Waldman, J. (2007) *ECDL Online Survey Report*. SWAP [online]. Available at: http://www.swap.ac.uk/docs/swap_ecdl_survey.pdf [accessed 24 April 2008]
Walker, H. (2008) *Studying for Your Social Work Degree*. Exeter: Learning Matters.
Ward, A. and Wood, P. (n.d.) *Writing dissertations: a guide for graduates*. Royal Literary Fund [online]. Available at: http://www.rlf.org.uk/fellowshipscheme/writing/diswriting/intro.htm [accessed 16 December 2008]

Warner, J. and Gabe, J. (2008) 'Risk, mental disorder and social work practice: a gendered landscape', *British Journal of Social Work* 38(1): 117–34.
Wenman, H. (2005) *Working towards full participation*. GSCC [online]. Available at: http://www.gscc.org.uk/NR/rdonlyres/CC4E1B8D-3883-44D8-80C9-E6C1D9E54AE1/0/Fullparticipationreportfinal05final.pdf [accessed 24 April 2008]
Wilson, K., Ruch, G., Lymbery, M. and Cooper, A. (2008) *Social Work: An introduction to contemporary practice*. Harlow: Pearson Education.
Young, P. (2003) *What is the scholarship of learning and teaching*? [online]. Available at: http://www.swap.ac.uk/research/introduction.asp [accessed 12 February 2007]

Index